The Politics of Migration: Managing Opportunity, Conflict and Change

Edited by

Sarah Spencer

Institute for Public Policy Research

Blackwell Publishing

First published 2003 by Blackwell Publishing as a special issue of *The Political Quarterly*

Blackwell Publishing, Inc., 350 Main Street, Malden, Massachusetts 02148–5018, USA
Blackwell Publishing Ltd, 9600 Garsington Road, Oxford OX4 2DQ, UK
Blackwell Publishing Asia Pty Ltd, 550 Swanston Street, Carlton, Victoria 3053, Australia
Blackwell Verlag GmbH, Kurfürstendamm 57, 10707 Berlin, Germany

First published 2003 by Blackwell Publishing Ltd

Library of Congress Cataloging-in-Publication Data has been applied for

ISBN 1–4051–1635–8

A catalogue record for this title is available from the British Library

Set in 9.5/11pt Palatino by Joshua Associates, Oxford
Printed and bound in the United Kingdom by Cambrian Printers Ltd, Aberystwyth
For further information on Blackwell Publishing, visit our website:
www.blackwellpublishing.com

CONTENTS

Notes on Contributors

Jeff Crisp is Head of the Evaluation and Policy Analysis Unit at the Office of the UN High Commissioner for Refugees.

Andrew Geddes is Jean Monnet Reader in the Government and Politics of the EU and Deputy Director of the Europe in the World Centre at the University of Liverpool.

Randall Hansen is a Fellow and Tutor at Merton College, Oxford and a University Lecturer in the Department of Politics and International Relations, University of Oxford.

Mark Kleinman, formerly Professor of International Social Policy, University of Bristol, is currently Head of Housing and Homelessness at the Greater London Authority and member of the Public Policy Group at the London School of Economics.

Will Kymlicka is Professor of Philosophy at Queen's University, Kingston, Ontario.

John Lloyd is Editor of the *Financial Times Magazine* and former Editor of the *New Statesman*.

Susan Martin is Visiting Professor and Director of the Institute for the Study of International Migration, Georgetown University. She was formerly Executive Director of the US Commission on Immigration Reform, which was mandated by Congress to make recommendations on changes in US immigration and refugee policy.

Tariq Modood is Professor of Sociology, Politics and Public Policy and Director, Centre for the Study of Ethnicity and Citizenship, at the University of Bristol.

Claude Moraes MEP was elected to the European Parliament for London in 1999. A member of the Parliament's Employment and Social Affairs Committee, he was previously Director of the UK-based migration NGO, the Joint Council for the Welfare of Immigrants, and a Commissioner of the Commission for Racial Equality.

Demetrios G. Papademetriou is co-director of the Migration Policy Institute, Washington DC. He is also the convener of the Athens Migration Policy Initiative, a task force of mostly European senior immigration experts that advises EU member states on immigration and asylum issues.

Shamit Saggar worked between 2001 and 2003 as a Senior Policy Adviser in the Prime Minister's Strategy Unit, Cabinet Office. He is a Reader in Politics at Queen Mary, University of London, and is currently a Yale World Fellow at Yale University.

Sarah Spencer is a Senior Associate at the Institute for Public Policy Research, a former adviser on migration to the Prime Minister's Strategy Unit, Cabinet Office, and former General Secretary of Liberty. She is a visiting professor at the Human Rights Centre, University of Essex.

Paul Statham is Research Director, Centre for European Political Communications (EurPolCom), Institute of Communications Studies, University of Leeds.

The Politics
of Migration

WITHDRAWN

Blackwell
Publishing

Acknowledgements

I WOULD like to thank the contributors for their collective effort in bringing this volume together, and Gillian Somerscales at *The Political Quarterly* for her skill and unfailing good humour during the inevitable hitches. I am grateful to my colleagues Heaven Crawley and Seamus Taylor for comments on parts of the text, and to the Joseph Rowntree Charitable Foundation and Atlantic Philanthropies for their support for the migration work at the Institute for Public Policy Research, which enabled me to edit this book. Finally, thanks to Demetrios Papademetriou and Gregory Maniatis for involving me in the Athens Migration Policy Initiative over the past year, the debates in which have been formative in my thinking.

Sarah Spencer

Published by Blackwell Publishing Ltd, 9600 Garsington Road, Oxford OX4 2DQ, UK and 350 Main Street, Malden, MA 02148, USA   vii

Introduction

SARAH SPENCER

THERE are few issues that are of such significance to civilisation, or so consistently present on international, state and local political agendas, as migration. The movement of people between nation-states has been a constant feature of history, but the recent pace and breadth of mobility have changed the face of Europe, bringing challenges and opportunities we have scarcely begun to address.

Migrants come to Europe from an ever wider range of countries, bringing diverse skills, values and experiences, creating a multicultural society that few envisioned when the first postwar migrants were encouraged to try their luck in our labour-hungry local economies. Around 8 per cent of the UK's residents are now from ethnic minorities, including 29 per cent of Londoners and more than one in ten of the UK's schoolchildren, most of them UK-born. They are future citizens of Europe.[1]

The global experience of migration may be long-standing; but few countries manage it well. It has been, as Randall Hansen says in his historical overview, a history of unforeseen developments and unintended consequences. Demetrios Papademetriou suggests that states fail to manage migration for three significant reasons, which resonate as themes throughout this book: that the speed and depth of change which migration brings challenge our sense of identity and continuity; that managing it requires difficult political and policy tradeoffs that have uneven distributional consequences; and that migration exposes weaknesses in a nation's governance arrangements, particularly in its ability to enforce the law, which sap the public's confidence in its capacity to govern in their interests.

The tensions to which these three challenges give rise catapult governments into reactivity, leaving little political space in which to explore optimal alternatives—still less the scope to demonstrate to the public that migration can be managed to their mutual advantage. The question—to which the essays in this book are addressed—is how to tackle this conundrum.

Migrants' motives and patterns of movement are complex; but we require them to enter through channels that label them: as student or asylum seeker, worker or family member; as either temporary or permanent. In each of those categories Europe has seen numbers grow over the past decade, notably those of asylum seekers, whom we have further labelled 'unwanted'.

Asylum determination systems set up to process the handfuls of applications from Cold War dissidents have near collapsed under the weight of requests received in recent years, leaving thousands waiting for a decision, disbarred in the meantime from working and thus dependent on support from the taxpayer. As one of the few channels of legitimate entry

Published by Blackwell Publishing Ltd, 9600 Garsington Road, Oxford OX4 2DQ, UK and 350 Main Street, Malden, MA 02148, USA

into Europe, the asylum route designed for those seeking protection has been taken also by those wanting a chance to better their lives in countries where their labour will be needed. Even those actually in need of protection create a tension, as Paul Statham argues, between the principle that liberal democratic nation-states provide sanctuary to those facing persecution, and the principle that they give priority to the citizens from whom their sovereignty derives.

Meanwhile we have seen growing demand by employers for overseas workers, with governments unsure how to respond. There is a global market for the highly skilled, and employers competing to attract them find the bureaucracy of visa controls and work permits an unwelcome regulatory burden. The UK, like the traditional countries of immigration, has responded by opening the doors to skilled workers, quadrupling the annual number of work permits issued since Labour came to power in 1997, and now approving 90 per cent within 24 hours. Most European states have been much more cautious.

All the evidence suggests that, at the global and national levels, labour migrants enhance competitiveness and boost economic growth, albeit to a modest degree. But there are winners and losers, with low-skilled older native workers more likely to see their job security threatened by mobile, younger migrant competitors. Their fears need to be understood in the context of the broader challenges that sections of European society face as a result of global economic and political restructuring. The visible presence of 'outsiders' is but a focus of wider insecurities for which they get the blame.

In the past, European states sought to maintain the pretence that they were countries of zero immigration; that they maintained high walls in which doors were rarely opened. As the number of asylum seekers grew, the right to family reunion ensured a continuing flow of entrants, demands from employers led to ad hoc schemes for overseas workers and evidence emerged of an unknown number of irregular residents, the public saw the fallacy of this claim and resented the presence of newcomers for whom no justification had been provided. Representatives of the populist right could claim that the public had been betrayed by political leaders ignoring their concerns, thus exploiting a vein of resentment which has at times led to violence against the newcomers, at others to electoral gain for those vocally hostile to them.

Management not denial

Now European states are waking up to reality: that migration is, at differing levels and in differing forms, a permanent part of our future. There is considerable scope for debate on how many labour migrants we might need—differing views are expressed in the pages of this book—or on the criteria on which family members might be welcomed—but the question is

2

not *if* we shall have migrants; it is *how* we shall meet that challenge. The object must now be optimal management, not denial.[2]

What, then, of the future? The demographic deficit—an ageing population with a declining number of workers—will hit Britain's European neighbours more quickly and more severely than it will hit the UK, where it is only from 2020 that the dependency ratio of older to younger people will be felt with full force. Yet there are skill and labour shortages in some sectors now, despite a level of unemployment, because skills are mismatched with demand, because job seekers are available in the wrong parts of the country, or because the pay and conditions on offer are at levels they are unwilling to accept.

Migrants are not the first answer to filling job vacancies, or to addressing the demographic deficit. The policy basket contains prior options, like raising the participation rates of women, ethnic minorities and older workers, and retraining those whose skills are out of date. But these options come with their own challenges: older workers will resist working until seventy before resorting to pension income; women can return to work after childbearing only if there is a carer—who may well be a migrant—to mind their children. Governments have already made strenuous efforts to enhance employability, but gaps remain, not least in vital public service jobs, for which migrants are needed. The health service in the UK would quite literally collapse without the overseas doctors and nurses who make up a third of its current staff; and some schools could not remain open.

The question, therefore, is not whether we accept migration, but how we manage it to maximise the opportunities it presents and minimise the costs it exacts. As the UK's Home Secretary put it in the White Paper that signified a turning point in the country's approach: 'Migration is an inevitable reality of the modern world and it brings significant benefits. But to ensure that we sustain the positive contribution of migration to our social well-being and economic prosperity, we need to manage it properly and build firmer foundations on which integration with diversity can be achieved.'[3]

This is not to suggest that some new managerialism could bring inherently anarchic migration flows within our regulatory control, enabling us to welcome those we need and turn back those we do not. Rather, it means we need to devise solutions as complex as the migration patterns themselves: understanding the multiple drivers and pull factors, the agencies that facilitate migration, and the full range of levers that we might deploy to channel it where it can do most good.

Drivers and tradeoffs

Managing migration—where it is involuntary or unwelcome—must start with tackling its causes. As Jeff Crisp argues in his essay on refugees, we are unbalanced in focusing so intently on the responsibility which receiving states have for asylum seekers, to the neglect of the responsibility of the states from which they flee.

Sometimes, addressing root causes may require forceful intervention by the international community, an approach which challenges the very sovereignty of nation-states. But in most cases, much can be achieved through partnership with countries of origin—if we are willing to do a deal from which they also gain, whether it be through work permits for their nationals or preferential terms of trade. We need their cooperation, so we must be willing to offer them something in return, not resort to penalising them by withdrawal of aid—an option discussed but rejected at the EU Seville summit in 2002—or return asylum seekers who reach Europe to transit camps in developing countries that already shoulder a disproportionate share of the responsibility. Partnership with countries of origin—through tradeoffs from which each benefits—is a prerequisite of the new comprehensive approach.

If we are to succeed in curbing illegal migration, we must also move beyond the old paradigm of ever tighter controls. Enforcement measures, while part of the package, can simply divert irregular migrants into new routes or towards new destinations. We need to be more subtle, more nuanced in our response. Creating legal channels that match demand for labour will provide alternatives to entry, or remaining, without permission. We also need to explore the potential for 'earned legalisation' schemes whereby those working without authority can regularise their status.

This does not mean going soft on illegality. Irregular migrants can undermine the pay and conditions of local workers, are vulnerable to gross exploitation, and distort public attitudes towards migration as a whole. But, as Papademetriou argues, governments cannot win the war on illegal immigration under the current rules of engagement. The trafficking networks have all the advantages—agility, resources and no compunction to abide by any rules. We need to do more than build better mouse-traps. We need to create incentives to comply.

Internal controls to detect irregular migrants carry particular risks. The public at large will resent checks on their entitlement to jobs and services; and, as we know from US experience, migrants will avoid essential services if they fear detection. Public health will be put at risk; children kept out of school.

Polarised debate

To reconcile the multiple tradeoffs that the management of migration requires, governments need to be clear on their high-level objectives: to acknowledge that managing migration is not simply about achieving labour market objectives, protecting national security, minimising public expenditure, promoting social cohesion, honouring human rights obligations, or promoting international development and cooperation—but all of these; and further to acknowledge that these goals can conflict.

The problem in the UK, as in other European states, is that the debate on migration is so polarised between those unwilling to acknowledge that migration brings benefits and those unwilling to acknowledge that it brings costs—that there is little political space for debate on the real choices facing policy-makers and on the decisions they are taking.

Governments are unwilling to lead an open debate on migration options, for fear of provoking public hostility. The real decisions—how to balance the demands of employers against those of the domestic labour force; how to reconcile our need for skilled workers against the costs this can impose on the developing countries that trained them; whether to allow migrants access to public services that will enhance their capacity to integrate or to cut benefits to save public expenditure—are taken behind closed doors. The result is that the public feel their concerns are not addressed and at the same time remain extraordinarily ignorant of the facts, with inflated perceptions of the numbers of migrants and the welfare benefits they receive. September 11 served only to enhance public fears of an 'enemy within', unjustly increasing hostility to, and the insecurity of, the 15 million or so Muslims living in Europe.

Welfare tension

September 11 led to a shift in focus in migration politics in the United States, in favour of security controls. But the 1990s had already seen legislative reforms ending the presumption that immigrants are citizens in waiting and, as such, should enjoy near full access to the same rights—prompted largely by their perceived responsibility for soaring welfare costs. The US, Susan Martin writes, still favours immigration, but is less welcoming of immigrants.

That migrants' access to welfare is equally a central point of contention in Europe is no surprise. Welfare systems, as Andrew Geddes shows, defined the boundaries of inclusion and belonging, and hence entitlement, long before the question of migrant recipients became contentious. Most migrants, young and eager to work, make few demands on services; but asylum seekers' dependency on welfare while they wait for a decision on their claim, coupled with their greater need for health services in particular, can—in those few areas where asylum seekers are congregated—create demands that over-stretched local services are ill-equipped to meet.

As Randall Hansen argues, one of the lessons of history is that we have failed to invest adequately in measures to promote the integration of those migrants who stay. Although there are significant differences between migrant groups, with some 'performing' better than other residents in education and the labour market, migrants, and their second generation, are disproportionately unemployed, in poorer health, achieving less well at school, and under-represented in our democratic institutions. It is in all our interests for the barriers to integration to be dismantled, and for migrants to receive the assistance—induction advice and language tuition, for instance—that they need. But such measures come at a price. We are back to tradeoffs, and government fears of public resentment at migrants being seen to receive assistance, at taxpayers' expense, for which the payback is not always apparent nor explained.

The public veto that governments fear is not, however, as immutable as they think. As Shamit Saggar shows, public attitudes now are more nuanced than in past decades, with opinion distinguishing between different categories of migrant. There is greater recognition of the benefits migrants bring and more acceptance of cultural difference, with some scope for redressing ignorance. Only a small hard core are implacably hostile.

Crucially, changing attitudes depends on restoring public confidence that migration is well managed, and in the public's interest. Assurances will be heavily discounted against past broken promises, recollection of unrealistic targets that could not be met. Statham argues that two crucial influences on public attitudes are government pronouncements—the source, he suggests, of the vast majority of negative coverage in the press—and local experience. The public will need not only to be told that migration is not harmful of their interests, but to see that in their daily encounters. To that end, it is disastrous for asylum seekers, not allowed to work, to be seen idle on street corners, or left to beg if denied access to benefits because they did not claim asylum on arrival.

While differing in their views on the impact of migration, the contributors to this book insist that public hostility to migrants cannot be dismissed as racism. Is there then a contradiction, if we say that governments should acknowledge public fears, but not reinforce them? The answer is that it can be a fine line to tread, with a trap for the unwary at the feet of every politician. The messages need careful thought, and governments need to build alliances with partners in civil society to share responsibility for their delivery.

Integration

Explaining the rationale for migration policy is but part of a wider investment in integration that cannot be left to chance. Integration is not simply about access to the labour market and services, or about changing attitudes or civic engagement; it is a two-way process of adaptation by migrant *and* host society at all of those levels. Members of a migrant community may be socially integrated through intermarriage, and the acknowledged role models of youth fashion and music, as are the UK's Afro-Caribbean population; but we have not succeeded when they are also disproportionately unemployed. Likewise, we have not succeeded if migrants are working but leading parallel lives, with little social contact or civic engagement in the broader community.

We have expected both too much from migrants and too little. We provide little support on arrival, expecting them to break down the language and institutional barriers to acceptance on their own. At the same time we have created few expectations that new migrants will engage with their neighbours and contribute to society, beyond their role as workers and taxpayers.

Across Europe and North America, states are reconsidering their approach to the integration of migrants and their second generation. Across the EU, there have been sharp differences in view on whether the focus of integration should be foreigners or ethnic minorities, whether the priority should be ensuring access to the labour market or cultural adaptation, whether migrants' diverse cultures are a barrier to be overcome or a contribution to be welcomed, and whether measuring ethnic differences reinforces the very barriers that we are trying to overcome or is an essential tool in delivering equality. The unresolved tension on formal endorsements of diversity reflects an underlying anxiety about the extent to which the nation-state and indeed the EU itself needs a level of common values to build social cohesion and stability. A common strategy at EU level is now emerging, reflecting some constructive convergence on these issues.[4]

The UK's 2002 White Paper, *Secure Borders, Safe Haven*, spoke of the need to build a common citizenship and described human rights as a key source of the values that its citizens could share. Across the EU, the twenty-five member states are formally united in their endorsement of the European Convention on Human Rights, which provides a set of minimum standards on human behaviour but also a framework within which conflicting rights can be reconciled. These principles, endorsed across nations, have a legitimacy and acceptance beyond those endorsed only by one nation-state, and could be promoted as the glue that binds us in our diversity.

Across Europe, states are indeed reconsidering their citizenship policies. In the UK, the government is introducing citizenship classes and ceremonies as a means to promote common values and belonging. In contrast to the consensus on this approach in North America, the British proposals met scepticism from those who feared that it was a means to promote assimilation—the abandonment of minority cultures—rather than a balancing of diversity with a recognition of common values. Will Kymlicka shows that the reception for these proposals in fact said little about the approach itself but rather reflected distrust arising from the context in which they emerged—not least the failure to endorse at the highest level, and promote acceptance of, the UK as a multicultural nation.

Governance

When enforcement was the sole response and zero immigration the aspiration, migration was left to law and order ministries, and their counterpart in the European Commission. The comprehensive, managed migration approach requires a new perspective on migration governance, in which departments as diverse as international development, employment and health have objectives to secure and relevant programmes to deliver. Migration cannot be solely in the tight grip of those whose primary objective is control.

Moreover, management requires an evidence base; evaluation of programmes to assess 'what works' and a willingness to resource innovation and adaptation. If governments are serious about this, they must be willing to invest in systems that can deliver. The earlier failure to resource the UK's asylum determination system, allowing backlogs to develop with consequent economic and political costs, is being reversed but needs transformation into a system capable of producing decisions that are respected by government and migrant advocates alike. Sound, fast decisions remove any incentive for those without a genuine claim to apply.

A final theme I want to highlight, before turning to the essays themselves, is the need to secure the support of civil society in managing migration. Governments cannot create the optimal range of incentives, deterrents and support networks in isolation; nor do they need to. Currently they face a barrage of criticism on migration, and have few friends. Yet employers, unions, churches, voluntary groups and community organisations are potential civil society partners who could be mobilised to share responsibility: by sponsoring refugees, matching schemes to recruit overseas labour with resources to retrain existing workers, providing induction and language training, running 'buddy' schemes to befriend new arrivals—and in numerous other ways as yet unexplored. If migration is a permanent part of our future—and it will be—we need to move beyond seeing it as an unwelcome intrusion imposed on us by government to acknowledge a shared responsibility for building and negotiating a positive future together.

These are the themes explored by the essays in this book.

Randall Hansen, in his essay on the history of migration since 1945, takes us through the two postwar movements of migrants into Europe that led to the emergence, thirty years later, of multicultural, multilingual societies. Focusing on the UK, France and Germany, he recounts the mistaken assumptions, tensions and tradeoffs that enabled states to secure sufficient political support for this transformation of society, and draws out some clear lessons for today.

The first, he says, is that temporary migration will almost certainly become permanent—and that this is as true for asylum seekers as for guest-workers. Support for migration must therefore be managed. Public opposition is rooted to a degree in ignorance and prejudice, but also in more reasonable concerns about the changes immigration will bring. If politicians give the impression ('as some pro-migrant academics are wont to do') that all fears of immigration are founded in racism, then that political debating ground is vacated to the benefit of the far right. But politicians must also be willing to lead public opinion. History, he assures us, provides occasions when the public have supported immigration—but only if none of the main political parties succumb to anti-immigrant sentiment.

The lesson from Europe's halting attempts to integrate migrants is that they have not worked. Many migrants who entered in times of economic boom did not have the skills to survive the subsequent economic downturn. Success in the labour market is key to integration; so states should give priority to skilled migrants, ensuring that they have both the skills and the flexibility to find alternative work if economic change eliminates the jobs for which they came.

The lesson from recent asylum history is that it is the most resourceful who make it to Europe and that, because deportation is an ineffective tool of immigration control, most will stay. Rather than perpetuate the myth that they will leave, governments should take advantage of this source of permanent migration and channel it into the labour market. Europe needs immigrants, and the pressure to emigrate from the poor and overpopulated South means that it will get them. European nations must therefore develop, collectively if they can and unilaterally if they must, a managed migration policy.

In his essay on managing change in this newest age of migration, **Demetrios Papademetriou** explains why states find the politics and governance of migration so problematic, before setting out the range of factors, including the demographic deficit, that will ensure that it is a permanent part of their country's future. Indeed, their economies would suffer if it were not. Part of the fascination in observing these debates, he writes, is seeing those politicians who have exploited public hostility to migrants in the past now having to acknowledge that their country needs overseas workers.

How governments will now respond to the competing pressures for and against migration is uncertain. Papademetriou sets out a number of options, each of which carries political costs. We are, he suggests, at a historical cusp. The impact of September 11 might have led the US and European states to close their doors. That they did not reflects the pressures *for* migration. Closure could yet happen if further attacks make current levels of mobility untenable. Should it not, states will need to manage growing levels of migration. They must do so by understanding its multiple causes and the full range of levers that can be used to manage it. They must understand the limits of unilateralism, and that enforcement alone cannot deliver.

In the UK, the need to address illegal migration has been one of the drivers behind the government's willingness to open up new legal channels to meet the demand for overseas labour. In his essay, **Mark Kleinman** investigates the nature of this demand and the outcomes for migrant and domestic labour.

Reviewing the research literature, he finds that the impact of labour migration on global and national economies is positive, though not large. Economies that are not highly regulated, and those that attract workers with different skills and characteristics from their own, benefit most. Migrants do the jobs where there are recruitment difficulties, whether at the high-skilled or the low-skilled end of the market.

While the overall impact on the receiving country is positive, there are winners and losers. It would be simplistic to say that migration is either 'good' or 'bad' for Western economies. Low-skilled workers may see their job security and wages suffer from migrant competitors, depending on their internal mobility and capacity to retrain—though the evidence in the UK is that any negative impact is marginal. Nevertheless, for governments there are real choices and tradeoffs to be made. They must give, and be seen to give, priority to securing jobs for existing residents, while responding to pressure from employers struggling to find the labour they need.

The evidence shows that migration improves the economic position of migrants themselves—that is, indeed, the most widespread motivation for moving—but that they are more likely to be unemployed, and to earn less. There is a paucity of evidence on the trajectories of migrants but we do know that, in North America, while immigrants continue to move up the economic ladder, recent migrants are doing less well than their predecessors. As economic integration is a key factor in social integration and community cohesion, this has to be a cause for concern.

Looking ahead, Kleinman finds it is not easy to predict the level of labour shortages, nor their likely skills breakdown. Most of the predicted areas of growth are for people with a degree or professional qualifications. Although there are some growth predictions for low-skilled jobs, overall the number needed will decline. In some sectors, wages are too low for there ever not to be shortages, and there is a danger that employing migrants could be a substitute for improving pay and conditions. He concludes, as did Hansen, that the government should be cautious about increasing the supply of low-skilled migrants, while expanding and streamlining the legal access routes for those with skills.

Asking whether Europe's ageing population points to significantly greater migration over time, Kleinman suggests governments should look first to raising the participation rates of existing residents, particularly those of women. Even in the UK, where participation rates are relatively high, there is scope to raise the employment rates of older people, not least by abolishing mandatory retirement. In contrast to Papademetriou, he sees migration as a relatively minor element of a policy portfolio to address the demographic labour market and pensions problem.

It is not only because of demand for overseas workers that migration will be a permanent part of Europe's future. Geopolitical instability will ensure that, at some level, people will continue to seek protection in the West. In his essay on the global politics of asylum, **Jeff Crisp** looks at the changing causes of human displacement and governmental responses to it. While the total number of refugees has declined in recent years (to 12 million), the number of those displaced by persecution, violence and armed conflict has increased: 25 million are uprooted within their own states, some half of whom are in Africa. Where once the primary cause of refugee movements was persecution by fascist or communist regimes, now it is armed conflict. Moreover, refugees are not only a by-product of that conflict: displacement is increasingly a deliberate weapon of war.

As the principal agency responsible for responding to involuntary movements, the office of the United Nations High Commissioner for Refugees (UNHCR) encounters an increasing unwillingness by states to admit and accommodate those forced to flee. No longer the victims of anti-colonial struggles, nor of communism, the new generation of refugees cannot rely on the support of Western governments, for which the receiving states no longer hold much geopolitical significance.

As Western countries pulled down the shutters, they set an example for poorer states that feel their past generosity was exploited by the international community. Their own populations, experiencing declining development aid and the pain of structural adjustment programmes, resented the handouts that the refugees received.

UNHCR has had to adapt to the changing patterns of displacement, increasingly working within areas affected by armed conflict and expanding its role from refugee protection to humanitarian action. In such circumstances, its neutrality may be challenged and the security of its staff put at risk, and the organisation can find itself embroiled in ethical choices—as in providing aid to the very people who had been engaged in genocide—to which there are no right answers.

As people move in response to a complex set of threats, hardships and opportunities, it has become increasingly difficult to draw a sharp distinction between 'refugees' and 'economic migrants'. Seeking asylum has been one of the few opportunities to obtain residence in the West, and numbers applying have soared—some 9 million over the past two decades. Less than one-third have been given permission to stay, fuelling the perception that the right to apply for asylum has been abused.

As asylum seekers have arrived in large numbers from countries associated with violence and terrorism, public perceptions have focused on the challenges they bring, not on the economic and cultural contribution they could make. A barrage of measures to deter their arrival has been erected, prompting these migrants to seek alternative routes, agents and destinations. Meanwhile, asylum determination and support systems exact significant costs on the public purse—money which could, it is often suggested, be better spent on looking after people in their region of origin, though the reality is that cutting back on protection at home is unlikely to lead to greater protection abroad.

The growth in human smuggling and its links to organised crime exacerbate the severity of the asylum problem for the governments concerned. Their failure to show leadership, falling instead into a downward spiral of tough measures justified by scapegoating the asylum seeker, compounds the difficulties faced by those who are given the right to stay. Thus the notion of the dependent refugee, relying on social welfare benefits, becomes a self-fulfilling prophecy.

The rise in the number of asylum seekers reaching Europe is one part of the context for the rise in support for the new populist parties, the subject of **John Lloyd**'s contribution. Populists demand that the nation-state protect the people from the rapid social and economic change that has a disproportionate effect on the working class, of which migration is only the most visible aspect.

The politicians of the far right who have been successful in exploiting resentment of immigration succeed because they are building on those deeper public fears about their nation's capacity to sustain its privileged position in the world, and their own standard of living within it.

Lloyd reminds us that the rise of the parties of the right in Europe has no single cause, nor any single political complexion. But there are similarities that transcend their differences. They are populist and anti-elitist, claiming a direct relationship with their public, while condemning their opponents as remote from (or even having betrayed) the people by being in thrall to immigrants, Brussels bureaucrats, or foreign powers.

While anti-semitism remains present among the far right parties, Lloyd argues that the evident rise in hostility to Jews is most strongly reflected in the outspoken anti-Jewish prejudices expressed by some Muslims in opposition to the oppression of the Israeli state. That this new virulence goes unchecked he attributes to a reluctance by European states to treat their Muslim citizens as responsible for their public speech and acts; and to an intellectual left determined to demonstrate 'Israelo-fascism' and blind to what he perceives as the much more potent danger of 'Islamo-fascism'.

Lloyd argues that, whereas prior to September 11 the problems within Europe's Muslim communities, and between them and the native populations, were rarely seen to be more serious than those affecting other minorities, 9/11 has both highlighted and changed those relationships. Emphasising what he sees as Muslims' unwillingness to integrate, and the involvement of an extreme minority in terrorism within their adopted countries, he argues that the failure of states to deal with that minority will alienate the public from their Muslim neighbours, and requires much more proactive Muslim civic leadership than has yet been evident.

Tariq Modood interprets the position of Britain's Muslims very differently. He attributes the anti-Muslim wind blowing across Europe to the perception that Muslims are making demands that are seen as culturally and politically unacceptable. On the contrary, he argues, Muslims emerging into identity politics are merely following in the tradition of earlier groups—ethnic minorities, women, gays and lesbians—in seeking space for their heritage and values in both the public and private spheres: a positive endorsement of group difference. Public attitudes and arrangements, national culture and the symbols of national membership, must adapt so that this heritage is encouraged, not contemptuously expected to wither away. Muslim identity is the legitimate child of British multiculturalism.

Muslims are not a homogeneous group but as internally diverse as 'Christian', 'Belgian' or 'middle-class'. Yet they are disproportionately among the most disadvantaged, and experience a sense of community, an actual or latent 'Us' that is partly caused by those who see Muslims as 'Them'. Because Muslims have been among the principal victims of the bloodshed that has led asylum seekers to flee to Europe, they have found themselves bearing the brunt of the hostility directed at them, while 9/11 and subsequent international events have exacerbated the doubts cast on their loyalty as citizens.

Muslim demands for recognition also need to be seen against the background of the differing attitudes to cultural difference in European states, not least in the UK (where multiculturalism is based on race, a black–white dualism that excludes religion), France (where insistence on assimilation and on secularism in public life posit Islam as the 'ideological foe') and Germany (where belonging is defined by descent and precludes dual identities). In that context it is mistaken to single out Muslims as an intractable group, unwilling to integrate. Integration is a two-way process, requiring give on both sides.

Notwithstanding legitimate criticism of some Muslim radicals ('as representative of Muslims as the SWP is of working-class politics'), Modood argues that much of what Muslims are demanding is merely 'catching up' with the earlier demands of racial equality. Focusing on the UK, he highlights the resentment caused by the failure (until 2003) to make religious discrimination unlawful, and to give parity to Islam with other religions, for instance in the funding of state schools. One of the criteria for judging the legitimacy of British institutions should now be that they fairly represent not only ethnic minorities and women, but religious minorities too.

Thus Muslim assertiveness, he argues, is primarily derived not from Islam but from contemporary Western ideas about equality and multiculturalism—ideas which need to embrace other equality-seeking movements. It is the secularism of British political culture which makes this extension so problematic.

Having argued for recognition of difference, Modood insists there must also be emphasis on commonality. It is anti-racists and multiculturalists who are, he says, more prone than Muslims to ignore this. He endorses the importance of learning English, and the rejection of forced marriages. The unacceptable views of some Muslim spokespeople, for instance on gender issues, can, he insists, be contested on a point-by-point basis. They are not objections to the Muslim identity itself.

The rise in the number of asylum seekers to Europe, September 11, and the success of the far right in exploiting public fears and resentment set the context for recent European Union migration politics, the focus of the essay by **Claude Moraes**, a Member of the European Parliament. A complex process of European cooperation has been under way since the early 1980s, first on freedom of movement for EU citizens within its borders, then in relation to those seeking to enter from outside.

Moraes describes a complex tension between drivers for cooperation and constraints. The drive to achieve a common policy has been a consequence both of changing patterns of migration to the EU and of EU integration itself. Its goal of internal free movement, driven not by idealism but for economic benefit, has necessitated a common approach to the question of who may enter.

In relation to asylum, the drivers have been the disproportionate numbers reaching particular member states, leading to calls for 'burdensharing'; and the recognition that individual states alone cannot address a situation where asylum seekers and trafficked migrants can enter at the weakest point on Europe's border. While agreeing that only EU-wide solutions will be effective, Moraes argues that some of the assumptions on which proposals have been based have not been sound. Assuming that harmonising welfare and reception conditions will stop asylum seekers 'shopping' between states, for instance, ignores the reality that their motivations for choosing a particular destination are more complex.

Moraes identifies a series of obstacles to securing European cooperation. Some are internal: political tensions between the Council, Commission and Parliament, and cumbersome decision-making procedures that reflect member states' unwillingness to cede control. Inevitably there are different views among member states on each area of policy. Meanwhile, the pressure from the public for immediate solutions is matched only by their resistance, stronger in some states than others, to EU involvement in bringing those solutions about.

The European Council in Tampere in 1999 finally saw agreement on a comprehensive migration strategy that begins by addressing the 'push factors' in developing countries, acknowledges the labour immigration needs of European states and the need for common entry and post-entry rules on asylum seekers, and, last but not least, supports integration. That agenda is still just about on track; but there was a noticeable shift in tone and emphasis at the Seville summit in 2002—responding in part to the then evident rise in support for the far right—to a focus on illegal immigration, asylum and enforcement.

The Greek presidency in the first half of 2003 sought to restore the broader agenda, including recognition of the need for labour migration and the emphasis on integration.[5] The Commission and Parliament think that labour migration schemes would benefit from a level of EU coordination. Member states are less convinced, or less willing to acknowledge publicly the reality that demand for labour will increase. The Commission and Parliament are equally convinced that there is a role for the EU to play in promoting the economic, social and political integration of migrants. The imminent enlargement of the Union to 25 countries raises the urgency of this issue up the political agenda.

While many in Europe still reject the suggestion that immigrants are needed, the perception is that, in the United States, support for immigration is less equivocal. In her essay, **Susan Martin** argues that, in practice, Americans have long held inconsistent views and that recent events have brought that ambivalence to the fore. Americans are proud to be a nation of immigrants, and there remains majority support for the admission of close family members, skilled workers and refugees. But a combination of factors— high levels of illegal immigration, what were perceived to be excessive welfare costs, and the 1993 World Trade Center bombing—all contributed to significant legislative reform to curtail the rights of immigrants, long before the terrorist attacks of September 11, 2001.

To disentangle the politics that led to a more exclusionary immigration policy, Martin separates the actors into four broad groupings, each forming alliances with others when their interests coincide. They can be categorised by their attitudes to immigration, on one dimension, and by their attitudes to the rights of immigrants, on the other. Thus the 'advocates' favour generous levels of immigration and full access for legal immigrants to public services and benefits; the 'free-marketeers' favour generous levels of immigration but little safety-net of welfare rights (a view well represented in the *Wall Street Journal*). 'Restrictionists' want to restrict the number of immigrants *and* their access to benefits, while 'integrationists' are less concerned about numbers than that those who do come should enjoy full access to services and support. The fragile alliances that form between these groups cross party divisions.

What emerged from the legislative battles of the mid-1990s was expansion in the potential number of legal (temporary) immigrants but simultaneous erosion in their welfare and legal rights, cut back further after 9/11. This, says Martin, sends a clear signal that immigrants are welcomed as workers but not as full members of the community. They must pay taxes and contribute to the economy, but society has no reciprocal obligations towards them. Yet she is optimistic that the 'Pennsylvania ideal'—that immigrants should be treated as presumptive citizens—will prevail.

Andrew Geddes explores this contradiction between pressures to expand migration and its impact on the welfare state, in the European context. He notes that while some focus on the costs migrants impose on the welfare state, others insist that, with Europe's ageing population, it is only migration that will plug the gaps in its resource base. Both arguments are, he says, over-drawn. Migration will neither sink nor save the welfare state.

The welfare state not only marks the boundary between inclusion and exclusion for migrants once they have arrived, but has become a means of regulating migration—denial of access being meant to deter those, not least asylum seekers, whose arrival would be unwelcome. This coercive side of the welfare state, endorsing norms of acceptability, has long been a feature.

Migration debates are merely exposing wider tensions in defining the community of legitimate receivers of state benefits, a debate in which *perceptions* of entitlement are crucial. Thus, Geddes argues, this is one argument that cannot be resolved just by resorting to 'the facts'. The question is not why migrants come, but how their arrival is perceived. In Germany the status of the *Aussiedler* shifted during the 1990s from that of ethnic co-belongers with full welfare entitlements to that closer to other immigrant groups; Denmark recently deemed that full entitlement to welfare support could be accessed only after seven years' residence. The former 'denizens' have, he says, become 'margizens'.

The shifting organisational and conceptual boundaries within welfare states, resulting from their own respective internal pressures, are playing a key role in shaping understandings of wanted and unwanted migrants; and this process, Geddes argues, is central to any analysis of changing migration policies. These debates can, nevertheless, be at their most intense when they focus on migrants, and the consequences of denying protection can be particularly negative for their integration.

In his essay on anti-asylum rhetoric in Britain, **Paul Statham** acknowledges the tensions caused by the costs of supporting asylum seekers. But his central thesis is that political leaders do not simply reflect, but lead, anti-migrant political sentiment. He sets his own empirical research evidence on the actors in this political debate in the UK against two theoretical interpretations of immigration politics—the 'interest group' approach (in which migration policy is seen as the outcome of competing interests whose negotiation takes place in the corridors of power) and the 'racist public' thesis (which sees restrictive policies as a response to anti-migrant public opinion).

The analysis of migration policies as the outcome of discrete negotiations conducted by political elites and organised interest groups fits Martin's description of America's shifting alliances, although there is greater open debate than the 'interest group' model would imply. Pro-immigration lobbies have been largely successful in keeping open immigration regimes, whereas the disadvantaged groups from the native population who have to compete with migrants for jobs and houses are, Statham argues, less well organised as a political constituency and less well able to compete. While the theory has more explanatory value for labour migration than on asylum, he argues that it provides insight on how this sensitive political issue could be managed by political elites if a strong civil society of interest groups exists to put across the pro-migration, pro-migrant perspective—acting as a buffer against their xenophobic competitors.

Statham argues that the current British government's approach is, in contrast, based on the 'racist public' thesis: namely, a perception that there are untapped resources of public grievances against asylum seekers and that government's policy proposals must compete for this political territory. But his analysis of 'political claims making' in the 1990s shows that this debate is shaped not by civil society actors, employers or ethnic community groups but by national state and executive actors, and that their position was largely hostile to migrants.

Moreover, to the extent that civil society actors do enter the British public debate they do so with a largely pro-migrant stance. It is thus not possible, he argues, to see the state's anti-migrant stance as the result of mobilised public pressure. He concludes that state actors definitively shape the public discourse on immigration and asylum and that civil society actors, to the extent that they mobilise at all, do so against this position.

Statham's qualitative research on the attitudes of people in their local setting found greater hostility to asylum seekers than to ethnic minorities; but those who lived in parts of the country with few asylum seekers shifted, in discussion, to express grievances about ethnic minorities in their area—that

16

is, hostility to asylum seekers was but a proxy. They felt able to use more openly racist language when talking about ethnic minorities in an immigration context than was perceived to be socially acceptable when talking solely about those resident in their area. Anti-immigration norms, he concludes, are sanctioned by government, whereas anti-ethnic-minority sentiment is not; and local experience of asylum seekers and minorities is one key factor in conditioning understanding of these issues.

Noting the public support for asylum seekers mobilised in some areas in which they are living, he concludes that it would be possible to mobilise such sentiment more widely should state actors choose to emphasise Britain's human rights values.

In the meantime, the government's anti-asylum rhetoric could be counter-productive, were public attitudes to turn against labour migrants in a period of economic downturn. Bringing in labour migrants while simultaneously promoting a political discourse hostile to asylum seekers, often people from the same countries of origin and finding homes in the same localities, is a risky strategy. The public may not share the government's perception of the difference.

In his essay on the politics of public opinion, **Shamit Saggar** acknowledges that anti-immigration attitudes have been a familiar feature of British public opinion, and an occasional feature in electoral contests. This 'race card' could be mobilised by politicians willing to exploit it to electoral advantage, with little obvious short-term cost—as their counterparts in the United States, Australia and continental Europe have done. As a consequence, there is a widely held assumption that governments have only limited scope to engage the public in rational debate on future options—an assumption his essay sets out to challenge.

To play the race card effectively, a significant majority must be anti-immigration, voters must be convinced that one of the major parties is aligned to their preferred position, and the issue must have high electoral saliency— voters must be willing to use it to reward or punish parties. Whereas this was the case in the UK in the 1970s, and has been elsewhere since (notably in the last Australian general election), Saggar shows that attitudes towards immigration in the UK have become more nuanced. The public now draw a distinction between labour migrants whose skills or labour are needed, and asylum seekers who are seen as a problem but also, where genuine, as deserving of protection. Moreover, voters are split on which party they think most likely to be effective. The asylum issue has not had sufficient saliency to be a determining electoral issue, although it could help shape political preferences.

Political attitudes are not merely the outcome of an individual's underlying beliefs but shaped by events, the media and—echoing Statham's evidence— by political leaders themselves. Saggar shows that public hostility or tolerance to immigrants mirrors attitudes towards other unpopular groups. There is a hard core of prejudice among a small minority (around 16 per cent), and a larger minority (some 36 per cent) do not feel hostile towards any particular group. Significantly, the greater the level of pluralism in an area and thus of the contact the public have had with minorities, the greater the level of acceptance.

It is the rising numbers of asylum seekers that have fuelled intolerance in the UK, while concern about former cohorts of migrants from the Commonwealth has slipped significantly down the agenda, with many now saying that that immigration had benefited the country. The young, women, the better-educated, Labour voters and those living in the south are most likely to take a positive view.

Significantly, the evidence underlines the importance the public attach to maintaining control of immigration and to transparency. Saggar concludes that, if governments can demonstrate both that they are managing migration and that they are willing to be transparent on the options, far right forces 'are toxic yet containable'. He calls in aid the arguments George Bush Jr used (pre 9/11) to convince those in his party hostile to immigration that such a position was contrary to American tradition, anti-business and not as electorally popular as they claimed. In contrast, the UK Conservatives, while not opposing Labour's move to open up labour migration, have not championed it—reflecting the legacy of Powellism and the dominance of social and cultural concerns about immigration over the economic benefits.

Given the inherent difficulty in managing migration, it is no longer an 'electoral albatross simply and solely for the left'. Immigration matters as an issue, but it matters above all else because of what it says about a party's ability to deliver. Governments must thus both convince the voters of their competence in managing migration, but also seek to shift public attitudes towards greater acceptance of the benefits of immigration, rather than the costs.

If the public are to accept migrants, they must come to terms with diversity, and be confident that migrants will respect the values that they hold most dear. Along with the acknowledgement that migration must be managed is the belated recognition that identity and the accommodation of difference must themselves be managed as part of a two-way integration process.

In the final essay, on citizenship, **Will Kymlicka**'s starting point is that most Western democracies are having to reconsider their approach to citizenship in response to the challenges raised by migration—not least because migrants now often also retain strong links to their countries of origin. While there are those who see the concept of national citizenship as increasingly obsolete, most perceive the need for states to revalue the rules and rhetoric of citizenship to promote common values and solidarity.

Current British reforms fall squarely in this category, with promotion of the English language, citizenship classes and ceremonies introduced as means of strengthening integration and social cohesion. Kymlicka sets out to explain why this move has been so contentious in the UK when very similar policies have long been accepted in North America. His argument is that it reflects the way in which citizenship policy is perceived in relation to those countries' policies on immigration on the one hand, and multiculturalism on the other.

Citizenship classes and ceremonies are uncontroversial in Canada because the requirements for naturalisation are not onerous; new citizens are not expected to renounce their previous identity or loyalty, and the legal status of non-citizens provides security and carries no stigma. It is accepted that access to citizenship helps Canada compete for the immigrant workers it needs. Moreover, there is a positive expectation that immigrants who become citizens will put down roots and make a greater economic and social contribution. In contrast to some European states, citizenship policy is thus seen as a mid-point in the integration process, not as the end goal.

Comparing the Canadian position to that in the UK, Kymlicka shows that many of the same conditions apply. The new citizenship test, for instance, will not be onerous and immigrants will be supported in preparation for it. The difference, which explains the controversy, lies in the context. Britain's colonial past means that some immigrants resent the implication that they need to be resocialised into a British culture that is already part of their heritage. Moreover, where the UK once had an open citizenship policy, the trajectory of policy has been to narrow entitlement, and the closing of the door was not seen as race neutral.

Finally, whereas Canada has a strong public commitment to multicultur-alism, built into its constitution and with broad public support, the UK government has always been more equivocal ('death by a thousand qualifica-tions'). People do not view citizenship policies in isolation but in the light of broader trends on the acceptance of newcomers and of diversity. So we need to see immigration, citizenship and multiculturalism as a 'three-legged stool'. Where one leg is weak, the public worry about the motives and consequences of the other two. Conversely, confidence in one leg can help build trust in another. If the UK is to secure a strong public consensus on citizenship policy, it will therefore need to develop a stronger consensus on managed migration and on multiculturalism.

Answering the sceptics

How, then, might one answer critics in the UK who say the pace of change is too fast, the number of immigrants too high, and that the threat this poses to our national culture, and the competition for resources to which it gives rise, could lead to conflict?[6]

First, we do not dismiss such concerns as motivated by prejudice. While their analysis may be misused by extremists, it can reflect genuine public concerns that need to be answered. Migration can indeed create conflicts of interest over jobs and services, and highlight differing views on acceptable behaviour. Much of this book is about how we manage and resolve those tensions; we should not pretend they do not exist. But the debate is not assisted by setting up straw men—insisting, for instance, that the UK does not need 'mass immigration' when no one is suggesting it does.[7] The record number of work permits issued in 2002, for instance—170,000—is a drop in the ocean (0.6 per cent) in a workforce of 29 million. The sometimes alarmist tone of writing on migration can, moreover, reflect a misunderstanding both about the nature of the society to which migrants come, and about the migrants themselves.

To take the UK as our example, it is mistaken, first, to portray it as having a static, monolithic and unified national culture with a common sense of identity, to which migrant diversity poses a threat. Britain has, as Jeremy Paxman wrote in his book on the English,[8] been a 'ragout' of people and cultures for a thousand years (in which context it is, incidentally, difficult to understand the criticism of the government's assertion that 'Britain has always been a nation of immigrants' as 'demonstrably false').[9] Long before postwar migration added new dimensions to the *mélange*, the UK already embodied diverse and evolving regional, religious, ethnic and gender identities. As Bob Rowthorn acknowledged in a *Prospect* essay, deciding who belongs to the 'native population' of Britain is not easy, but it is precisely because of the country's long history of migration that we cannot, as he suggests, 'define as a native any inhabitant of Britain who is neither a post-war immigrant nor the descendant of such a person'.[10] On that arbitrary definition, the Jewish refugees who arrived during the war are 'native' but the displaced east Europeans who arrived in 1946 are not. Britain's population cannot be divided into insiders and outsiders in that way.

Critics also place considerable emphasis on numbers. Immigration on a 'modest scale' is acceptable, even beneficial, but 'too many' is a problem. This is a misunderstanding. It is not the numbers per se that are relevant, but the context. Where there are plentiful jobs, services are not overstretched and the population is familiar with diversity, migration is not a contentious local issue. It is striking, as Saggar demonstrates, that the public is least concerned about migration in those areas that are already the most diverse, and most concerned in those areas where there are few minorities living: that is, there is an *inverse* correlation between numbers and public concern. The exception is where there is a localised concentration, not of migrants per se but of that particular category of migrant who are both not allowed to work, and thus not seen to contribute, while having significant welfare needs: asylum seekers. Thus we cannot say that a continuation of net migration to the UK of around 172,000 per annum is either too many or too few:[11] it will depend on the socio-economic conditions into which they arrive, and how well their entry and integration are managed. The notion that, regardless of these conditions, the UK is nevertheless 'full up' falls when we recall the recent plea from the Scottish Executive for more immigration to Scotland because its declining population, over three decades, is jeopardising economic growth.[12]

In some of the critiques of migration policy there is an underlying sense that it is not numbers per se that are the problem, but ethnicity. The unspoken fear is not that the proportion of the population who are foreign-born, but that of ethnic minorities, will rise in coming years. The rare occasions when public disorder divides on ethnic lines are highlighted—not the daily experience of positive social interaction between colleagues, friends and family across communities; nor the vast economic, professional, social, civic and cultural contribution that individuals from ethnic minorities make as equal citizens. Practices such as genital mutilation and forced marriages are seen as evidence that ethnic cultures are incompatible with liberal values, ignoring the daily reality of compatible coexistence in which sharply conflicting values are the exception, not the norm. What does matter is that there is sufficient common ground among the population as a whole to ensure social cohesion, to which initiatives promoting integration and citizenship contribute.

There can, finally, be an underlying assumption that, if only we can secure agreement that there are 'too many', we can curtail immigration to the number, and hence rate of social change, that we want. Yet all of the evidence demonstrates that, while we can channel and modify migration, numbers cannot be determined with precision. The essays in this volume explain the many reasons why. Hence we should not conduct debate on the basis of a false premise; nor should governments promise to the public what they cannot deliver.

Looking ahead to a managed migration agenda

The contributors to this book differ in the solutions they put forward. But all emphasise the need to manage migration more effectively, to reap the economic, social and cultural opportunities it offers while limiting its costs. Recognising and reconciling the tensions and tradeoffs is a constant theme. The following proposals on how we might do that, informed by those put forward in these essays, are my own.

First, migration is no longer, if it ever was, simply a matter of enforcement. Migration has significant economic and social impacts—touching multiple areas of government policy from international development through to health, education and social cohesion. Governance arrangements are thus needed that bring migration into mainstream planning across policy domains. Stakeholders, including those at devolved and local levels, need to be given a voice in future migration policy and commensurate responsibility for delivering it.

At EU level, this could mean greater use of the 'open method of coordination' which promotes cooperation among, but does not bind, member states, along with joint working between the European Commission directorates responsible for migration, foreign and development policy, employment and social affairs. In the UK, it could mean a Public Service Agreement target shared across departments; or consideration of a Department of Migration and Citizenship—as in Canada—that could potentially embrace cohesion, equality and human rights issues, while providing a means of coordination with departments, like health and education, responsible for essential services.

Second, governments need to invest in robust migration management systems, and evaluate their effectiveness in delivery, refining their policy levers to maximise results. First priority in the UK would be investment in the asylum determination system to provide well-founded, faster and fairer decisions in which both government and migrant advocates have confidence, so that the huge incentive the current system provides to make unfounded applications is removed.

Third, governments need to provide sufficient legal channels for migration to undercut the people smugglers. This is not to say that we need to allow employers to have free access to global labour markets, nor any prospective worker to enter. But the potent combination of labour shortages, a willing supply of migrants and few legal entry routes will inevitably lead migrants to come, or stay, without permission.

Governments should give priority to enhancing the employability of their existing workforce, but allow migrants to fill the gaps. In devising schemes and safeguards, governments can look abroad for ideas and good practice. But no scheme is transferable, in its entirety, to a different setting. The least-cost option is to create schemes only for the highly skilled, whose adaptability is high and need for services low. But it is vacancies for low-skilled labour that are drawing in irregular workers; and increasing the participation rates of women can in practice require migrants to take their place as carers. We need a level of access for the low-skilled too.

We should consider whether migrants should be able to apply for work permits when already in the country, so that the potential asylum applicant who is not actually in need of protection can choose that more appropriate route. This should not act as an incentive to enter illegally if the applicant's chance of getting a work permit is as good or better if they apply abroad. Even some of those whose current status is irregular should have the option of 'earned legalisation', recognising that it is not realistic to assume that all those in Europe without permission will or could be deported. While enforcement is an essential part of a managed migration system, governments should avoid controls that would be counterproductive, such as those at gateways to essential medical services and schools.

Fourth, governments need to engage source countries as partners in optimising the benefits of legal migration, for both sides, and in curbing illegality. But this means making cooperation worthwhile. Incentives in most cases are likely to be more effective than sanctions.

Fifth, governments need to harness their critics—in the market and in civil society—to devise solutions and become partners in delivery. Employers could take some responsibility for induction of workers and their accommodation. Voluntary organisations are under-utilised as a resource for meeting migrants' needs, while equally denied a voice in policy deliberation. Churches, unions, community groups—all could play a part.

Tensions over migrants' access to public services and benefits cannot be resolved without a fundamental rethinking of the rationale for providing—or denying—services to different categories of people. Should entitlement reflect immigration status, length of stay in the country, level of need or, as now in some cases, the existence of a reciprocal arrangement with their country of origin? Should public policy take into account the interests of the wider society—protection of public health, for instance, or social cohesion; the impact on the public purse; or the wish to deter future migrants from coming to the UK? Whom do we want to include within our 'community of legitimate receivers', as Geddes puts it; in essence, to whom do our social justice principles apply?[13]

Sixth, governments, employers and civil society must invest in integration. It cannot be left to chance. New arrivals need information on their rights, and on their responsibilities. Assistance in securing language skills and access to jobs may require investment upfront but will be repaid in self-sufficiency, social integration and public acceptance. Integration strategies must be directed not at foreigners *or* at ethnic minorities, but at all those facing barriers to inclusion and acceptance; with particular attention to Muslim communities, for whom the new EU-inspired provisions to combat religious discrimination in employment will be one step forward, if implemented effectively. Firmly endorsing the value of multiculturalism, and promoting a broader human rights culture, would both encourage respect for difference and provide a common framework of values within which we can negotiate our future together.

Finally, governments must be truthful with the public, explaining—in a proactive and consistent exercise in communication—the rationale for managed migration, including the values that underpin the protection of refugees and allowing families to live together. They should be open about the benefits and the costs, and realistic about the limitations of what can be delivered. As Lloyd argues, the two views of migrants—the negative and the positive— produce parallel discourses in Europe which rarely engage. Politicians must attempt to bridge that chasm, to secure a consensus that migration is here to stay and must be well managed, within which we can discuss together how this can be achieved.

Politicians must tread the fine line between acknowledging the public's fears and reinforcing their prejudices much more carefully than some do now. Rather than suggesting that migration policy is a tightrope walk in which one false move could lead to disaster, governments must try new initiatives and give citizens the confidence that the risks are not life-threatening, and are worth taking. The states that have not faced a crisis over immigration are those where the public are confident that their governments have the capacity to resolve whatever difficulties arise.

In this, the greatest challenge may be how to explain the tradeoffs. Kymlicka criticises the current British government for presenting labour immigration not as a policy which outweighs the costs but as a policy in which there are no costs. The public will not buy that. But it will require skill to disentangle the real costs from unfounded prejudices, a task in which much of the media will be of no service. The goal, as Papademetriou says, cannot be perfection because that cannot be achieved. The result of a successful managed migration programme will still mean living with imperfection, and managing uncertainty. But channelling migration is a more realistic course than denying its existence or seeking total control. Yet this approach is more than a pragmatic response to the inevitable. It offers the real prospect of harnessing the diverse, positive contribution that migrants can make to Europe's future in a way that builds public confidence, while preserving human rights and social justice principles. Creating the political middle ground in which it is possible to pursue a reasoned debate on these terms is the first challenge for political leaders at the European, national and local levels.

Notes

1 Census data April 2001 on www.statistics.gov.uk.
2 The case for this approach in the UK was first made, in a different economic and political climate, by the Institute for Public Policy Research in S. Spencer, *Strangers and Citizens: A Positive Approach to Migrants and Refugees*, London, Rivers Oram/ IPPR, 1994.
3 Home Office, *Secure Borders, Safe Haven: Integration with Diversity in Modern Britain*, Cm 5387, London, Home Office, 2002.
4 European Commission, *Communication from the Commission on Immigration, Integration and Employment*, COM(2003)336 Final. See also A. Rudiger and S. Spencer, 'Meeting the Challenge: Equality, Diversity and Cohesion in the European Union', paper presented to European Commission/OECD conference on 'Economic and Social Aspects of Migration', Brussels, 21–22 Jan. 2003.
5 To that end it set up the Athens Migration Policy initiative. See www.migrationpolicy.org/AMPI.
6 See e.g. Bob Rowthorn, 'Migration Limits', *Prospect*, Feb. 2003.
7 Anthony Browne, *Do We Need Mass Immigration?*, London, Civitas, 2002.
8 J. Paxman, *The English: A Portrait of a People*, London, Penguin, 1998.
9 D. Coleman, 'Demographic, Economic and Social Consequences of UK Migration', in M. Azurmendi et al., *Work in Progress: Migration, Integration and the European Labour Market*, London, Civitas, 2003.
10 Rowthorn, 'Migration Limits'.
11 See website of National Statistics Online, http://www.statistics.gov.uk/cci/ nugget.asp?id=260. In 2001, 480,000 people arrived in the UK to live for at least a year; 308,000 left to live elsewhere.
12 Scotland's First Minister, Jack McConnell, reported in *The Times*, 25 Feb. 2003; *Guardian*, 26 Feb. 2003.
13 See also S. Spencer, *Migrants, Refugees and the Boundaries of Citizenship*, London, IPPR, 1995.

Migration to Europe since 1945: Its History and its Lessons

RANDALL HANSEN

WHEN vast swathes of Europe were rubble, and the United Kingdom teetered on the verge of bankruptcy, few expected that the largely white and ethnically cleansed old world would emerge thirty years later as a multi-ethnic continent. The history of migration to Europe is one of unforeseen developments and unintended consequences. This was true of labour migration, of colonial migration and, most recently, of asylum-related migration. Adopting a broad—probably too broad—postwar historical sweep, this essay reviews past patterns of migration to Europe and tentatively draws a number of lessons from these experiences. It refers in particular to the experience of France, the United Kingdom and the Federal Republic of Germany.

The legal frameworks through which the postwar migration occurred were varied, but they can be grouped in two: colonial migration regimes and 'temporary' guest-worker policies. Migrants passed through these two streams for one reason: to satisfy labour shortages created by a booming European economy. The story of migration up to the early 1970s is one of economic shortages interacting with prewar colonial migration and citizenship laws in the UK, France, the Netherlands and Belgium, and with postwar guest-worker policies in Austria, Switzerland, Germany, Belgium, the Netherlands, France, Denmark and Sweden.

Labour migration 1: guest-worker policies

After the 1948 currency reform the German economy began to recover, and recover quickly. By the mid-1950s, Germany and the rest of continental Europe had a level of demand for labour that could no longer be satisfied domestically (or, in Germany, by expellees from eastern Europe). In a pattern common to most continental European countries, Germany looked first to southern Europe (believing that such migrants could be assimilated more readily into the labour market), later to Turkey and finally to North Africa. The German government negotiated guest-worker schemes with Italy (1955), Greece and Spain (1960), Turkey (1961), Morocco (1963), Portugal (1964), Tunisia (1965) and Yugoslavia (1968). In 1964, an apparently bemused worker identified as Germany's one-millionth *Gastarbeiter* was given a motorcycle; a decade later, he was one of over two million.

German trade unions—which often privilege those in work to the detriment of those out of it—were highly suspicious of guest-worker migration, fearing that it would lead to downward pressure on wages. The German government

© The Political Quarterly Publishing Co. Ltd. 2003
Published by Blackwell Publishing Ltd, 9600 Garsington Road, Oxford OX4 2DQ, UK and 350 Main Street, Malden, MA 02148, USA

appeased them by guaranteeing the guest workers the same basic conditions as their German counterparts, and the former were integrated into the unions. The basic idea behind the guest-worker schemes was simple: the workers would remain so long as there were jobs for them, and they would return home once the economy soured. When Germany experienced its first recession in 1967, the policy appeared to work: large numbers of guest workers returned home, knowing that they could come back when the labour market picked up again.

By the early 1970s, however, numbers were rising in the context of a slowing economy, and the SPD–FDP government responded by issuing a migration stop in 1973. Among its other consequences, this had the unintended effect of locking in Germany's foreign population. In the absence of a guarantee of easy return to Germany, most guest workers did not opt for repatriation. They stayed in Germany and, with the aid of churches, NGOs and sympathetic academic activists, secured a number of legal judgments that guaranteed their right to remain. Austria, Belgium, Switzerland, Sweden, Denmark, the Netherlands and France adopted variants of this guest-worker scheme. After 1973, all countries ended or sharply reduced labour migration.

Labour migration II: colonial migration regimes

In countries without a colonial history, bilateral guest-worker agreements were the only source of migrant labour. Europe's former colonial powers—the UK, France, Belgium, and the Netherlands—were, by contrast, able to draw on a vast supply of unskilled workers. Some scholars of migration have maintained that European policy-makers deliberately sought to tap the reservoir of colonial labour to feed the postwar boom; this is a misunderstanding. It was rather the case that an inability to secure workers (especially white workers) from Europe meant that policy-makers had little choice but to rely on (or, which was more often the case, to tolerate) colonial migrants. The United Kingdom and France present the clearest examples of this trend, but it can also be found in the Netherlands and Belgium.

After the war, the UK briefly tried its own version of the guest-worker schemes, bringing in workers from eastern Europe. The Iron Curtain put paid to this effort, and the sluggishness of the British economy soon meant that France, Germany, Switzerland and Austria were more attractive destinations for migrants from southern Europe. Nevertheless, in the 1950s, the UK may have lacked the German and Swiss economic buoyancy or the French cultural affinity with southern Europe, but it had a citizenship regime encompassing some 600 million colonial subjects.

In 1948, for reasons unrelated to migration,[1] the British government had adopted legislation that transformed all colonial British subjects into citizens of the United Kingdom and Colonies, confirming their right to enter the UK and to enjoy all social, political and economic rights. From the early to mid-1950s, the British economy, though unstable, delivered full employment and labour shortages resulted. Following classic 'pull' incentives, first West Indians, then Indians and Pakistanis, began to migrate to the UK. When restrictive legislation was first introduced in 1962, some 500,000 non-white migrants had entered the UK; a decade later, when the government curtailed the migration privileges attached to UK citizenship, the figure was closer to a million.

France's experience was in some ways similar, although Algeria was legally not a colony but (in the oft-repeated phrase) an integral part of France. In the 1950s, France sought to avoid recourse to migrants from Algeria and the rest of North Africa by having the National Office of Immigration (ONI) set up bureaus exclusively in southern Europe. German/Swiss competition and sustained economic growth soon rendered this supply inadequate. Algerians exercised their right to enter in ever larger numbers (especially in the run-up to Algerian independence) and, from the 1960s, French companies looked to Algeria, and to Morocco and Tunisia as well. In contrast with the tightly regulated system in Germany, Switzerland and Austria, the common practice in France was for companies to hire colonial migrants directly and to regularise their status later through the ONI.

Family reunification

As another indication of how similar the postwar migration experience has been across Europe, all countries ended (or all but ended) primary migration in the early 1970s. The UK acted first in 1971, France and Germany followed in 1972 and 1973, and everyone else did the same within a year or two. By then, however, the deed was done. Colonial migrants had entered in the main as citizens, and as such claimed a right to family reunification. For the others, governments attempted to limit family reunification, and even to encourage repatriation, but all such efforts failed.

There is a debate within the literature about the source of migrants' security, but the most convincing explanations hold that domestic courts, on the basis of domestic constitutions, blocked state efforts to limit family reunification.[2] As a result, in admitting young men in the 1950s and 1960s, European states committed themselves to admitting wives, children and sometimes grandparents later. At the same time, in the short to medium term, migrants almost always have a higher birth rate than the indigenous population. The result, for every nation in Europe, was the emergence of multicultural, multilingual societies.

The politics of immigration

In France and Germany, the first two decades of immigration were relatively uncontentious. A strong economy and full employment meant that indigenous workers did not feel especially threatened by the new arrivals. In many cases, the new workers took jobs that no French or German national wanted anyway, and when they did obtain better-paid industrial jobs the unions ensured that the terms were equal to those offered to domestic workers.

Altruism was not the motivation: ensuring equality of wages and conditions prevented migrants from acting—as they do in the United States—as wage depressors. Above all, Germany throughout the period, and France until the late 1950s, could harbour the illusion that migrants were temporary, and that they would politely return to their countries of origin if and when the boom ended. To be sure, migrants to both countries faced discrimination in housing and in daily life, but their arrival was for the most part not a national political issue.

Perhaps because Britain could harbour no such myth, immigration became politicised much earlier in the United Kingdom. In the 1950s, Labour—motivated by imperial guilt and optimistic internationalism—was largely in favour of colonial migration. The Conservative Party, in power throughout the decade, was much more divided, but a sort of pro-migration deadlock emerged: the imperialist right was unwilling to exclude Canadians, Australians and New Zealanders, while the moderates were unwilling to exclude solely non-white colonial migrants.[3]

The TUC equivocated on the issue, but ultimately decided that its commitment to the international worker took precedence over workers' concerns about foreign labour. Partly because of its limited ability to enforce its policies, there was widespread discrimination on the shop floor, and the closed shop was used to lock black migrants out of certain trades. No one asked the public what it thought until 1958, but the festooning of London hotels with 'No Coloureds' signs suggested a less than enthusiastic welcome.

This elite consensus was shattered in 1958. In the late summer, a group of white thugs in Notting Hill, London, and in Nottingham went on 'nigger hunts', attacking West Indians with knives and broken bottles. No one was killed, but the 'race riots' shocked the public; from then on, immigration and race were high politics. Public opinion polls taken shortly after the riots indicated strong majority support for immigration control, and MPs in constituencies with a high concentration of migrants lobbied publicly for it. The government itself remained divided—the Minister for Labour was strongly in favour of controls, the Colonial Secretary against—but an increase in arrivals after 1959 eventually carried the argument. In 1962, the Commonwealth Immigrants Act ended the open-door policy towards the Commonwealth.

The new controls did not end the debate on immigration; if anything, they relaunched it. In the 1960s immigration became the source of bitter national debate, often punctuated by the sudden arrival of significant numbers of migrants following a decolonisation crisis. Opponents of immigration in the Conservative Party and the press made liberal use of the aquatic metaphors associated with migration—waves, floods, swamping—and from 1964 to 1972 migration politics in the UK reached their nadir.

In 1964, in the midlands constituency of Smethwick, a Tory challenger unseated a prominent Labour MP, Patrick Gordon Walker, through a shameless appeal to racism. He offered an apologist interpretation of the slogan 'If you want a nigger for your neighbour, vote Liberal or Labour,' and painted nightmare scenarios of an immigrant takeover of the UK. As the hapless Gordon Walker drove off after conceding defeat, Conservative supporters jeered at him: 'Where are your niggers now, Walker?'

A few years later, a conservative Shadow Cabinet member and leading Tory intellectual, Enoch Powell, threw a match onto the tinderbox. In an infamous 1968 speech, he told the story of an elderly English lady who suffered the taunts of grinning immigrants, saw excrement pushed through her door and feared to leave her house. Filled with much 'foreboding', Powell saw the 'River Tiber flowing with much blood', a prediction of interracial violence.

This speech, by a cultured student of classics and modern languages with no obvious connection to the man on the Clapham omnibus, galvanised working-class support: Conservative Central Office was flooded with letters backing Powell, and thousands of workers marched through London in his defence. Edward Heath sacked him, but this only gave Powell the freedom to launch an impassioned, and at times demonic, campaign against immigration. Throughout the 1970s immigration crises repeatedly flared up; the National Front enjoyed some local electoral successes (but no national ones), and immigration was only removed from national politics in 1979. The issue stayed away until the 1990s, when asylum applications brought it back with a vengeance.

In France and Germany, immigration became politicised only later, when it became clear to both countries, and especially Germany, that migrants were there to stay. In France, the issues were first local—appalling housing conditions for North Africans, local mayors' opposition to immigration, specious arguments about a 'threshold of tolerance' pegged at a certain percentage of migrants—but they later became national. They did so for one reason: the Front National. In the early 1980s, the Front secured a derisory result—less than a single percentage point—in national elections. By 1988 its support had reached 15 per cent, and its indefatigable leader, Jean Marie Le Pen, scored 17 per cent in the 2002 presidential elections. Divisions among the left meant that the far-right party knocked the socialists out, and Le Pen went on to the second ballot.

The sources of his support are too varied to be fully covered here, but the major parties themselves have played a role in the Front's rise, or at least its consolidation. The Socialists did so in part by retreating, after 1983, from their radical heritage and by embracing a neo-liberal macroeconomic policy. With the Communists out of government and mired in decline, the Front constituted the only radical alternative in national politics. The point is often exaggerated, but a substantial portion of Front National support comes from disaffected Communists. More importantly, Mitterrand encouraged the introduction of proportional representation (PR) for the 1986 legislative elections in order to divide the right, but thereby ensured Front National representation in the National Assembly.

Although PR lasted for only two years, it is likely that holding parliamentary seats helped the Front to stabilise its support at around 15 per cent. For its part, the centre-right (Gaullists, UDF) attempted to siphon off Front National support by itself politicising immigration and nationality. It adopted a series of restrictive immigration measures and more rigorously enforced existing regulations (notably the French equivalent of stop-and-search, especially of North Africans). Following a somewhat tortured debate about what it meant to be French, in 1993 the centre-right coalition passed a restrictive nationality law that ended the automatic acquisition by foreigners born in France of French citizenship at the age of majority. These measures did nothing to undermine Front National support; if anything, they conceded part of the Front's argument.

In Germany, a different sort of dynamic has shaped immigration politics. Even more than in France, the debate about immigration has been a debate about citizenship. Germany allowed itself to believe for longer than did France or (especially) the UK that guest workers would one day return home. Once it became clear that they would remain, Germany's citizenship law, founded almost exclusively on ethnicity, became untenable. The debate on immigration—like the debate about everything else in Germany—was and is shaped by the country's history.

Germany's (pre-1989) uncertain borders, the 16 million East Germans held hostage by the GDR, and the still substantial number of ethnic Germans facing discrimination in eastern Europe all argued in favour of a descent-based citizenship. Ethnic citizenship was also supported by an unholy alliance between the right, which opposed the integration of migrants except under the most stringent of terms, and the left, which saw in any attempt to integrate migrants a new form of *Zwangsgermanisierung*, the National Socialist policy of 'forced Germanisation'. At the same time, the CSU (Christian Social Union), partly because it takes a particularly robust view of German citizenship, and partly to prevent the far right from making any inroads into Bavaria, consistently blocked nationality reforms from within the centre-right. As the Germans fought each other about what it meant to be German, the non-Germans—Turks, Yugoslavs and others—were excluded from the debate, from full acceptance by Germans and from political citizenship.

The deadlock was overcome only in the early 1990s. The fall of the Iron Curtain was followed by German unification, a final settling of the border question—and an explosion in asylum applications (many from Yugoslavia), reaching 438,000 in 1992. Germany's processing machinery was overwhelmed, and in Hamburg there were literally accommodation centres floating on the Elbe. At the same time, a series of brutal attacks on asylum seekers and other foreigners horrified Germans, and created unwarranted fears of a return to the violence and instability of the Weimar period.

The CDU/CSU (especially the latter) wanted to restrict asylum; the FDP, SPD, Greens (and a few CDU members) wanted to reform citizenship. As asylum was a constitutional right, cross-party agreement was needed to make any change in the law. The left agreed to restrictive asylum measures in return for more liberal citizenship provisions. After reforms in 1990 and 1993 failed to increase substantially Germany's naturalisation rate, the left turned to support for dual citizenship. After coming to power in 1998, the SPD–Green administration proposed a highly liberal nationality law including full acceptance of dual citizenship.

The CSU, however, now saw its chance, and it spearheaded a campaign against dual citizenship that helped to tear the heart out of the Schröder government's nationality reform. The campaign garnered something like 5 million signatures, and helped bring the CDU to power in 'Red Hessen', thus robbing Schröder of a majority in the upper house of parliament. Although its tone has moderated somewhat lately, the CSU remains a significant impediment to a reformed nationality law and immigration policy. It is the first voice raised to warn of the dangers of multiculturalism, or to seize on some especially heinous crime committed by a foreigner resident in Germany.

In sum, by 1980, the labour shortages of the 1950s and 1960s had led— through guest-worker schemes and/or colonial migration and citizenship regimes—to a core of non-white settlement in Europe. Family reunification and higher birth rates locked this population in and expanded upon it, and the result in Europe is a non-white citizenry/permanently resident population of some 10 per cent. In Britain, France and Germany alike, immigration was transformed from a non-issue or a local matter to a national issue, often when an individual politician or party sought to make it one. In the UK, immigration occurred through the mechanism of citizenship; in France and especially Germany, the politics of immigration became bound up with the politics of citizenship. Finally, in all three countries, immigration occurred against the wishes of the public. All hard measures to foster immigration, and quite a few soft ones, have attracted majority opposition.[4]

Permanent migration and public opinion

In this abbreviated history lie a number of observations relevant to immigration. The first is that temporary immigration will almost assuredly become permanent. This is as true for asylum seekers at is for 'guest workers'. Politicians should not—as they have at times in all three countries examined here—give the impression that immigration can be turned on and off like a tap, or that migrants will merely resolve labour shortages or do jobs that Europeans do not want to do before going quietly on their way. When we ask for hands, to paraphrase Max Frisch, we get people.

As immigration tends to be permanent, reactions to it must be managed. The default position of public opinion across Europe, and indeed across the West, is anti-immigrant. This opposition is at times rooted in ignorance, prejudice and hysteria; at others, it reflects a more reasonable concern that newcomers will alter the culture of local communities. In both cases, politicians need to recognise and address public fears. If they give the impression—as some pro-migrant academics are wont to do—that all fears of immigration are founded in racism, then the argumentative ground will only be vacated to the benefit of the far right.

At the same time, politicians must be willing to lead public opinion. European publics can at times be persuaded to support immigration, but it requires exceptional events (Kosovan refugees fleeing soldiers burning their houses) or exceptional actions (Edward Heath taking a principled stand in favour of the admission of Ugandan Asians in 1972). If politicians of any party play to anti-immigrant sentiment, then there is little hope of turning European publics towards immigration. The history of immigration to the UK makes it clear that public suspicion can quickly be transformed into loud, ugly opposition if a politician or party lends its support. This is true everywhere in Europe; in the UK, there is the added difficulty of the gutter press, which compares immigrants in generous moments with thieves, in less generous ones with sewage.

Finally, if anti-immigration sentiment is to be countered or at least controlled, politicians must start by stopping: they must end their habit of making promises they cannot keep. When Tony Blair or Jack Straw claims that their government will deport 30,000 failed asylum seekers, they raise expectations that they know—or should know—will be disappointed. If politicians can stop playing to prejudice, they can then take the next step: outlining to the public the case in favour of migration. As the history of the integration of Europe (though not in the UK) shows, governments willing to argue their case can turn sceptical public opinion around, or at least persuade it to give the government the benefit of the doubt.

The integration of Europe's ethnic minorities

As permanent migration to Europe was unexpected and unwanted, integration policies developed belatedly and inadequately. The UK adopted anti-discrimination legislation as early as 1965, but its aims were purely 'negative'—keeping first public then private bodies from discriminating in employment, housing and services. It did little positively to promote the integration of new migrants. The Netherlands, which has the closest thing in Europe to an integration policy, adopted it only in 1981; in France and Germany, integration measures are piecemeal and often left to localities and/or intermediate institutions (such as unions and churches).

Perhaps unsurprisingly, the integration of Europe's ethnic minorities has proceeded in a halting and unsatisfactory manner. Migrants and their descendants are poorly represented in national parliaments; they suffer from disproportionately high levels of unemployment; and they thus draw disproportionately on welfare services. The latter points admit of several exceptions (such as the Indian community in the United Kingdom), but there is nonetheless worrying evidence of a racialisation of unemployment across Europe.

In the United Kingdom, the employment rate among whites of working age is 75.1 per cent; the average for black and Asian people is 57 per cent (1998 figures). Within this second category, the rates for Pakistanis and Bangladeshi Britons were 35 per cent and 41 per cent respectively. On a positive note, the average hourly earnings of Indian men and white men in 1988/9 were almost identical (£9.34 for Indian men, £9.29 for white men); they were £1 lower for black men and £1.50 lower for Bangladeshi and Pakistani men.

In Germany, the picture is equally bleak. In the year 2000, the unemployment rate among foreigners, at 16.4 per cent, was double that of the national population at 8.8 per cent.[5] Low educational levels and a poor grasp of German are contributing factors. Looking at a particular severe case, a study of the Berlin district of Wedding (which contains a large foreign population) showed that 75 per cent of the children required additional German-language instruction to compete at a primary level, and 40 per cent needed intensive German-language lessons. While many German students were found in the first groups, foreign children dominated the latter. In France, a strong aversion (based on the Vichy experience) against ethnic monitoring makes it extremely difficult to know with certainty, but anecdotal evidence from Paris's northern suburbs and the south of the country suggests a much higher unemployment rate among France's North African communities.

These unemployment levels exist among communities that have lived in Europe for some time. The chances that more recent migrants, including refugees, will integrate into the labour market remain lower still. In part (but only in part) because European policy-makers restrict asylum seekers' access to the labour market, the costs of their housing and support fall almost entirely to the taxpayer. Figures are disputed, but it is estimated that in the United Kingdom alone, asylum-seeker support in 2000 cost £835 million, or £34 per UK household.[6] Once processing is added, the total bill comes to almost £2 billion per annum.[7] Although most studies confirm that migrants make a net economic contribution to the economy, these figures are worrisome.

Europe's experience with immigration has been an unhappy one in part because the entry of immigrants was, until the 1970s, largely market determined. The state's role has been limited to (often heavy-handed) control, largely negative forms of integration policy (anti-discrimination legislation in France, the UK and the Netherlands),[8] and mass legalisation programmes (Italy). The result was that the market chose low-skilled immigrants who found themselves disproportionately penalised by the restructuring of the

European economy after the oil crises of the 1970s. Migration patterns in the 1950s, 1960s and 1970s make it clear that immigration policy needs to ensure a greater integration of future immigration streams and domestic labour markets.

Priority for skilled workers

Part of this effort would involve placing an emphasis on skilled migration, and both Germany and the UK have taken steps in this direction. Britain has adopted a more liberal attitude to work permits for the high-skilled, and policy-makers are debating (though they have been debating for some time) a complete overhaul of the 1971 immigration legislation. Germany in 2000 launched a 'green card' programme for 20,000 high-skilled workers, and an ambitious immigration law fell in late 2002 for procedural reasons.

When privileging skilled immigrants, governments should not—as they have done in the past—place the emphasis on matching particular jobs with particular people. They should rather ensure that workers have the skills that make them flexible and adaptable, so that they may find other work if economic change eliminates the jobs for which they came. The higher ethnic minority unemployment rate in France, Germany and Britain in part reflects the fact that these people arrived to fill particular positions in the early postwar years but were unable to cope with the economic restructuring that followed the oil shocks.

Europe should also—and Germany is particularly guilty in this respect—adopt a more liberal attitude towards foreign higher education qualifications. A trip through migrant communities in London, Frankfurt or Paris will find trained doctors driving buses and engineers sweeping floors. This sort of brain waste is both demoralising for the individuals themselves and maso-chistic for the European economy. There are no doubt gaps between Euro-pean degrees and (some) non-European ones, but to allow the professions to use a white-collar version of the closed shop to lock out fully trained foreigners is in no one's interest.

As part of this emphasis on skilled migration, Europe should open the immigration door fully to the developed world. Nothing more than a misguided liberal sentimentality justifies the claim that a young American accountant seeking to work in London, or a Québécois journalist with an eye on a career in Paris, presents the same immigration problem as an impover-ished peasant from Vietnam or an unskilled worker from Russia. Yet such a claim underpins all European immigration regimes.

Language acquisition

A related policy shift would involve a clearer emphasis on language and language acquisition. Evidence from all countries of immigration makes it

© The Political Quarterly Publishing Co. Ltd. 2003

clear that mastery of the national language(s) is fundamental to economic success, especially in the service sector. European policy-makers must ensure that new migrants have or can quickly acquire it.

There are several ways to do this. In the case of family reunification, policy-makers should encourage new migrants to bring their spouses and children and to integrate their children into local schools as quickly as possible, as young children have the greatest hope of becoming bilingual. They should thus replace work permits with immigration schemes for long-term settlement, pure and simple. If migrants are unsure whether they will be able to remain after four or five years (which is now the case in Germany and Britain), they will be more reluctant to bring spouses and children and more tempted to place the latter in international schools.

In every case, all efforts should be directed at ensuring that migrant children master the language quickly and succeed in school. This would involve both positive measures (providing easy access to language training) and negative ones (preventing an excessively high concentration of non-native language speakers in particular schools). European policy-makers should above all avoid the madness—supported in the past by some German *Länder*—of allowing or encouraging migrant children to be educated in their native language. Even bilingual education, depending on what is meant by this term, should be viewed with suspicion.

Asylum

Following labour migration and family migration, the third link in the migration chain is composed of asylum seekers. For much of the postwar period, asylum was a Cold War sideshow. Applications were low, and the majority of the world's refugees came from the Soviet Union and eastern Europe. Accepting rare large-scale outflows (such as from Hungary in 1956) and the occasional Soviet ballet dancer allowed the West to assert, without much financial cost, its moral superiority.

From 1980, numbers began to increase—they passed the 100,000 mark in West Germany in that year—and after 1989 they exploded. Violent conflict, falling transportation costs and the fall of the Berlin Wall all made travel to Europe more attractive and easier. The result was a sharp increase in asylum applications. Between 1989 and 1992 total applications in Europe more than doubled, from 320,000 to 695,000, declining to a still-high 455,000 by the end of the decade. In 1992, almost two-thirds of all applications in Europe were lodged in Germany, which received a still unmatched record of 438,000. The UK, by contrast, in that year received 32,000. By the end of the decade, the UK had overtaken Germany as a destination country, receiving some 100,000 applications.[9]

I shall leave the future of asylum policy to other essays in this volume, but it is worth making one comment on the evolution of asylum policy since 1980. In the past two decades, EC/EU member states and the Community/Union itself have constructed every barrier to asylum consistent with their obligations under the 1951 Geneva Convention relating to the status of refugees (and some that are probably not). Yet, numbers to Europe remain, in most EU countries, at intolerably high levels. At the same time, only the most resourceful—generally the young and male—can make it to Europe's shores, and they are by definition not always the most deserving. The vast majority of the world's refugees are in the South, rotting in refugee camps or suffering internal displacement.

In a shrill and caricature-ridden debate, asylum seekers are seen as either genuine or 'bogus'. Yet there is no clear distinction between desiring freedom and desiring material security. Asylum seekers coming to Europe want a better life, to use an American phrase, but they come in the main, as Jeff Crisp describes elsewhere in this volume, from lands afflicted by political instability and violence. They are fleeing death and destruction and seeking a land of stability and prosperity.

At the same time, postwar and more recent history suggests that the majority of asylum seekers—50–70 per cent—will be denied refugee status but remain in Europe. As they cannot prove an individual well-founded fear of persecution by the state (in France and Germany) and/or by a non-state actor (in the UK), the majority will see their applications turned down. Because deportation is an ineffective tool of immigration control, the majority will nevertheless stay.[10]

Rather than perpetuating a second postwar myth—that asylum seekers, like guest workers before them, will eventually go home—governments should recast policy to accept and take advantage of this permanent migration. Above all, they should seek to channel asylum seekers into the labour market through a mix of carrots (language training, job placement) and sticks (tight controls on entry, and limits on access to welfare).[11]

Conclusion

Three steps in a historical migration chain have brought us to where we are today: the arrival of guest-worker/colonial migrants; the arrival of their families; and the post-1980 (and especially post-1989) surge in asylum seekers. European publics did not want immigration at all; European policy-makers did not expect it to be permanent; and the policies developed to manage it have been reactive and, in terms of integration, less than entirely successful.

This would be disconcerting in itself, but it is doubly so because, as Demetrios Papademetriou explains in this volume, Europe needs immigrants. Whereas the United States has a birth rate at replacement levels (2.2 per cent), Britain, France, Italy, Germany and Spain all have birth rates below the replacement rate and, all things being equal, face an ageing population and probable population decline over the next fifty years. The problem is especially severe in Spain, Italy and Germany (in that order).

In 2000, the UN's Population Division released a report entitled 'Replacement Migration: Is it a Solution to Declining and Ageing Populations?'[12] It provided estimates, based on different scenarios, of how much migration would be required in certain countries to maintain the overall population and its working-age component. To retain its current population of 82 million by the middle of the century, Germany would need to accept 17.8 million net migrants, or 324,000 per year. To maintain the current size of its working-age population, it would need many more: 6,000 migrants per one million inhabitants per year, or approximately 480,000. The latter figures, and possibly the former, are beyond what Germany could absorb. Immigration is thus only a partial solution to the demographic problem, and it will have to be accompanied by an increase in the retirement age and measures to ensure, outside Scandinavia, a higher female employment rate. A partial solution is nonetheless immensely preferable to none at all.

Europe's emergence as a multicultural continent was unforeseen and largely unwanted. It has given Europe's capitals and other large cities an added international flair, and it has undoubtedly enriched European life. There are also many Europeans who appreciate and defend multicultural Europe, though too many of them live in west London or north Oxford rather than the eastern neighbourhoods of either city.

At the same time, however, immigration policy has been poorly thought out, has served short-term economic interests, and has failed to ensure sufficient life-chances for first- and often second- or third-generation migrants. This is regrettable in itself, but it bodes extremely ill in the context of Europe's demographic development. In a post-9/11 world, there is much that stands in the way of a rational policy. Justifiable fears about security, and genuinely held but unjustifiable fears about Muslim migrants' capacity to integrate, may tempt policy-makers into silence or, worse still, anti-immigration rhetoric. Either step is a great mistake. Europe needs immigrants, and the emigration pressures emanating from a poor and overpopulated South—manifested already in asylum applications—mean that it will in all likelihood get them. Europe must develop—collectively if it can, nationally if it must—a proactive, managed immigration policy.

Notes

1 See Randall Hansen, *Citizenship and Immigration in Postwar Britain*, Oxford, Oxford University Press, 2000, ch. 2.
2 See Christian Joppke, 'Why Liberal States Accept Unwanted Immigration', *World Politics*, vol. 50, 1998, pp. 266–93.
3 Hansen, *Citizenship and Immigration in Postwar Britain*, ch. 3.
4 On this, see J. Simon and L. Lynch, 'A Comparative Assessment of Public Opinion toward Immigration and Immigration Policies', *International Migration Review*, vol. 30, no. 2, 1999, pp. 455–67. Even in the United States, only twice in its history has a majority of the public supported more immigration. See Phillip Martin, 'The

Impacts of Immigration on Receiving Countries', in E. Uçarer and D. Puchula, eds, *Immigration into Western Societies*, London, Pinter, 1997, pp. 17–27 at p. 22.

5 R. Süssmuth (chair), *Zuwanderung gestalten, Integration fördern: Bericht der Unabhängigen Kommission Zuwanderung*, Berlin, Ministry of the Interior, 2001, p. 42.

6 http://news.bbc.co.uk/1/hi/uk_politics/1261116.stm (accessed 13 Aug. 2002).

7 http://society.guardian.co.uk/asylumseekers/story/0,7991,727599,00.html (accessed 13 Aug. 2002).

8 See Erik Bleich, *Race Politics in Britain and France*, Cambridge, Cambridge University Press, 2003.

9 Randall Hansen, 'Commentary', in Wayne A. Cornelius, Philip L. Martin and James F. Hollifield, eds, *Controlling Immigration: A Global Perspective*, Stanford, Stanford University Press, 2002.

10 In the latter case, mainly because of limits on deportation. See Matthew J. Gibney and Randall Hansen, http://www.unhcr.org/ (accessed 20 Feb. 2003).

11 On the latter, see Matthew J. Gibney and Randall Hansen, 'Asylum Policy in the West: Past Trends and Future Possibilities', http://www.wider.unu.edu/conference/conference-2002-3/conference2002-3.htm.

12 United Nations Population Division, 'Replacement Migration: Is it a Solution to Declining and Ageing Populations?', March 2000, on website: http://www.un.org/esa/population/publications/migration/migration.htm (accessed 1 June 2002).

© The Political Quarterly Publishing Co. Ltd. 2003

Managing Rapid and Deep Change in the Newest Age of Migration

DEMETRIOS G. PAPADEMETRIOU

AT the dawn of the twenty-first century, international migration touches the lives of more people, and looms larger in the politics and economics of more states, than at any other time in the modern era. With more than 160 million people estimated to be living outside their country of birth, almost no country is untouched by international migration or is immune to its effects. This reality alone guarantees migration's place as a top agenda item in national and international conversations for the foreseeable future.

Recorded human history is dotted with 'ages of migration'. From the Greek colonies and Roman military conquests through the Byzantine and Ottoman empires, and from the European colonisations to the great migrations of the nineteenth and early twentieth centuries, migration has been consequential to civilisations as few other large social phenomena have. Yet, considering that the process is as old as humankind, crucial to human progress, and integral to the rise and decline of organised political entities, it is remarkable that virtually no society seems capable of managing it particularly effectively.

This paradox is explained in part by the fact that large-scale migration, by challenging the receiving society's sense of identity and exposing the weaknesses of its social and economic governance, as well as its capacity to enforce its laws, quickly leads to political contention. Deeply fractured politics, in turn, interfere with the ability of governments to pursue domestic and foreign policies that deal with the phenomenon thoughtfully and, more importantly, to systematic advantage.

When support for immigration collapses (which, historically speaking, occurs with pendulum-like regularity), the duration and depth of a society's engagement with the process does not seem to inoculate it against excessive reactions. This is as close to a 'law' of migration as anyone might posit. And, as with most laws, it seems to hold independently of such factors as the size of immigration's imprint on a society's evolution and economic progress, or the benefits and experience that society has gained from it.

This essay is addressed almost exclusively to policy-makers in the advanced industrial world. As a result, and with regrettable loss in comprehensiveness, it at times papers over issues that are best pursued with a solid grounding in the circumstances and perspectives of the less developed world, whose nationals are migration's protagonists. The essay discusses some of migration's causes, elucidates some of the principal reasons why the issue is difficult to manage well, and speculates about migration's size and most likely evolution over the next two decades.

© The Political Quarterly Publishing Co. Ltd. 2003
Published by Blackwell Publishing Ltd, 9600 Garsington Road, Oxford OX4 2DQ, UK and 350 Main Street, Malden, MA 02148, USA

The essay argues that the conceptual softness of current immigration classifications and administrative practices contributes to a loss of policy focus and coherence. It outlines some of the philosophical and practical issues that policy-makers must understand as they search for more effective interventions. And it makes the case for being more realistic about the capacity to change important and deeply embedded social processes exclusively through tougher domestic regulations, and to do so unilaterally in an increasingly interdependent world.

The essay sets the policy target instead at drawing out the benefits of immigration more systematically, while controlling its most negative consequences. Managing international migration to advantage can be done best through laws and regulations grounded in a realistic policy vision, a sensitivity to domestic requirements (itself a balancing act of the first order), and clarity about international obligations and objectives.

The ambitiousness of these requirements suggests that managing uncertainty and learning to deal with imperfection may be the only realistic policy goals in a policy domain as complex as international migration. The essay concludes that there is no single blueprint for success and points out that learning from other states—even those as closely related to one another as many advanced democracies are—requires extreme care lest borrowed policy responses prove counterproductive in their new sociocultural and political contexts.

The supply side: triggers, drivers and facilitators of international migration

Wars and large-scale disasters, whether natural or man-made, are obvious migration triggers as people flee for their lives. Beyond them, the roots of international migration can be found in the quest to protect oneself and one's family from sustained physical jeopardy and to escape dramatic declines in economic opportunities that have become chronic. The latter cause of migration is qualitatively different from the search for economic improvement, which is a constant feature of migration.

Two elements within those broad causes are likely to remain important drivers in the next two decades. The first is political, social and cultural intolerance; at the extreme, gross, group-based violations of human rights. The second is the systematic failure (some will say wilful indifference) of governments to redress issues of cumulative disadvantage: the various forms of economic exclusion and ethno-racial, religious or linguistic discrimination that systematically disadvantage certain segments of a population.

Both of these migration drivers are always present, to a greater or lesser extent. In most instances, however, they are not sufficient either to start a large new migration flow or, suddenly, to expand substantially an existing one. For that to happen, a number of preconditions ('facilitators') must be in place. Most notable among them are:

- The pre-existence of a long-term political, social and economic relationship between a sending and a destination society that includes a tradition of migration.
- Economic benefits from migration substantial enough to motivate economic elites in the receiving country and their political allies to organise themselves in support of significant flows.
- The presence of a mature and influential 'anchor' ethnic community in the country of destination which, in response to sharp reversals in the circumstances of their coethnics/coreligionists in another country, mobilises itself to become the 'enabler' of a substantial migration flow. This typically includes offering to assist with the initial integration of the newcomers or, if the receiving society is unresponsive, providing the essential 'lubricants' for the unauthorised migration of their brethren through the provision of capital for their travel and entry, and of an incubating social and economic environment within their own community upon arrival.
- The presence of key constituencies in the prospective destination country, such as religious and human rights activists, who stand in strong philosophical opposition to the circumstances migrants are attempting to escape and are willing to use their political capital in support of a migration 'solution'. Such constituencies and their civil society allies, in coalition with ethnic and economic interests, become the undeniable stakeholders that can sustain an opening to migration to the point where it becomes a permanent feature. Once such alliances mature, unilateral efforts by state bureaucracies to change the terms of the migration bargain stand low probabilities of success.

At the dawn of the twenty-first century, and looking ahead to the next two decades, three additional causes require separate mention because they have recently gained in both virulence and importance. The first is outright ethnoracial and/or religious conflict in which forcing the targeted group to abandon the contested area is not simply a by-product of the conflict but a major policy objective. The second involves the deterioration of ecosystems to the point of making life unsustainable—prime instances are endangered water security and extensive degradation in water quality, the contamination of basic foodstuffs and the consequences of desertification. The third concerns the flight from various forms of natural and man-made disasters. These last two causes are related in that climatic change and the deterioration of the ecosystem can affect both the frequency and the catastrophic potential of natural disasters.

When concepts and language fail us

Categories of social analysis do not develop *sui generis*: they are developed by analysts trying to get a handle on 'a problem'. Once established, however, such categories are very difficult to change. The complex, shifting terrain of international migration, the growing complexity of its causes, processes and consequences, and the radically new global context in which it takes place all demand that we review both the usefulness of our conceptual and analytical tools and the administrative categories and structures that have grown from them.

Such a review suggests that, the danger of oversimplification notwithstanding, the existing international migration system is organised around ideal constructs that are both dated and disturbingly binary. States are designated as either 'sending' or 'receiving'; people who move are classified as either permanent settlers or temporary residents; and reasons for flight are categorised either as the improvement of one's economic condition or protection from various form of persecution.

Such gross dichotomies shed increasingly little light on the reality of today's migration patterns. Today, people move for a variety of reasons simultaneously. Many states both send and receive substantial numbers of migrants, and may also act as routes of migrant transit. Large proportions of permanent immigrants move back from or on beyond their adopted country of residence. And temporary residents (such as students and professionals) often settle in their host countries.

It is essential that we come to understand these behaviours better, for at least two related reasons. First, since policy responses and administrative practices typically reflect the accepted classifications, bringing the latter closer to actual behaviour improves the opportunity to manage flows better. Second, since states and individuals participate simultaneously in multiple 'systems' of movement, the attempt to manage what amounts to complex transnational processes through unilateral and single-purpose policies will be of ever-diminishing value in the years ahead.

The core issues: change, complexity and distributional effects

If traditional analytical tools, existing administrative categories, and the menu of policy responses developed during the second half of the last century are no longer adequate to address today's migration flows, what accounts for this inadequacy and what might be the alternatives?

Three sets of factors lie at the root of the difficulty governments and, more generally, societies, have in managing the effects of large-scale immigration well. The first is found in immigration's relationship to sudden and deep social and cultural change; the second concerns immigration's complexity;

and the third stems from its deeply uneven distributional effects. All three sets of factors require governments to engage in delicate balancing acts in which the cost of failure is often measured not only in severe social and economic consequences but also in political ruin.

Managing change

All living organisms evolve at leisurely, almost glacial, rates. Societies are no exception. Large-scale immigration accelerates that pace and deepens its effect, while its ethnic, racial or cultural 'visibility' makes changes caused by immigration more difficult to deny. Immigration makes change, rather than constancy, the rule.

Most organised societies are built around the concept of constancy. Their nation-building symbols and myths emphasise commonality and often invent 'facts' that support it, reinterpreting or condemning 'non-conforming' facts to the dustbin of their version of history.

Most Western states have also spent enormous quantities of time, capital (of all types) and blood before finding workable formulas for managing their diversity—whether religious, linguistic, ethnic or racial. Their public mythologies recall vividly the costs their not so distant ancestors incurred in building their current political edifices. Most European societies fit this model all too well. Large-scale immigration challenges these societies' dominant systems of social, economic and political governance to open up and, in effect, 'renegotiate' their power allocation formulas. Significantly, this is not the case for the so-called 'traditional' countries of immigration—the US, Canada, Australia and New Zealand—that built themselves through immigration and for whom the only social and cultural 'constant' is change.

Deep and profound change carries within it the seeds of instability. The rate at which international migration has grown since the early 1990s and the degree to which it has spread throughout the advanced industrial world constitute a large part of the explanation for the issue's prominence. There are at least four major components to that change.

First, the rate at which immigrants have been entering advanced industrial societies has grown geometrically. Gross annual immigration intakes by the US and Canada have more than doubled in the past twenty years. Migration to Europe grew by comparably large rates but, significantly, did so in about half the time and mostly without active immigration selection systems in place. In fact, in most European instances, such growth occurred despite sustained efforts to minimise the numbers gaining entry. In much of southern Europe, the growth rate has been nothing less than extraordinary.

The second component of change, the national composition of these flows, reinforces its impact. Immigrant streams now originate from virtually all states, making the flows truly global.

The third element of change also concerns composition. Today, increasing proportions of the flows comprise immigrants who enter and/or stay in destination countries without authorisation. Attempted entry though the asylum system is considered by some as a variant of that phenomenon.

The final component of change relates closely to the third in that it focuses on the process through which would-be immigrants reach their destinations. It concerns the emergence of a new industry: the organised smuggling of people. Two challenges appear to be particularly daunting about this development. The first is that these syndicates use constantly shifting organisational frameworks in order to protect themselves from being penetrated and dissolved by the authorities. The second is much more consequential. Illegal immigration controls have spawned lucrative black markets for all types of products and services that are highly profitable and can corrupt officials at any level—pointing again to the basic flaw of single-focus regulatory practices.

Managing complexity and negotiating difficult tradeoffs

Sudden and deep change is always difficult to manage, but the complexity of migration presents policy-makers with a particularly challenging set of political and policy tradeoffs. Three examples of such tradeoffs—one reflecting competing economic and social policy perspectives, the second concerning the pros and cons of alternative policy interventions, and a third concerning international cooperation—offer a sense of that complexity.

Migration juxtaposes a philosophy of economic competitiveness that seeks ever greater access for employers to the global labour pool, with social democracy's more traditional interests in training its own workers and maintaining generous social and labour protections. In such a binary framework, the economic interests supporting immigration are put on a collision course with the interests of the broader society. Although, as posited, a large part of this tension is artificial, policy-makers are nonetheless asked to make virtually instant calculations about complex cost–benefit ratios across a maddeningly broad array of policy domains—and to do so with grossly inadequate information and crude policy tools.

The second tradeoff involves making informed choices between different but equally complicated forms of interventions. An example is finding the proper balance between the furtherance of human rights and economic opportunities in developing countries and offering opportunities to their citizens in the form of immigration. Both alternatives have merit and carry substantial costs. The former requires international activism and substantial and sustained investments of physical, diplomatic and political capital. The latter ('immigration slots') demands significant expenditure of domestic political capital, primarily in the form of an unceasing effort to explain to one's public the rationale for and benefits from this course of action.

A third type of tradeoff resides in the area of international cooperation to tackle irregular migration. It focuses on the challenge of engaging key sending countries in sharing in the management of migration, based on agreed policy outcomes. Accomplishing such a 'joint management' objective involves difficult choices on the part of both parties to the negotiations. Simply put, if the advanced industrial democracies want the assistance of immigrant sending and transit states in a common front against organised forms of illegal migration, they must place on the table items of high interest to those countries in exchange for their 'organic' cooperation. Among the items receiving countries must offer are *conditional* opportunities for liberalising trade in areas such as agriculture, textiles and garments (sectors that are highly protected by all rich countries), substantial physical and social infrastructure assistance, *and* far greater access to the advanced world's labour markets.

The political challenge of such a negotiating stance is obvious. Policymakers must trade off one set of public goods, such as work visas or preferential treatment in a traded good, in return for a joint effort against illegal immigration. While the policy objective is an important one, the costs of making such a 'deal' are measured both in jobs and short-term economic well-being for some sections of society, and in political pain, as the affected domestic constituencies organise in opposition to such a bargain.

Managing migration's distributional effects

The third part of the issue's complexity can be traced to its distributional effects. Migration's economic and social impacts are distributed unevenly across policy domains (such as human resources, trade and tax) and among investors, producers, consumers and workers—an issue explored, in the context of labour migration, in Mark Kleinman's contribution to this volume. Those effects, unless managed well, create distinct categories of 'winners' and 'losers' and thus sow the seeds for negative political reactions to migration. Failure to address these reactions quickly and decisively can and does make immigration politically contentious, as we are observing throughout the advanced industrial world.

Managing political tensions in the context of economic interdependence

The domestic tensions that arise from migration cannot be separated from the winners and losers from broader global trends. The globalisation of capital, production and markets has meant that well-capitalised and highly competitive global firms have been able to exploit global opportunities with fewer and fewer risks, in part through international agreements to liberalise trade and capital flows. These instruments advance the objectives of the business sectors that promote them and, as a result, most producers and consumers benefit.

At the same time, such agreements blur the lines between opportunities and risks for some segments of the societies that are parties to them. Opening foreign markets, for instance, creates new opportunities for Western businesses from which they, and those employed up and down the economic stream in those sectors, benefit. The opening of foreign markets, however, requires roughly commensurate concessions by advanced industrial democracies. Opening up protected sectors in those countries often has substantial adverse consequences for affected businesses and their workforces. Thus, for nearly every opportunity that trade accords create, some social and economic sectors 'win' while others are asked to absorb a significant amount of risk.

The adverse effects of increasing economic interdependence and consequent restructuring impact most directly on non-competitive industries and the holders of uncompetitive skill sets. Probably more significant for this analysis, however, are the *social* consequences of this restructuring. It is these consequences that are at the root of the popular uncertainty and fear that globalising forces have created; and they are at the root of much of the reaction to immigration as well.

Economic and other forms of interdependence place countries and entire geographical regions in the grasp of an increasingly global migration system, in which economic and sociopolitical events have direct migration consequences. Witness, for example, US fears in the mid-1990s that the failure to 'rescue' the Mexican peso would greatly increase immigration pressures from that country; or Europe's concerns that, under some circumstances, the Iraq war might have substantial refugee consequences for the EU—just as the Balkan conflicts did in the 1990s.

Domestic tensions

Anxieties about such global forces over which single countries have little control have turned large-scale and, in particular, poorly regulated migration into a social and political tinderbox in many localities. The animus against immigration has at times manifested itself in street violence and, as Shamit Sagger suggests in his essay below, is thought to have led to several extraordinary upheavals in local and national elections. In a perverse way, unwanted migration may thus be transferring instability from 'source countries' to 'destination countries', where it threatens to (or actually does) adversely affect the lives of ordinary people.

These developments have put immigration policy and management regimes throughout the West under the policy microscope. The challenge now is how to deal with the fact that the crisis of legitimacy fuelled by poorly managed immigration threatens to infect the broader governmental edifice. At issue is regaining the public's confidence that their governments can *and will* manage immigration competently, address public grievances relating to it effectively, and defuse the growing xenophobia and violence.

Given that poorly managed migration, in conjunction with the other large phenomena identified here, can affect people's livelihoods significantly, it should not be surprising that the political resonance of the issue ebbs and flows most consistently with an economy's overall performance. An example may suffice to make the point clearer. When entire industries retrench radically, invest heavily or relocate abroad, or attempt to change their labour relations in a quest to enhance their global competitiveness, there seems to be little that the affected workers and their organisations can do. But they can—and do—speak out against the one visible and tangible element of that change: immigrants.

Often enough, politicians seize upon the divisive potential of immigration to bolster support for explicitly extremist agendas. Such opportunism has often pushed mainstream political parties into positions about immigrants and immigration that may be inimical to their societies' longer-term economic interests. In fact, one of the issue's unfolding paradoxes (and one that is fascinating to watch) is how mainstream political parties, which have sought to accommodate the minority appeal of xenophobic impulses by adopting restrictionist rhetoric and policies, deal with the emerging realisation that immigrants are fast becoming demographically and economically indispensable—and the policy U-turns such realisation entails.

The more general point, however, must not be forgotten. One of the most notable by-products of this crisis has been that parties of protest (at this historical juncture they are mostly parties of the right) have been able to exploit public fears and discontent about *several* issues, initially in local and regional elections. But it is in their ability to whip up anti-immigration fervour and then use it as a political weapon that most such parties have excelled, thus catapulting immigration to the forefront of public debate and electoral politics.

The point here is that to call these important phenomena a reaction to legal and illegal immigration may miss an important part of the story. The reactions from which fringe parties and movements benefit go much deeper. Most fundamentally, they go to the very fears and anxieties of both governors and governed about the capacity of their countries (individually and collectively) to make the policy adjustments that will allow them to retain their privileged standing in the world community—and with it, their political and economic well-being and the social order that flows from it.

One 'new' variable, however, may make future reactions to immigration less extreme. With immigrants attaining a politically significant 'critical mass', a class of ethnic power-brokers is emerging. This critical mass will likely make it more difficult for mainstream politicians to be as blatantly anti-immigration in the years ahead. Their reluctance is likely to come only in small part from the fear of being tagged, and punished, by those constituents as 'anti-*immigrant*'. The biggest challenge to their political careers is likely to come instead from the leadership of their own party. Most mainstream party leaders are becoming increasingly aware that the political power of immigrant and ethnic groups can only grow as large-scale immigration and active citizenship drives increase the electoral power of such constituencies; and that a party's position on immigration can influence these constituencies' voting behaviour.

Conundrums

In public policy terms, it follows that there are a series of issues that policy-makers need to understand if they are to manage immigration more effectively in the years ahead.

First, we need greater knowledge of the factors that cause or at least substantially affect migration 'events', as well as those that merely mediate them; and of the levers that a policy-maker can pull, and in what sequence, in order to bring about a desired outcome.

Second, we need to understand the reasons why some people react to certain events by emigrating while so many others under similar or worse pressures stay put—and how governments can intervene in each instance so as to shape the outcomes.

Third, we need to acknowledge the critical role of organised people-smuggling syndicates in the growth in unwanted migration, and the imperative of reallocating resources and using shifting patterns of detection and enforcement in order to tackle them.

Finally, policy-makers need to recognise the limits of unilateralism (or of multilateralism that does not include sending countries as partners) in responding to unwanted migration. Migration ties sending, transit and receiving countries—as well as immigrants, their families and their employers—into intricate systems of interdependence. It takes determined efforts by virtually all these actors to make real progress in that area.

Failure to understand these matters will place governments further behind in the migration management effort—especially in view of the continuous adaptations unwanted migrants make to their entry strategies. Making things worse are the public's impatience with experimentation and its intolerance for anything but near-immediate results. The obsession with controlling international migration through unilateral law-and-order measures continues to distort the public debate and allows governments little leeway to demonstrate that immigration is not at the root of the North's major problems; that the problems to which migration contributes can be managed; and that immigration, properly managed, can in fact provide important answers to some of the North's most intractable longer-term economic, social protection and demographic dilemmas.

There is clear agreement that reform is long overdue. What is less clear is whether such reform will be the product of a judicious effort to address all of a nation's interests, as well as to balance those interests with international obligations—or will be little more than the typical knee-jerk yank on the control levers.

The outcome is likely to be influenced over the next two decades by a profoundly important factor: demographic change.

The demand side: demographics, economic competitiveness and migration to 2020

Because of low rates of native population growth across the advanced industrial world, migration is already a large demographic force. Between 1985 and 1990, international migrants accounted for about one-quarter of the developed world's population growth. That figure grew to around 45 per cent during the period 1990–5: a function of increased immigration and relentlessly low fertility. It likely stands at about two-thirds of growth today. Of course, averages typically hide enormous regional, subregional and national variations. Nevertheless, international migration now accounts for nearly all of western Europe's overall population growth. But what will the future bring?

The demographic facts are not in dispute. Most of the advanced industrial world has failed to reproduce itself adequately for a generation. As the post-Second World War baby-boomers leave the labour market over the next decade or so, most Western democracies will experience substantial declines in their native-born working-age population. Countries with significant migration inflows in the last decades will also notice the evolving racial and ethnic composition of their workforces as much larger proportions of those joining the labour market will be immigrants and their offspring.

It is the bulge in the retirement-age population, however, that is of special interest to this analysis. The number of retirees will reach absolute and relative sizes unlike anything we have witnessed in history. With people living much longer than ever before, the taxes of fewer and fewer workers will have to support ever larger numbers of retirees—a ratio known as the old age support (or dependency) ratio.

The evidence is nothing less than compelling. The OECD estimates that by 2020 most of its member states will have old age support ratios that range from a low of about 30 per cent for some of the traditional countries of immigration to about 42 per cent for Japan.[1] (More recent reports from the European Commission, as well from the UN's Population Division, validate these findings completely.) This means that for OECD states with tax-supported, pay-as-you-go retirement systems, the taxes of between 3.3 and 2.4 workers will have to support the cost of each retired person to the public purse. For the relatively few countries where tax-financed pensions are supplemented by private pensions or mandatory occupational retirement schemes, the picture is slightly better.

The data become more troubling when *total* support ratios are examined: that is, the ratio of the number of persons in the workforce to the sum of those who are already retired *and* those who are too young to be working. Nor does the bad news for the next two decades stop here. Most estimation models assume that young persons 'enter' the workforce at age 15 and that retirement occurs at age 65. Both of these conventions are at gross variance with actual behaviour in advanced industrial countries and bias the estimates systematically in favour of greater optimism—and complacency.

The greatest challenge may be securing adequate living standards for pensioners without putting crushing tax burdens on workers—a challenge that will worsen every decade. In 1998, the OECD projected that by 2020 its members would experience substantial increases in pension expenditures, rising to more than 12 per cent in the cases of Germany and Japan. More significantly, some private economists' estimates of the developed world's size of unfunded pension liabilities stand at about $34 *trillion*; paying for elderly medical care adds another $30 *trillion* to that amount.[2] Both figures will increase at first geometrically and later exponentially as the aged cohort bulges and medical consumption patterns explode.

These are not the only implications. The decline in the population of working age will lead to increasingly severe labour shortages that will go beyond the mismatches between needed and available skills that characterise many labour markets today. The labour market implications of this demographic conundrum will be felt most directly in economic sectors of particular interest to the aged. Among the most vulnerable sectors are those in which the nature of the work (often difficult jobs with physically demanding conditions and undesirable hours), as well as their social standing and wage structure, make them unappealing to native workers. These jobs include care of the elderly and tending to the personal service needs of the affluent. More workers will also be needed to help, through their taxes, to keep retirement and public health systems afloat; and, in many cases, to keep both production and consumption systems humming.

This analysis suggests that societies that address these demographically centred challenges sooner and more definitively will enhance their prospects for economic stability and growth. Those that do not can expect to experience greater economic instability and, under certain extreme scenarios, economic decline. Both scenarios also imagine a spillover into *social* instability; accordingly, responses must factor in the requirement of social cohesion.

Faced with this challenge, states find that every potential policy response entails significant pain for important segments of society. Governments are thus likely to attempt first to prolong the status quo. This tactic will prove both inadequate and harmful in the longer run.

Among the stop-gap measures that are certain to be relied upon will be mandating longer working lives (Japan and the United States are already moving in this direction); attempting to increase labour force participation of such groups as women, minorities and the disabled; reducing retirement benefits and introducing additional forms of retirement systems; experimenting with greater efficiencies in state-supported health care delivery systems (including the introduction of competition from private sector care providers); and the mechanisation and 'exportation' of labour-intensive industries.

Most states are already experimenting with several of these approaches. However, the political resistance to the most promising 'innovations' is already strong and will intensify as the inevitable service cuts begin to be felt by ever larger population cohorts. It is the judgement of this essay that only three long-term solutions are truly salient: gradual changes in retirement age; significant and long-term changes in fertility; and immigration on a far larger scale.

The first will pit the government against retirees and those nearing retirement, two groups that hold a disproportionate share of a country's wealth *and* political power. The government is not likely to win that battle except at the margins—and even that will take much longer than the crisis can allow. The second solution, changes in fertility, implies a reversal in long-term trends and would require nothing less than a revolution in prevailing social norms and economic logic.

The final option is immigration. No reasonable analyst believes that immigration alone can 'solve' this policy dilemma. Maintaining 2010-level old age support ratios in 2020 through immigration alone would require intakes several times the size of most states' actual immigration intakes for the period 1985–95. That is clearly neither socially nor politically viable.

More to the point, perhaps, unless a state admits primarily very young or mostly temporary immigrants, one would need ever larger foreign-born populations to maintain reasonable old age support ratios. An alternative 'immigration' option, larger numbers of temporary workers, is thus likely to become more popular for many advanced industrial societies, and thus gain in significance relative to permanent immigration. Introducing age biases in permanent immigration formulas—as do Canada and Australia—may also become more common.

Larger immigration intakes will require even sharper attitudinal changes to overcome the age-old resistance to large-scale immigration and the social and cultural change it implies. Can societies that appear to value tradition and continuity virtually above all else, as the Europeans (as well as the ancient Asian societies) do, make the leap that larger immigration levels require? Will the traditional destination countries start preparing the political ground for the larger immigration intakes they will need—as they must also do? Will both types of societies be able to manage the social and political reactions this solution will generate? These are difficult adjustments indeed; yet none of these societies can remain meaningful international players if they fail to address the demographic issues outlined here or if they attempt to address them without the required wisdom.

September 11 and controlling illegal migration

The terrorist attack on America of September 11, 2001 may yet play a bigger role than it has to date in reshaping the environment in which international migration has thrived in recent decades. In that regard, terrorism and the 'war' against it have introduced a wild card into the calculus that underlies this essay. It raises the possibility, but not yet the likelihood, of extreme state reactions to most migration.

If we are entering a new era of nihilistic conflict rooted in resurgent nationalism (not only in the developing world), politically expressed religious fundamentalism, and various other nearly forgotten 'isms'—and if the casualties on both sides grow at rates commensurate with the capabilities of our era's instruments of destruction—the scenario outlined herein may indeed be nullified. If such a conflict and chaos scenario comes to pass, the only reasonable projection is that national security will trump all other migration policy priorities for an indeterminate period, and that most forms of international migration to the developed world will be cut dramatically.

Otherwise, immigration's reach during the next two decades will expand and go beyond the advanced industrial West, to Japan and the other East and South-East 'Asian Tigers', as well as to emerging market societies everywhere. Initially, the government-assisted part of this expansion will most likely take the form, primarily, of regulated temporary entry for high- *and low*-skilled foreign workers. But it will not stop there. 'Front gate' provisions for converting valued 'temporary' legal immigrants into permanent ones will also proliferate, turning temporary admission streams into filtration systems for selecting permanent immigrants. In addition, opportunities for admitting better-skilled foreigners outright as permanent immigrants will also increase, particularly when the world economy rebounds and global competition for talented foreigners intensifies.

At the same time, pressure from unauthorised migration is also likely to remain robust, and managing it will continue to be a major preoccupation. Efforts to change the status quo in this area, however, must show a willingness to move beyond the 'tried and failed' paradigms of simply putting ever more resources into border and interior controls. It must add to them interventions that are as multifaceted as the problem itself. Effective management will require unusual degrees of coordination across policy competencies and between countries of origin and destination.

Setting realistic policy goals

Perfection must not become the policy goal, particularly when dealing with the complex social and economic issues associated with unwanted immigration. The standards it demands are too high, and any policy designed to meet them will ultimately be judged a failure. 'Zero immigration', the publicly stated goal of some European states in the early 1990s, was no more realistic than defeating illegal immigration exclusively through law-and-order responses is today. That principle stands even if such responses are coordinated to include tougher border controls, greater labour market regulation, enhanced intrusiveness in interior policing, and minimising the demand for asylum by making it ever more difficult to succeed in the adjudication process.

Three reasons make the point obvious. First, immigration systems create their own self-feeding dynamic that encourages ever more migration (through family reunification and the continuing need for more immigrant workers). Second, unless a state buries itself in isolation, all transnational contacts (economic, political, social and cultural) result in some migration consequences. Third, people fleeing circumstances that *they* consider intolerable will enter the illegal migration stream and test various receiving states' 'defences' again and again, whether they subvert the asylum system or enter through other means to insert themselves into the underground economy.

The approach to managing all migration—and not just its illegal variant—better has four interdependent parts that must be pursued and implemented in concert:

- First, legal immigration channels of various forms must be widened and deepened.
- Second, internal controls must be systematically reviewed with an eye to reducing opportunities for unauthorised immigrants to gain footholds in the domestic economy. In this regard, regulators should work *with* the market and key stakeholders must be turned into partners in what should become 'national projects'.
- Third, the state's border control stance must be reviewed with an eye to making only those investments that make sense. Agreements between major countries of origin and destination that focus on sharing responsibility for the management of migration flows should be pursued simultaneously and in earnest. Such agreements must be truly bidirectional and balanced in terms of what each party gives and what it gets in return. A good rule of thumb should be that the benefits to each party must be substantial enough to alter behaviour, while the costs do not undermine either party's fundamental legitimacy to the point where delivering policy outcomes in accordance with the agreed terms becomes impossible.
- Fourth, the task of solving the immigration and domestic, intergroup relations puzzle must be addressed with uncharacteristic imagination and rigour, in part by creating level playing fields for the economic, social and political integration of immigrants—new and old.

Public education will be key to making real progress towards any of these objectives. Specifically, governments must move gradually but firmly away from the rhetoric of just keeping immigrants out and toward language that extols the benefits of pursuing migration management policies that address contentious issues directly, encouraging all relevant societal actors to participate in public/private bargains with terms that make sense. In so doing, the debate will move from the enforcement of unilateral and typically arbitrary rules that continue to fail, to sharing responsibility for implementing the mutually agreed terms of a bargain.

Taking on the smuggling syndicates

This is not to suggest 'going soft' on illegal immigration. In addition to subverting a society's legal order, illegal immigration can also undermine other policy priorities. Arguably, however, the most significant consequences of illegal immigration may stem from the fact that the trafficker's 'cargo' is made up of desperate people. They are willing to work long hours under virtually any conditions, or engage in illegal activities under various forms of duress, to pay passage fees of up to tens of thousands of dollars for a contract that includes delivery to a specific destination.

Smuggling networks are thought to prefer only part of their fees up front—a 'preference' that reflects, in part, the reality that few migrants can amass the funds needed to pay for passage. As a result, increasing numbers of unauthorised immigrants mortgage their very lives and futures to their smugglers—turning themselves into peons at the beck and call of unscrupulous syndicates and their clients. This class of modern-day indentured servants undermines the receiving society's system of wages and working conditions, as well as its legal and social order, and dilutes support for all immigration.

Nonetheless, it is the contention of this essay that, as with efforts to combat many other lucrative illegal activities, the global 'war' on trafficking in people is not winnable under the current rules of engagement. The agile, transnational and relatively small trafficking networks have an advantage over the much larger, slower and more bureaucratised government agencies whose roots and organisational culture are in a single state. Governments are at their worst when they must act across borders. Moreover, relative to their opponents, government agencies tend to be grossly under-resourced, not least in their access to appropriate technology. Moreover, governments have to observe rules that hamper their ability to respond—rules that do not apply for the transnational criminal syndicates that run the trafficking networks. The government also faces domestic political obstacles: economic interests dependent on cheap, undocumented labour and humanitarians reluctant to see even so problematic a migration channel closed.

Hence, the best approach is to let the market find its own equilibrium within the rules set by society and enforced jointly by the government and key stakeholders.

Living with imperfection and managing uncertainty

Instead of seeking perfection, then, with its inevitable disappointments, immigration policies of any type must proceed from the premise that uncertainty and imperfection will be a way of life. Immigration policy is an exercise in the inexact, as migration always locates the path of least resistance. Channelling it is a better and more realistic course than either denying its existence or articulating policy goals that seek total control or exclusion. Both of those goals create unrealistic public expectations and fuel climates of intolerance.

Similarly, no policy can simply be transferred from one country to another. Successful immigration rules must instead be compatible as much with a people's sense of themselves as with a country's social, economic, labour market and demographic realities. Successful national goals flow from the specific political realities of countries, from important social and cultural myths about nationhood, and from the international environment, which at times dictates what is and what is not possible.

Countries (or regional groupings) might then start with some modest experiments in cooperation—a learning by doing approach—that are continuously evaluated. These experiments must test a variety of market-based responses (such as fees and bonds for migrants and their employers, incentives to employers for hiring native workers, and the establishment of migrant-funded trust funds for providing most social support in the early years of migration) and introduce ideas that go beyond simply building better mousetraps. Specifically, they must also delve into areas that address the long-term needs of emigrant-producing countries. Only by systematically setting up and assessing the performance of new policies, testing the durability of new regulatory frameworks, and laying out menus of policy alternatives can initiatives on migration stand a decent chance of bearing the desired management fruit.

From vicious circles to virtuous cycles: managing migration to advantage

What, then, might the advanced industrial world be doing differently to capture and maximise the many benefits of migration while controlling its most adverse consequences? Moving beyond the often narrow perspective of the developed countries of immigrant destination, how might migration's role as a critical resource for human progress—through migrant remittances, the dissemination of new ideas, and the transfer of economic and non-economic skills—be enhanced?

Mindful that policy prescriptions are always easier to offer the further one sits from the 'real' world of politics and policy, the following ideas are offered with the necessary amount of deference. The objective is simple-sounding but extremely complicated to accomplish in managing complex social processes: to regulate international migration in ways that escape the vicious circle of failed unilateral and single-purpose controls and move state actors towards cooperative policies that promote the virtuous cycles of disciplined pragmatism and good governance. I suggest that states must:

- Recapture control of migration from the two groups that are posing the most imminent and clearest threat to this valuable instrument of progress: the demagogues, irrespective of party affiliation and regardless of whether they are in or out of government, who are riding the issue for political advantage; and the international criminal syndicates, which are substituting their interests for those of the societies in which their cargo ends up and those of their hapless cargo itself.
- Be more truthful and transparent. While all governments use facts and truth much more sparingly than they should on politically complicated issues, on immigration, wilful distortions and outright lies play directly into the hands of immigration's opponents.
- Explain to the public what they are doing and why; and seek out a national debate in which they make the case for immigration policies that maximise benefits while minimising costs. Consistently applied rules-based actions and predictable outcomes are essential to building public confidence in complex and divisive policy realms.
- Build robust management systems, fund them properly (under-resourcing the management of migration has become endemic across most advanced industrial countries), review and adjust them frequently—so that they are always aligned with policy objectives—and pay attention to delivery, because it is in implementation that most systems stumble. Building and maintaining capacity in the management of migration should thus become a policy priority of the first order for all immigrant destination countries.
- Understand that single-purpose policies, just like single-cause explanations, are poor guides in setting policies on complex issues.
- Make immigration decisions part of the policy mainstream across domains and responsibilities. Government competencies are typically single-issue-focused, and bureaucracies are organised vertically in order to deliver the necessary function. Yet immigration, in terms of both benefits and consequences, cuts across policy domains; a partial list must include public order, social welfare, education and training, and foreign and development policy. Accordingly, the responses to it are stronger when they are considered and implemented across multiple policy domains.
- Finally, turn two of the most determined 'critics'—the market and organised civil society—into partners in a common effort to create win–win situations on managing migration. Working against, rather than with, the former is often an exercise in futility; working without the benefit of the latter—a system's main stakeholders—makes the task of governance on complex issues tougher than it needs to be. Working with critics on difficult issues makes it possible to share responsibility for what succeeds rather than always being blamed for what fails.

Measuring success

So far, dealing with migration has taught most advanced democracies how to deal with failure. It is now time to look to the future and consider how to measure success. The issues outlined in this essay represent enormous hurdles along the path to greater policy coherence. The point here, however, is not to dwell, Cassandra-like, on doom-and-gloom scenarios. Rather, it is to recognise that coherence is a process (and not an event), to understand what policy-makers are up against when they talk about 'reining in' illegal immigration and managing legal immigration more effectively, and to set realistic benchmarks against which to measure progress.

Many countries have had success with different types of legal, organised immigration. Furthermore, the past decade has shown that good management practices can prevent immigration from becoming a runaway policy and political 'problem' that requires extreme measures to control. The willingness of Australia and Canada to adjust their policies regularly and to invest systematically in policy research and evaluation has enabled these countries to derive substantial benefits from immigration while minimising its down-side. Similarly, US actions in the mid-1990s in support of Mexico's currency showed a particularly sophisticated understanding of the complex linkages between economic and political stability and unwanted migration, while pointing to the mutual obligations and liabilities that NAFTA-like relation-ships impose on all the parties involved. The negotiations between Mexico and the US on sharing responsibility for managing their bilateral migration relationship (until the events of September 11 took the energy out of them), showed extraordinary promise towards developing a new bilateral regulatory paradigm with implications well beyond North America.

These and similar responses, the exceptions in a sea of rhetoric and action that emphasises unilateral controls, do represent a ray of hope that advanced industrial democracies appreciate that most migrants, including many unauthorised ones, have been essential to their prosperity. It ill behoves them now to forget that migrants have basic human, social and economic rights, and that these rights should not be withdrawn unilaterally.

Conclusion

Given the significant economic, political, human rights and demographic differentials that continue to divide the world, the realistic response to migration cannot be denial. Advanced industrial societies cannot exhort people to stay at home without a serious commitment to a long-term and costly endeavour to improve conditions there. Open and democratic societies must also understand that attacking the root causes of flight, while worthy and necessary, has a long horizon that will exact substantial domestic political costs before it yields measurable long-term benefits.

In the interim, advanced industrial societies must resist the temptation to retreat in the face of immigration's challenge and retrench behind increasingly restrictive, and ultimately undemocratic, controls. As is becoming apparent, unilateral actions and fortress mentalities misread the complexities of the migration system while denying receiving societies an essential ingredient for their own economic success and social enrichment. Policies designed within such naïve frameworks are destined to fall short of even relative long-term success.

A more insightful set of policies would take into account the variety of the experiences of advanced industrial societies and their different levels of success—while appreciating that 'success' is overwhelmingly a function of effort, resources, commitment, flexibility, and consonance with a state's culture and history. This is true both for the control of illegal flows and for the broader management of legal flows. Success in solving the immigration puzzle also requires confidence, sure-footedness, leadership and vision in the public arena. These are surely precious commodities, but they are well within the realm of realistic possibility in the advanced democratic world.[3]

Notes

1 Organisation for Economic Cooperation and Development, *Maintaining Prosperity in an Ageing Society*, Paris, OECD, 1998. See also United Nations Population Division, *International Migration Report 2002*, New York, UN, 2002.
2 Dora L. Costa, *The Evolution of Retirement: An American Economic History, 1880–1990*, Chicago, University of Chicago Press, 1998.
3 Further analysis by the author and his colleagues at the Migration Policy Institute in Washington DC can be found at www.migrationpolicy.org.

The Economic Impact of Labour Migration

MARK KLEINMAN*

IN recent years we have seen a considerable change in the scale and nature of labour migration flows to the UK and other European countries, and in the policy stance of these countries towards migration. These developments have been driven by global structural changes as much as by specific local circumstances, including the continuing integration of the world economy, the falling real cost of international travel, and the impact of global mass media on knowledge flows and aspirations. Within the European Union there is now a cross-border labour market for millions of workers. Globally, there is effectively a single labour market across the OECD and beyond for an elite of the most highly skilled.

Policy, in the UK and elsewhere, has shifted to open up channels for both high-skilled and low-skilled migration. In part, governments are responding to pressure from employers experiencing skill and labour shortages in particular sectors, as well as to a more general concern to reduce inflationary pressures through better matching of demand and supply in the labour market. But increased migration gives rise to social and economic tensions: both because there are winners and losers from this economic restructuring, and because of impacts on public services and broader concerns about national identity.

Governments are thus subject to competing pressures to which they must respond. As well as such domestic concerns, they need to take into account the reactions of their partners in the EU and of the governments of developing countries. Those governments *may* welcome easier access for their nationals to the labour markets of the developed world, because of the benefits from migrants' remittances; equally, they may not, because of the negative impacts of the 'brain drain'.

In this essay, I explore the nature of the demand for migrant workers and the impacts of migration on outcomes for both migrant and domestic ('native') workers, focusing on the UK. I also examine the impact of the 'demographic deficit' and draw out some policy implications. In broad terms, the economic impact of migration is positive for the destination country; but the size of the impact is not great, and there are distributional consequences to consider. The implications for policy are that there are real

---

* The author is Head of Housing and Homelessness at the Greater London Authority. This article is written in a personal capacity and does not reflect the views of the Greater London Authority.

© The Political Quarterly Publishing Co. Ltd. 2003
Published by Blackwell Publishing Ltd, 9600 Garsington Road, Oxford OX4 2DQ, UK and 350 Main Street, Malden, MA 02148, USA

choices and tradeoffs to be made; it is not a question of labour migration being either 'good' or 'bad'. The policy debate would benefit from a better understanding of the economic impacts of migration. But the economic arguments alone will not be (and should not be) decisive. Governments will have to balance the economic case against other policy objectives, including those relating to social inclusion, public protection, human rights and international development.

The overall picture

Migration has a range of economic impacts:

- on the employment rate and wages of native workers;
- on the employment rate and wages of immigrants;
- on productivity and the growth rate of the economy;
- on entrepreneurialism and innovation;
- on the fiscal balance of government.

In this essay I concentrate on the first two of these; that is, on the labour market impacts of migration.

For most economists, it is clear that increased migration brings economic gains at the global level:

If we consider both the sending and the receiving countries as part of the same world, then—and on this every economist agrees—the overall effect of migration on the average standard of living of the world's people is positive. The reason for this is that the migrant goes from a place where he or she is less productive to a place where he or she is more productive. The increased production benefits the standard of living of the community as a whole, as well as that of the migrating individual.[1]

In principle, one can estimate the size of the potential gain to the world economy from completely open borders; or, to put it the other way around, estimate the current economic loss from immigration controls. In practice, such an exercise involves rather heroic assumptions. Moses and Letnes build on earlier work by Hamilton and Whalley to estimate the efficiency gains from lifting global immigration restrictions. They find the gains to be in the range of 15–40 per cent of world GNP, noting that 'In all cases, these gains exceed current levels of official foreign aid and foreign direct investment to the developing world.'[2]

The authors concede that their study is 'highly speculative . . . and relies on a number of contentious assumptions'. Nevertheless, the magnitude of the gains indicates that immigration should be considered 'as an important means for bridging the income gap that separates the world's richest and poorest inhabitants . . . Moreover, a substantial proportion of these gains can be reaped without open borders. Even small changes in international migration controls could produce significant economic gains.' Conversely, the restriction on the movement of people across regions imposes economic costs on both developed and developing countries which far exceed those of trade restrictions on goods.[3]

At the level of individual countries, the vast majority of studies find that the effects on the *overall* economic welfare of the destination country are positive:

Using a basic economic model, with plausible assumptions . . . immigration produces net economic gains for domestic residents, for several reasons. At the most basic level, immigrants increase the supply of labour and help produce these new goods and services. But since they are paid less than the total value of these new goods and services, domestic workers as a group must gain.[4]

Domestic (or 'native') workers will not in fact be the only winners: some of the gain will also go to shareholders via return on capital and to government via taxation.

At the same time, however, there may be important distributional consequences. There will be losers as well as winners from migration. If the losers are mainly unskilled native workers, and the gainers mainly native skilled workers and employers, there will be significant impacts on the distribution of income, unless compensating policies are in place.

These costs and benefits are not independent of other aspects of the economy. Its flexibility, openness to world trade and other factors will affect the size and distribution of the gains from migration. Highly regulated economies will find it harder to reap the benefits migration can bring.

Economic gains from migration are also higher if migrant workers are *complements* and not *substitutes* to the existing workforce—that is, if migrants have different skills and characteristics from native workers. Indeed, it is from the *complementary* nature of the new workers, not necessarily from their skills level, that the benefits to the destination country flow. A country consisting entirely of skilled workers would benefit from migration of unskilled workers, not from more skilled workers. In the real world, there are labour market inflexibilities, so migrants end up doing the jobs wherever there are recruitment difficulties, whether at the high-skilled end (a recent example being a shortage of IT workers) or at the low-skilled end, such as cleaning.

In the long run (assuming constant returns to scale) immigrants will affect economic growth rates only if they are different from the existing labour force, primarily if their skills mix is different. Also, these differences must persist over generations. If immigrants are just like existing workers (or rapidly become so) then immigration simply augments the population. This may of course be a desirable policy goal, especially in the light of current demographic projections. But the key point is: having a larger population does not of itself change the rate of growth of income per capita.

Most studies also conclude that the overall economic impacts of immigration, while positive, are relatively modest—for winners *and* losers. For the United States, 'the most plausible magnitudes of the impacts of immigration on the economy are modest for those who benefit from immigration, for those who lose from immigration and for total gross domestic product.'[5] Recent studies estimate the gain to the US economy at between $1 billion and $10 billion. Gains for the UK are likely also to be small relative to the size of the economy, as Britain is a very open trading economy with imports at 30 per cent of GDP.

A key question, with significant political implications, is whether the costs of migration are simply short-term adjustment costs on the way to a long-run equilibrium in which all workers are better off, or whether there are labour market effects which permanently worsen the position of some workers. In a world of perfect information and perfect mobility, changes in wages will induce shifts in labour supply to more productive uses. With perfect foresight, local workers would choose to raise their own level of skills, as the return on that human capital would outweigh the short-term costs of retraining.

In practice, labour markets are not characterised by perfect information, workers do not have perfect foresight, there are structural inefficiencies in labour and housing markets, and there is pervasive state intervention in markets, not least through the welfare system. In reality, therefore, the short run turns out to be not so short—so less skilled native workers (including those currently unemployed or inactive) can suffer semi-permanent disadvantage from the arrival of migrant competitors.

These distributional aspects of immigration are broadly similar to the impacts of increased trade or globalisation, or indeed any type of economic restructuring. In addition, the gains to labour market flexibility and improved resource allocation partly derive from immigrants' willingness to take or acquiescence in taking low-skilled, low-paid jobs—including jobs which are below their own education or skills level.

In some cases this will be perfectly acceptable, for example for the young people on the UK's Commonwealth Working Holiday Scheme who do office jobs in exchange for a couple of years in London. Other examples, such as highly qualified immigrants who work for years as minicab drivers because their overseas qualifications are not recognised or they face racial discrimination, represent an economic and human waste.

Wages and jobs of existing workers

Theory thus suggests that there may be negative effects from migration on particular types of workers. In particular, high-skilled migration will impact on the wages of high-skilled workers, low-skilled migration on low-skilled workers. Even if the overall balance from immigration is positive, there can be concern about the impact, particularly from low-skilled migration, on those most disadvantaged in the labour market. Immigration may make it harder for less educated workers to find work, and may reduce the wages they can obtain in work. These groups are, of course, the focus of much government policy in the UK, through the New Deal and other programmes.

Looking first at the experience of the United States, evidence shows that there is only a weak relationship between native wages and the number of immigrants in a city or state.[6] This holds true for both skilled and unskilled workers. Part of the explanation for this lies in the different geographical location of international and domestic migrants. US Census data show that domestic migrants do not move to the same cities as international migrants. Places in the US that grew through international immigration in the 1990s showed a net *outflow* of domestic migrants. The fact that domestic and international migrants in the US are not found in the same locations reduces the competitive downward impact on wage rates.

At the national level, US research shows that, since the 1980s, immigration has increased the supply of unskilled workers (lacking a high-school diploma or equivalent) by 15 per cent relative to the more skilled. This probably lowered the wages of these workers by about 5 per cent, just under half of the fall in wages for this group between 1980 and 1994. But bear in mind that this group represented less than 10 per cent of the US workforce by 1995. Immigration thus plays some role in explaining wage decline for the least skilled in the US, but very little in explaining increased wage inequality for other native workers.

While it may be true that unskilled immigrants take jobs that natives do not want, 'we still need to ask why natives do not want these jobs . . . Almost every job that immigrants do in Los Angeles or New York is done by natives in Detroit and Philadelphia . . . the reason is that by local standards the wages are abysmal.'[7] Similarly in Britain, many of the jobs (in hotels, cleaning, catering) performed by international migrants in London and the south are carried out by local people elsewhere in the UK.

A key difference between the UK and the US is the level of internal mobility. The UK and other European countries are characterised by low mobility. The US is a very mobile society, with very flexible labour markets. In those circumstances, the local impacts of immigration will be attenuated because workers and firms adjust their behaviour to take it into account. The impact of the increased supply of unskilled workers is diffused throughout the whole regional (or even national) labour market—not just locally.[8] So increased immigration of unskilled labour into a local labour market will lead to an increased net outflow of native unskilled labour—those workers looking elsewhere for jobs because of the increased competition from immigrants.[9]

In the UK the housing and labour markets, particularly for less skilled workers, are far more rigid. This suggests that increased immigration, particularly at the low-skill end, may have a greater local impact on the existing low-skilled workforce because those workers cannot move on to find better jobs elsewhere.

The evidence base on the economics of migration in the UK is far smaller than in the United States. But recent research commissioned by the Home Office explored the impact on native workers in local labour markets.[10] The main conclusion is that there is no strong evidence that immigration has any large adverse effects on employment prospects or wages. Rather, immigration to the UK has a small and often not statistically significant effect on the unemployment of native workers. The effect of immigration on wages seems, if anything, to be positive: using the most robust data source, an increase in immigration of 1 per cent of the non-migrant population leads to a nearly 2 per cent increase in non-migrant wages. However, the statistical reliability of these estimates is sometimes weak.

The findings are consistent with a large body of evidence for other countries which finds that there is no large discernible impact of immigration on native wages or employment. Hence: 'on current evidence fears of large and negative employment and wage effects on the resident population are not easily justifiable. The perception that immigrants take away jobs from the existing population, thus contributing to large increases in unemployment, or that immigrants depress wages of existing workers, do not find confirmation . . . in this report.'[11]

Wages and jobs of immigrants

In looking at the economic impacts on immigrants themselves, it is often difficult to separate out the effect of migration per se from effects related to differing characteristics of ethnic groups, or from the effects of labour market discrimination. What we can say in broad terms is that immigration most directly benefits the economic welfare of migrants themselves. That is, indeed, their main motivation in moving.

In Britain, migrants benefit despite the fact that the foreign-born overall tend to 'perform' worse than the native population, with lower employment and labour market participation rates and higher unemployment. These outcomes differ considerably across migrant groups and are more marked for women than men. White migrants have similar labour market outcomes to the existing population, but ethnic minority migrants are less likely to be employed or to participate, and tend to have lower wages. Ethnic minority migrants also do worse on these indicators than people from the same ethnic group who are born in the UK.

Even when socio-economic characteristics are controlled for, ethnic minority migrants are found by one study to have lower levels of employment and participation and lower wages than the UK-born population. Another finds this true only for Bangladeshis and Pakistanis. Female migrants from these groups have participation rates 54–57 per cent below the white population, and still 31–34 per cent below when individual characteristics (such as education and skills) are taken into account.

'White' immigrants generally have higher wages than UK-born whites with the same characteristics, but ethnic minority migrants have lower wages. This is true for men and women, but more so for men. Wage differentials are considerable, reaching about 40 per cent for male Bangladeshis.

The main factors affecting labour market outcomes for migrants are the following:

- Education has a positive effect on employment and participation.
- UK qualifications are more valued in the market than overseas ones.
- English-language fluency enhances probability of employment by about 20 per cent and increases wages. Labour market premium to fluency is greatest for those ethnic minority migrant groups with the least success in the labour market and the lowest fluency rates.
- Participation and the employment rate differential gradually reduce with length of stay. After twenty years' residence, participation and the employment probabilities of male minority immigrants are similar to those of UK-born whites. But differences for women from ethnic minority communities are much more pronounced. Female immigrants do not appear to reach parity of employment rates no matter how long they have been in Britain.

Among existing British minority ethnic communities (the majority of whom are now UK-born), there is considerable heterogeneity across ethnic groups in terms of educational and labour market outcomes.[12] Indian men are the least disadvantaged; Pakistani, Bangladeshi and black men and women the most. Evidence suggests that there is insufficient economic integration either for first-generation immigrants or their children. All ethnic minorities remain disadvantaged in relation to employment and occupational attainment and, with some exceptions, also disadvantaged in relation to earnings. Observables such as educational attainment account for some of the differences in outcomes, but other factors are also relevant, including discrimination.

In general, we do not know enough about the *trajectories* of migrants— economic, educational or residential—in the UK. Current and proposed research within and outside government, such as analysis of the lifetime labour market database, should improve the state of knowledge on this in the future. But it is likely to be the case that the progress or otherwise of migrants will depend on several factors: the characteristics of the migrants themselves; external economic circumstances, such as the strength of the national and local economies; the strength of the occupational and industrial sectors in which migrants are working; structural barriers in the labour market; and discrimination. The variation in outcomes across different minority groups (and differences between men and women within ethnic groups) is likely to be true also for new migrants. They themselves comprise a more hetero-geneous group in terms both of geographical origins and skills levels than earlier cohorts.

Recent immigrants do less well

In the United States, immigrants do continue to move up the economic ladder, but the rate of progress is falling, and the research consensus has moved from an optimistic to a somewhat pessimistic view.[13] An influential early study was that of Chiswick who, using census data, showed that immigrants began with a disadvantage but that their prospects quickly improved. After around twenty years, immigrants' earnings surpassed those of natives of the same ethnic background. Thus, Mexican immigrants advanced more slowly than European immigrants, but over time did better than comparable Mexican Americans. Borjas challenged these findings on methodological and substantive grounds. Chiswick had assumed the characteristics of more recent migrants to be similar to those of earlier ones.[14] But migrations are selective. It is hardest at first, so the early movers are likely to have higher skills, greatest resources, best connections and highest risk propensity. It is also the case that, from the mid-1960s, legislative barriers to migration to the US were lowered.

Empirically, the gap between foreign-born and native workers has widened recently. Using 1980 data, Borjas shows that 1970s migrants were moving ahead more slowly than earlier cohorts, and the picture for 1990 was worse still. Recent immigrants do not catch up with, let alone surpass, their native-born counterparts. So recent Mexican migrants fare worse than Mexican Americans generally, who are themselves a disadvantaged group.

Recent arrivals to the US and those migrating from Latin America (both men and women) earn the lowest wages. Recent migrants are better educated than earlier waves, but the education levels of natives have increased more—so the skills (and hence wages) gap has widened. 'This relative decline in immigrant skills and wages can be attributed essentially to a single factor—the fact that those who have come most recently have come from poorer countries, where the average education and wage and skill levels are far below those in the United States.'[15]

In Canada, recent immigrants are also doing less well than their predecessors. Recent immigrants—especially 'visible minorities'—have experienced high unemployment and underemployment in low-wage jobs that do not reflect skills and qualifications: 'In 1995, 35 percent of immigrants who arrived in Canadian cities after 1986 were living in poverty . . . rising to 52 percent of those who arrived after 1991. Other analysts have documented a lengthening catch-up period between immigration and convergence to average rates of employment, earnings and family incomes.'[16]

The reasons for this are complex, but include the effect of recession in the first half of the 1990s; the changing mix of refugees, family-class immigrants and skilled migration; non-recognition or under-valuation of foreign education, skills and credentials; and discrimination. With the return of economic growth between 1995 and 1998, the gaps in employment and income opportunities between recent immigrants and other Canadians narrowed considerably.

The economic integration (or exclusion) of migrants will have a key influence on social integration and community cohesion. Labour markets in the UK and elsewhere are today characterised by growing inequality. This contrasts with earlier phases of migration in the postwar period which took place against a backdrop of increasing *equality* in economic terms, and (in the UK) alongside the establishment of a welfare state. The UK has moved in the direction of the United States where, over the past twenty years, real wages among *all* less skilled workers have fallen sharply, and hence 'Less-skilled immigrants are striving to make it in a labour market oversupplied with poorly educated workers and in which the terms of compensation have shifted sharply against the less skilled.'[17] This is not a problem for the highly educated, skilled immigrant—indeed, it is to his or her economic advantage—but makes life more difficult for the less skilled.

The migration paradigm, at least for long-term migrants, is that initial hardship will be followed by economic and social progress, if not for the original migrant, then at least for succeeding generations. In the United States, many researchers now think it unlikely that the children and grandchildren of current immigrants will reach the pinnacle of US society, as was the case with children of earlier waves. The historical circumstances for new migrants, at least in the US, are now less favourable. In the early twentieth century, the economic gap between immigrants and natives was not great: 'Most immigrants were poor, but so were most natives.' Now, Borjas estimates that the wage gap between immigrants and natives is three times as large as it was in 1910. 'Only half the Mexicans living in America have attended secondary school, and only a third have graduated. Only one in eight claims to speak English very well. Italians and Poles had similar handicaps in 1910, but Americans are far better educated today than they were a century ago, so the gap between Mexicans and American-born workers is wide.'[18]

Demand for migrant labour

Labour markets both in the UK and across many OECD countries are relatively tight at present: 'all the available data and research confirm that labour markets are tight in several OECD member countries, principally in the areas of advanced technology, but also relating to some unskilled occupations.'[19] Coupled with projected demographic change, this is often taken to imply that the demand for migrant labour will increase. There are currently relatively large numbers of vacancies in many occupations in the UK, including low-status jobs such as care assistants and home carers, general office assistants and labourers. Such vacancies coexist with unemployed workers for a variety of reasons including geographical mismatch, attitudes of unemployed workers and employers, barriers to employment (such as transport and childcare costs) and some aspects of the benefit system.

The persistence of unfilled vacancies suggests a case for at least temporary migration schemes aimed at the low-skilled. But what about the future demand for migrant labour? This is not at all easy to predict. With most OECD countries committed to a more market-based approach to labour market balance, 'manpower planning' on a command economy basis is no longer appropriate. It is not straightforward to estimate future labour shortages overall, nor the skills breakdown of these shortages. Part of the reason for this is that, in the UK and elsewhere, reported shortages can coexist with pools of unemployed or inactive workers. In the UK, projections show that the occupations expected to show the largest growth to 2010 are caring personal services (up almost half a million jobs) and business and public service associate professionals, projected to rise by 360,000.[20] Other occupations showing large increases are business and public service professionals (+260,000), teaching and research professionals (+257,000), science and technology professionals (+252,000) and health professionals (+95,000). Most of these categories require a degree or professional qualifications.

Conversely, declines are projected for less skilled jobs. The number employed with qualifications below NVQ level 2 is expected to fall by 229,000 between 1998 and 2009. Moreover, unemployment rates for unskilled workers are far above those for more skilled categories, and this differential has increased over the past twenty years.

There are a number of occupational groups where there are projected increases for staff with low levels of training or qualifications. These include plant and machinery operators, and sales and clerical occupations. Bivand comments: 'Many of these jobs will be suitable for those moving from welfare into work, with lower levels of skills or qualifications.'[21] Data from the Institute for Employment Research at Warwick University suggest that the numbers employed in catering, domestic staff and related occupations will also rise between 1999 and 2010, as will those of food, drink and tobacco process operatives. A total increase of some 62,000 jobs is anticipated in these sectors. But this is more than outweighed by a loss of 247,000 jobs in 'other elementary occupations'.

It is also important to remember that persistent unfilled vacancies may be a consequence of the characteristics of the sector rather than any real deficit in the number of available workers. In some industries, the wages may be too low for there ever *not* to be vacancies. In some parts of the hospitality sector, for example, this appears to be built into the structure. For example, a recent study of the sector in London argued that 'for some employers, competitiveness depends on low-cost service provided by a primarily young, mobile workforce. Far from being a problem, employee "transience" is integral to the business strategy. Quality is a secondary issue.'[22] In these circumstances, an increased supply of migrant workers should not be used as a substitute for improving the pay and conditions in the sector which are the underlying driver of high turnover and high vacancies.

The general conclusion must be to urge caution with regard to increasing the supply of migrants in response to supposed shortages of low-skilled labour. Evidence from other countries suggests that current migrants are finding it harder to advance economically than previous cohorts, while projections for the UK suggest a continuing shift towards a more skilled economy and hence reduced long-term demand for unskilled labour.

Demographic impact

The report by the UN Population Division entitled 'Replacement Migration: Is It a Solution to a Declining and Ageing Population?' generated considerable publicity through its suggestion that very high levels of migration into EU and other OECD countries would be needed to counteract their ageing population. The study considered whether replacement migration could in fact be a solution to declining and ageing populations, exploring different scenarios for the migration needed to achieve specific population outcomes.

As the study makes clear, for 'France, United Kingdom, the United States and the European Union, the numbers of migrants needed to offset population decline are less than or comparable to recent past experience.'[23] For the UK, net migration flows of 125,000 per annum between 1995 and 2050 would keep the size of the working-age population constant. This figure only slightly exceeds the central government projection of 100,000 net migration per annum, and is below the actual net migration figures for recent years.

The migration flows needed to keep the potential support ratio (workers to non-workers) constant are vastly higher. For the UK, this would require net migration of around 1.2 million each year; for the EU as a whole the flow would be 13.48 million. Korea's population would rise to more than 5 billion! Clearly this scenario is not realistic, but rather a statistical device to demonstrate the scale of demographic change.

Analysis of Eurostat figures by Feld does 'not support the alarmist tendency' of the UN report but rather suggests, on Eurostat's median scenarios, a relatively gentle fall in the size of the European labour force from 175.82 million to 172.96 million between 2000 and 2025 (1.6 per cent over twenty-five years). Moreover, the question of whether increased migration is necessary depends not only on demography, but also on factors that affect the participation rates of different components of the existing labour force. Within Europe, labour force participation varies greatly (in 1995 from 36.7 per cent in Italy to 67.1 per cent in Sweden, for instance). Hence, 'some EU countries will experience no difficulty ensuring continuing growth in the size of their labour force over the next 25 years, while others will be faced with stagnation and for a few of them a slight fall.' This will mean 'very different assessments of the need for, importance of and scale of recourse to migratory flows among the countries'.[24]

This analysis implies that countries with currently low labour participation rates have scope for mobilising higher rates as a response to demographic change, for instance by encouraging or enabling more women to work. This option is less apparent for the UK, with its currently relatively high participation rates (by European standards). However, even in the UK the employment of older men has been falling, and there are estimated to be 2.8 million men and women aged between 50 and state pension age who are economically inactive, providing a potential reserve of additional labour. The government is indeed actively engaged in initiatives to increase their participation rates, including plans to legislate to make age discrimination in employment unlawful by 2006.

On current migration trends, the size of the working-age population in the UK will remain roughly constant. Moreover, over the next twenty years the demographic impacts on dependency are relatively small. It is in the period 2020–40 and beyond that the position deteriorates significantly. The number of pensioners per 1,000 persons of working age is expected to increase only slightly (from 291 to 301 per thousand) between 2001 and 2021. Indeed, the number of *all* dependants (pensioners and children) *falls* over this period.

Higher net migration is projected by the government to have a marked impact on the overall size of the UK population (from 60 million to 70 million in 2035). But higher net migration will not prevent the old-age dependency ratio rising sharply from 2020 onwards. The conclusion must be that migration can at most mitigate the population ageing process; it cannot be a solution to the problem. Britain, along with most other OECD countries, is currently undergoing a transition in the age structure of the population. If the real value of income in retirement is to be maintained for current and later cohorts of workers, people will need to work longer, or more productively, or save more—most likely, some combination of all three. Migration policy can at best be one element, and a relatively minor one, within a policy portfolio addressing the demographic/pensions problem.

Migration policy can never be as effective as changes to, for example, retirement age. At root, this reflects the difference between averages and marginals: raising the retirement age by one year affects the entire labour force and the entire retired cohort, while changes to migration policy work at the margin. This is implicit in the UNPD calculations. To achieve in 2050 the same potential support ratio in the UK as in 1995 would, we have seen, require an increase in *net* migration to 1.2 million per annum over the whole of the period: ten times the historically high level of 126,000 in 2001. With zero migration, the same effect could be achieved by raising the state pension age to 72; that is, extending working life by around 16 per cent. While neither of these is a realistic policy option, the exercise makes clear the difference in orders of magnitude in their effects.

The statistical analysis thus supports the intuitive position that migrants can only be a 'one-off' fix, because they will age too. There are just two exceptions to this. The first is the institution of guest-worker programmes, in which migrants are sent elsewhere once they are no longer economically productive. Such schemes raise practical as well as moral questions. The second is the trend for migration increasingly to be a short-term process in which people choose to live and work in one country for variable periods of time, and then move on.

The demographic argument is a specific instance of the general proposition that immigration changes things only to the extent that migrants are different from natives. If immigrants quickly become like natives (for instance, acquiring similar fertility rates) migration can only provide a once-and-for-all boost to population and dependency ratios.

Policy implications

Migration policy is concerned not only with the needs of the labour market but also with social cohesion, public protection, international development goals and human rights. The challenge for migration policy is getting the balance right both *within* and *between* these objectives.

A modern, productive economy undoubtedly requires labour as well as capital mobility. The UK is an attractive destination for skilled workers from across the world, and it will need to compete to attract and retain workers in a more globalised system with additional players. While some low-skilled shortages will also remain, overall numbers of such jobs are projected to fall. Sectors which rely on a continuing supply of low-skilled jobs, unless there are clear seasonal or similar factors at work, may not be sustainable in the long-term in the UK.

Higher net migration can at most mitigate the process of population ageing. It cannot provide a long-term solution to the problem. In order to preserve the real value of income in retirement, changes will be needed to the length of working life, to productivity, and to the balance between consumption and saving. Migration policy can at best be a minor element in the policy portfolio responding to demographic change.

Higher migration generates gains in production. We have seen that in general the effect is found to be positive, but not large in relation to the size of the economy of the destination country. Migration also redistributes income between domestic labour groups, between labour and capital, and between natives and immigrants—but again these effects are unlikely to be large.

In order to maximise the economic benefits from migration, the evidence suggests that the UK government needs to build on the success of existing managed migration routes in order to establish a comprehensive and clearly specified set of entry channels which will:

- prioritise medium- and high-skilled workers;
- continue to expand existing schemes but also look at ways of simplifying the range of current schemes for economic migrants;
- use a mixture of sector-specific and points-based schemes;
- make better use of existing and future migrants to meet public sector recruitment needs.

The recently expanded work permit system, in which employers are given permits for specific migrants to fit particular hard-to-fill jobs (anticipated to total about 200,000 in 2003), and schemes such as those for Commonwealth Working Holidaymakers and Seasonal Agricultural Workers appear to be working well. Nevertheless, there is a plethora of existing schemes, with new initiatives being announced regularly, including most recently a new channel for low-skilled migrants to work in hotels and catering and the food production industry. Paucity of research means that these policy innovations can not be sufficiently informed by rigorous evaluation of existing schemes and hence new developments cannot always learn from experience.

Low-skilled migration is a complex policy area. Some argue that there is a strong case for a major expansion of 'temporary' low-skilled schemes, in part to reduce the incentive for irregular migrants to come and work without permission. However, how 'temporary' can such migration be? There are good reasons on both the demand and supply sides to think that the underlying drivers are for permanent migration. On the supply side, there is an extremely large potential supply of low-skilled economic migrants. On the demand side, many of these temporary jobs do not arise in response to strictly seasonal or cyclical factors, but rather follow from working practices in particular sectors which rely on a permanent supply of rapid-turnover, unskilled labour. Moreover, evidence from many countries suggests that 'guest-worker' schemes almost always turn into permanent migration.

Of course, it is always possible in theory for governments to enforce the temporary nature of schemes, through rigorous monitoring, policing and deportation of over-stayers, or enforced destitution for those refusing to leave. However, such policies would conflict with both social cohesion and human rights goals.

The downside risks are thus greater with low-skilled than high-skilled schemes. The rationale for expansion of low-skilled economic migration routes is unclear: there are still large numbers of unemployed and inactive UK residents, and unemployment rates are higher among ethnic minorities. Moving the majority of unemployed and inactive workers from benefits to work implies improving their access to, and willingness to take, low-skilled jobs.

There are a variety of domestic policy responses to labour shortages (both skilled and unskilled), including active labour market policies, education and training initiatives, and housing and transport policies. There is a strong policy implication for caution with regard to the possible expansion of channels for low-skilled migration. Rather, current and existing schemes, for both low- and high-skilled migration, should be subject to more rigorous programme evaluation, including a wide definition of costs and benefits, to cover the costs of promoting the social inclusion of migrants, of monitoring the scheme, and of provision for detection and removal of over-stayers. Consideration should be given to other government objectives for the labour market, particularly policies regarding workforce development and training; and schemes for temporary and/or seasonal workers should be clearly distinguished, in terms of objectives, operation and evaluation, from permanent migration.

One unequivocal finding from much research is that the acquisition of English-language skills is crucial for the economic and social integration of migrants. Its importance is not yet adequately reflected in policy. In some cases there also needs to be better recognition of existing skills and overseas qualifications. Support to secure faster labour market access will help integration and social inclusion of migrants more generally.

The economic impact of migration on the UK is positive, but probably not large. Hence, the argument for immigration restriction on the basis of 'unsupportable' economic costs is wrong. But at the same time, there is not a compelling long-term case for increased immigration purely in terms of economic benefits. Understanding the economics of migration is crucial for an informed rational policy debate. However, the economic case alone will not be conclusive. Future UK migration policy will need to be determined through a careful balance which includes economic costs and benefits alongside social concerns, human rights obligations and public protection goals.

Notes

1 J. L. Simon, *The Economic Consequences of Immigration*, Ann Arbor, Mich., University of Michigan Press, 1999, p. 299.
2 J. W. Moses and B. Letnes, 'The Economic Costs to International Labor Restrictions', paper presented to WIDER conference on Poverty, International Migration and Asylum, Helsinki, 27–28 September 2002; B. Hamilton and J. Whalley, 'Efficiency and Distributional Implications of Global Restrictions on Labour Mobility', *Journal of Development Economics*, vol. 14, 1984, pp. 61–75.
3 T. L. Walmsley and L. A. Winters, 'Relaxing the Restrictions on the Temporary Movement of Natural Persons: A Simulation Analysis', 2002, http://www.gtap.agecon.purdue.edu/resources/res_display.asp?RecordID=949.
4 J. P. Smith and B. Edmonston, eds, *The New Americans: Economic, Demographic and Fiscal Effects of Immigration*, Washington DC, National Academy Press, 1997.
5 Ibid.
6 David Card, 'The Impact of the Mariel Boatlift on the Miami Labour Market,' *Industrial and Labour Relations Review*, vol. 43, no. 2, Jan. 1990, pp. 245–57; Smith and Edmonston, *The New Americans*.
7 C. Jencks, 'Who Should Get In?', *New York Review of Books*, 29 Nov., 20 Dec. 2001.
8 G. J. Borjas, 'The Economics of Immigration,' *Journal of Economic Literature*, vol. 32, no. 4, 1994, pp. 1667–1717.
9 The net outflow of native workers is increased not only by native out-migration but also by reduced levels of *inflow* of native workers, compared with what would happen in the absence of immigration.
10 Christian Dustmann et al., *The Local Labour Market Effects of Immigration in the UK*, London, Home Office, 2002, using data from the Censuses of 1971–91, the Labour Force Survey 1983–2000 and the New Earnings Survey 1980 and 1990.
11 Dustmann et al., *The Local Labour Market Effects of Immigration in the UK*, p. 46.
12 Cabinet Office Performance and Innovation Unit, *Ethnic Minorities and Labour Markets: Interim Analysis Report*, London, Cabinet Office, 2002.
13 R. Waldinger, ed., *Strangers at the Gates: New Immigrants in Urban America*, Berkeley, Calif.: University of California Press, 2001, p. 12.
14 B. Chiswick, 'The Effect of Americanization on the Earnings of Foreign-Born Men', *Journal of Political Economy*, vol. 86, 1978, pp. 897–921; G. Borjas, 'Assimilation,

Changes in Cohort Quality, and the Earnings of Immigrants', *Journal of Labour Economics*, vol. 3, 1985, 463–89, and *Heaven's Door: Immigration Policy and the American Economy*, Princeton, NJ, Princeton University Press, 1999.

15 Smith and Edmonston, eds, *The New Americans*.

16 A. Jackson and E. Smith, 'Does a Rising Tide Lift All Boats? Recent Immigrants in the Economic Recovery', *Horizons Newsletter*, vol. 5, no. 2, 2002, Policy Research Initiative, Government of Canada.

17 Waldinger, *Strangers at the Gates*, p. 14.

18 Jencks, 'Who Should Get In?'; Borjas, *Heaven's Door*.

19 M. Doudeijns and J.-C. Dumont, 'Immigration and Labour Shortages: Evaluation of Needs and Limits of Selection Policies in the Recruitment of Foreign Labour', paper presented to OECD conference on the economic and social aspects of migration, Brussels, 21–22 Jan. 2003.

20 P. Bivand, 'Future Skills and Qualifications Needs', *Working Brief* 125, June 2001.

21 Ibid.

22 London Skills Forecasting Unit, *London's Recipe for Success: The Challenge for the Capital's Hospitality and Leisure Sectors*, London, LSFU, 2002.

23 UN Population Division, 'Replacement Migration: Is It a Solution to a Declining and Ageing Population?', March 2000.

24 S. Feld, 'Labour Force Trends in the European Union (2000–2025) and International Manpower Movements. Initial Outlook', paper presented at the International Union for the Scientific Study of Population General Conference, Salvader, Brazil, 2001.

Refugees and the Global Politics of Asylum

JEFF CRISP

THROUGHOUT human history, people have been obliged to flee from their own communities and countries as a result of political persecution, social violence and armed conflict. And in almost every part of the world, governments, armies and rebel movements have resorted to moving people by force in order to attain their political and military objectives.

The people who are most frequently and seriously affected by these forms of involuntary migration are the most vulnerable and marginalised members of society: minority groups, stateless people, indigenous populations and others who are excluded from the structures of political power. Even if they have managed to find a safe refuge in another country, they may never know if or when it will be possible for them to return to their place of origin.

This essay examines the politics of human displacement, and the role of the international community, especially UNHCR (the Office of the UN High Commissioner for Refugees) in responding to their plight. The opening section examines the changing causes of mass displacement. The second section explains why countries in developing regions have proven increasingly reluctant to accommodate large numbers of refugees, and the third examines the constraints on and limitations of humanitarian action in areas affected by armed conflict. The fourth section focuses on the movements of asylum seekers, refugees and other migrants from poorer and less stable regions to the industrialised states. The essay concludes with an examination of governmental responses to this phenomenon, identifying and assessing some of the alternative approaches that have been proposed.

Causes of mass displacement

It would be inaccurate to suggest that the refugee problem is more serious now than it has been in the past. In fact, the statistics demonstrate that the global refugee population has actually been in decline in recent years, from just under 15 million in 1995 to around 12 million at the beginning of 2002. Nevertheless, the issue of human displacement has assumed some particularly important—and in certain respects new—characteristics in the period since the end of the Cold War.

First, while refugee numbers may have declined, the total number of people displaced by persecution, violence and armed conflict appears to have increased substantially. Rather than crossing an international border, however, a growing proportion of these uprooted people now remain in their own

© The Political Quarterly Publishing Co. Ltd. 2003
Published by Blackwell Publishing Ltd, 9600 Garsington Road, Oxford OX4 2DQ, UK and 350 Main Street, Malden, MA 02148, USA

country, usually because they are unable, or in some cases unwilling, to seek asylum in another state. The most recent figures suggest that up to 25 million people are now displaced within their own state, around half of this number in Africa.

Second, the root causes of refugee movements appear to have changed. When UNHCR was established at the beginning of the 1950s, the European refugees for whom it assumed responsibility were primarily people who had fled from actual or feared persecution by fascist and communist regimes. The political persecution of dissidents and minority groups continues to be an important cause of refugee movements. But in recent years, the largest and most speedy population displacements have taken place in countries affected by armed conflict and communal violence, such as Afghanistan, Burundi, Colombia, Liberia, Sierra Leone and Somalia.

Third, while mass displacement most frequently takes place in the context of armed conflict, refugee movements are not simply a by-product of war. Indeed, one of the most disturbing developments in recent years has been the extent to which displacement has been used as a weapon of war, instigated by governments and other entities with the objective of expelling their enemies and population groups whose loyalty cannot be guaranteed.

As well as inflicting terrible suffering on civilian populations, this military strategy enables the protagonists in an armed conflict to gain control of territory and to ensure that it is populated with their coethnics or political allies. It was for this reason that the wars in former Yugoslavia, especially Bosnia-Herzegovina, led to such large-scale movements of people.

By way of contrast, in post-genocide Rwanda a massive exodus of people was engineered not by the victorious army of the Tutsi-led rebels, but by the leaders of the defeated and Hutu-dominated regime. As they lost their grip on power, these leaders persuaded and induced more than a million of the country's citizens to leave the country and to take up residence in internationally assisted camps located in eastern Zaire and Tanzania. The aim of this strategy was simple: to deprive the new administration of a population to govern, and to establish large concentrations of exiles on Rwanda's borders, where they could engage in a campaign of intimidation and destabilisation.

Asylum under threat

As the international organisation mandated to protect refugees, UNHCR has been at the forefront of recent efforts to respond to mass population movements of the type witnessed in the Balkans and the Great Lakes region of Africa. In doing so, UNHCR has encountered a serious problem: a declining willingness on the part of states to admit and accommodate large numbers of refugees.

In 1995 the then UN High Commissioner for Refugees, Mrs Sadako Ogata, observed that 'many countries are blatantly closing their borders to refugees' while others were 'more insidiously introducing laws and procedures which effectively deny refugees admission to their territory'. 'The threat to asylum', she observed, 'has taken on a global character.'

Since those words were spoken, the situation has not improved. In recent years, a number of countries have refused or granted only limited entry to people fleeing from armed conflict in neighbouring states. Pakistan, for example, which granted asylum to millions of Afghan refugees throughout the 1980s and much of the 1990s, pursued a restrictive policy during the US-led war against the Taleban at the end of 2001. African states such as Tanzania, which have historically pursued very liberal refugee policies and allowed large numbers of exiles to take up long-term residence on their territory, now make it very clear that they want the refugees to go home as quickly as possible. Throughout the world, developing countries routinely deprive refugees of basic rights, confining them to camps in remote border areas where they have no prospect of becoming self-reliant or integrating with the local population.

The declining commitment to asylum among the world's developing countries is a consequence of several political and economic trends. In the 1960s and 1970s, many refugees were the product of independence struggles and wars of national liberation, and were therefore welcomed by neighbouring and nearby states that had shared the same experience. The relative prosperity of many former colonial states in the early years of independence, coupled with the modest size of the refugee movements that took place at that time, also enabled those countries to bear the burden of refugee influxes without too much strain.

These favourable conditions for asylum were reinforced by the generous provision of international aid. In most developing regions an implicit deal was struck, whereby states admitted refugees to their territory and provided land for them to farm, while Western donor states provided the funding—much of it channelled through UNHCR—that was required to feed, shelter, educate and provide healthcare to the exiled populations. As well as being an important humanitarian gesture, such assistance played a useful role in the efforts of Western states to establish friendly relations with developing countries, thereby containing the global communist threat.

Since the late 1980s, the political and economic underpinnings of asylum that existed in the 1960s and 1970s have been progressively dismantled. Sheer numbers have played a part in this process. As noted above, the scale and speed of refugee movements increased significantly in the 1980s and 1990s, as a result of the new forms of armed conflict and communal violence that flared up as the Cold War came to an end. No longer the victims of anti-colonial struggles, the new generation of refugees could not always count on the sympathy of host states and societies.

Other factors have played an important part in weakening the commitment to asylum and refugee protection in the world's less prosperous states. As a later section of this essay will suggest, the industrialised countries took a lead in attempting to keep refugees and asylum seekers away from their territory, and in so doing set an important example for states in other parts of the world that were less well placed to assume responsibility for large numbers of refugees.

During the 1990s countries such as Malawi and Pakistan, which had previously admitted very large numbers of refugees, began to feel that their generosity was too easily and quickly forgotten by the international community. Once the emergency was over or the refugees had gone home, they were left to cope with the environmental and economic impact of the influx.

With the end of the Cold War, donor states had less political interest in financing generous refugee assistance programmes. Indeed, many of the world's largest refugee populations were to be found in countries which were of little geopolitical significance and had not shared in the expansion of the global economy.

At the same time, these very same countries were confronted with a wide range of interrelated political, economic and social problems: high levels of population growth and unemployment, declining levels of official development assistance, environmental degradation, the HIV/AIDS pandemic, and the imposition of structural adjustment programmes that led to cuts in public sector spending, services and jobs. Not surprisingly in this context, local populations began to resent the fact that refugees received free food, education, healthcare and other essential services from the international community.

The increasingly hostile reception accorded to refugees in developing regions can also be attributed to political developments at the national level. Prior to the 1990s, authoritarian governments and one-party states were relatively free to offer asylum to large refugee populations when they considered such a policy to be consistent with their own interests. But with the end of the Cold War and the introduction of pluralistic systems of government in many parts of the world, the refugee issue has achieved a new degree of political salience.

As in the industrialised states, both governments and opposition parties are prone to mobilising popular support by promoting nationalistic and xenophobic sentiments, and by blaming their country's ills on the presence of refugees, asylum seekers and illegal immigrants. In countries where large numbers of people are living at or below the poverty line—Côte d'Ivoire, Guinea, Pakistan and South Africa provide four good examples—such messages can have a potent appeal to voters.

The scenario is consequently a gloomy one. While certain civil wars have recently come to an end or diminished significantly in intensity (in Angola, Sierra Leone and Sri Lanka, for example), the likelihood is that new conflicts will erupt, forcing people to abandon their homes and to look for safety elsewhere. Increasingly, it seems, that 'elsewhere' will be in another part of their own country, where they may well remain vulnerable to the persecution or conflict from which they have fled, rather than to the relative safety of a neighbouring or nearby state.

In this context, it should be noted that the international community's approach to the problem of mass displacement continues to focus on the responsibility of those countries to which refugees flee, rather than on the responsibility of those states which generate large population movements. For a brief moment in the early and mid-1990s, when traditional notions of sovereignty and non-intervention came under growing scrutiny, it appeared that this situation might change. UNHCR itself argued that international responses to the refugee problem were becoming less 'exile-oriented' and more 'homeland-oriented', and it was thought that this trend would be reinforced by the appointment of a UN High Commissioner for Human Rights.

The predictions made at that time have not been entirely confounded, as demonstrated by those situations (in northern Iraq, Kosovo and East Timor, for example) in which military forces have intervened to halt human rights abuses and to enable the return of refugees or displaced populations. At the same time, only limited progress has been made in the broader effort to establish the principle that states and non-state actors alike have a responsibility to desist from actions that force people to leave their own countries and communities. While this principle may be invoked in relation to leaders who have suffered a political and/or military defeat (as is the case in former Yugoslavia) it appears that those who have been able to remain in power will continue to enjoy a significant degree of immunity.

The limitations of humanitarian action

Until the 1990s, UNHCR and other refugee relief agencies were primarily concerned with cross-border population displacements. They consequently focused their operations in countries of asylum, where conditions were relatively secure and stable. Humanitarian action in countries of origin and in areas of active conflict was largely the preserve of the International Committee of the Red Cross (ICRC).

Over the past decade, UNHCR's traditional reluctance to work in such locations has effectively been abandoned, and the organisation now frequently finds itself working in countries of origin and in areas that are affected by armed conflict. This development can be ascribed to a number of different factors: the declining willingness of states to admit large numbers of refugees; the growth in the number of internally displaced people; and the changing notions of national sovereignty, which have allowed for greater international intervention in the affairs of unstable states.

UNHCR's willingness to change its approach has also been conditioned by the growing degree of competition in the humanitarian sector. Recent years have seen a proliferation of international and local NGOs alongside long-established international agencies such as the ICRC, UNHCR and the World Food Programme, and a growing interest in humanitarian relief from the private sector. At the same time, military forces, acting with or without a

United Nations mandate, have assumed a leading role in the delivery of assistance and the provision of security to relief operations, as witnessed in places such as northern Iraq, Somalia, the former Yugoslavia and East Timor. In this environment, everyone is competing for market share.

A final reason for UNHCR's expanded involvement in areas of violence and instability derives from the fact that many refugee-hosting countries are themselves in the throes of armed conflict and political violence. Thus in West Africa, for example, Sierra Leonean and Liberian refugees have come under attack in Guinea, while Liberian refugees have been threatened by the wars in Côte d'Ivoire and Sierra Leone. In these and other parts of the world, refugees have left their own country to seek safety in another state, only to find that their country of asylum is equally dangerous.

UNHCR's experience in moving from the realm of 'refugee protection' to that of 'humanitarian action' has been a salutary one. As indicated earlier, in the 1990s there was a widespread belief that the international community, freed from the bipolar paralysis inflicted by the Cold War, would use the anticipated 'peace dividend' to maintain security and protect vulnerable populations in the world's less stable states; and, for a period of time, such hopes were realised, as witnessed by the joint military and humanitarian operations that were launched in a number of conflict-affected countries.

Before very long, however, the problems associated with such interventions became manifest. In Somalia, US and other external forces were confronted with intense local hostility; in Bosnia, UN troops were evidently unable to provide adequate protection to minority groups; in Liberia, West African peacekeepers were responsible for inflicting human rights violations on the local population. Not surprisingly, the enthusiasm for such initiatives began to wane. While operations of this type have not been entirely abandoned, it seems clear that in future such deployments are most likely to take place in situations where humanitarian concerns are matched by the geopolitical interests of the Western states.

Since the early 1990s the difficulties and dilemmas associated with human-itarian action in situations of armed conflict have become increasingly evident. In violent operational environments, where resources are scarce and where the displacement of civilian populations is an objective of the combatants, humanitarian action may not be regarded as a neutral or impartial activity. Humanitarian agencies and their employees may be targeted if they are known to be providing assistance to groups of people who are associated in some way with the enemy. Aid organisations may have their assets appropriated by the parties to a conflict, or be faced with demands to hand over a proportion of their relief supplies in exchange for access to displaced and war-affected populations.

As well as facing additional danger and pressure from political and military actors, humanitarian actors such as UNHCR have been confronted with increasing moral dilemmas. During the war in Bosnia-Herzegovina, for example, the organisation feared that if it helped endangered minorities to move out of harm's way, it would simply be facilitating the process of ethnic cleansing. In the African Great Lakes crisis of the mid-1990s, many critics called on UNHCR to withdraw from the Rwandan refugee camps established in Tanzania and Zaire, alleging that the organisation was feeding the very people who had been responsible for the genocide, and thereby supporting them in their military and political objectives.

Another conclusion to be drawn from UNHCR's recent experience is that humanitarian action has a limited role in situations of armed conflict and political violence, and must not be used to absolve states of their rightful responsibilities. The organisation's experience in theatres of war such as the Balkans, the Caucasus and West Africa has demonstrated that humanitarian action can help to meet the basic needs of vulnerable populations. In some situations humanitarian agencies may be able to reduce levels of tension and even limit the scale of human rights violations by acting as an international witness. But humanitarian action cannot bring wars to an end, force governments and rebel groups to sit at the negotiating table, or protect civilians who are confronted with forces determined to destroy or displace them.

Asylum seekers and migrants

Most of the people who abandon their homes to escape from persecution, armed conflict and violence either remain in their own country as internally displaced people or seek asylum as refugees in a neighbouring or nearby state. Between 1992 and 2001, for example, developing countries accommodated on average more than 70 per cent of the world's refugee population. At the beginning of 2002, around 9 million of the world's 12 million refugees were to be found in Africa and Asia.

Other people, however, look for safety and security further afield, by seeking asylum in the industrialised states of western Europe and North America. In doing so, they join a broader stream of international migrants whose primary objective is to look for work, to attain a better standard of living, or to join family or community members who have already moved to another part of the world. In fact, it has become increasingly difficult to make a sharp distinction between 'refugees' and 'economic migrants'; for in many cases people move from one country and continent to another in response to a complex set of threats, hardships and opportunities.

Irrespective of their exact motivation, a large proportion of those people who have managed to move from poorer and less stable parts of the world to one of the industrialised states have sought to secure the right of residence there by submitting a claim to refugee status. Indeed, given the very limited opportunities that have existed for legal or regular migration from the 'South' to the 'North' since the 1980s, it is the one route that has been available to them.

Over the past twenty years, almost 9 million asylum applications have been submitted in the states of western Europe and North America. In the early

1980s the number of applications filed each year stood in the region of 150,000, but thereafter the number increased very rapidly, from 250,000 in 1987 to a peak of 850,000 in 1992. While the annual totals have since subsided, they have remained at a relatively high level—between 500,000 and 600,000—in each of the four years from 1999 to 2002.

The arrival of so many asylum seekers has not met with a favourable reaction from politicians and the public. Governments have pointed out that less than a third of all applicants for asylum in the industrialised states are eventually recognised as refugees or given permission to remain on other grounds. On the basis of such statistics, they argue that the asylum procedure has been abused by large numbers of economic migrants who have no need of international protection.

Public reaction to the arrival of asylum seekers has also tended to be hostile. International migration, it would appear, is acceptable to the electorate when it is modest in scale and orderly in nature, and imposes few pressures on the public purse. But it is not appreciated when it involves large numbers of people who enter the country in an irregular manner and who appear to bring little financial or social capital with them. When asylum seekers arrive from distant and unfamiliar countries that are associated in the public mind with terrorism, radical Islam and political violence, then the public reaction is likely to be even more negative.

In this political and social climate, it is not surprising that the industrialised states have in recent years tended to ignore the economic and cultural contribution that many refugees make to their countries of asylum. Instead, they have introduced a barrage of measures intended to deter or prevent the arrival of people who intend to request refugee status. These include visa requirements, carrier sanctions, preboarding documentation checks at airports and readmission agreements with transit countries, as well as the interdiction and mandatory detention of asylum seekers.

As demonstrated by the statistics presented earlier in this section, these measures appear to have had some success in first reducing and subsequently stabilising the volume of asylum applications submitted in the industrialised states. But there is also evidence to suggest that these restrictive measures have simply prompted asylum seekers and other migrants to find new destinations and new migratory routes, and to make more extensive use of professional human smugglers. In certain cases migrants have been particularly successful in remaining one step ahead of states and their security services. Over the past decade, for example, the UK has introduced an almost constant stream of legislative and administrative measures, all of them designed to limit the number of asylum applications the country receives. And yet the figures have risen relentlessly, from just over 30,000 in 1992 to more than 110,000 in 2002.

Impact on Western states

As such figures suggest, for many of the governments and politicians concerned, asylum has become something of a nightmare, an issue which appears relatively impervious to the usual instruments of public policy.

First, despite a considerable expenditure of resources, the industrialised states have generally found it very difficult to establish effective and expeditious procedures to process claims to refugee status. This problem has been manifested in a number of ways: in the prevalence of asylum application backlogs, in delays in status determination, in the failure to ensure the removal or deportation of people whose claims to refugee status have been rejected, and in the periodic declaration of amnesties for irregular migrants. On the one hand, these difficulties appear to have made asylum seeking a less risky and thereby a more attractive proposition for potential migrants. On the other hand, they have communicated an impression of governmental incompetence and incapacity.

Second, the salience of the asylum issue in the industrialised states has exerted significant pressure on public finances. While the accuracy of the figures is somewhat suspect, the industrialised states claim to spend in the region of $10 billion each year on asylum-related activities—a figure massively greater than the $800 million that UNHCR spends on almost 20 million refugees and other displaced people around the world. At national level, the sums of money involved can be very significant. In March 2003, for example, the British Chancellor of the Exchequer was obliged to make an emergency payment of around $1.5 billion to the Home Office to help it cope with the rising number of asylum applications—not a welcome commitment for a government that is struggling to juggle all the other demands made on public finances.

A third concern for Western governments is to be found in the way asylum seekers have been able to evade the increasingly restrictive immigration controls which they have introduced in recent years. As indicated earlier in this section, as it has become increasingly difficult to cross international borders in an open and legal manner, so a commercial (and in many instances criminal) industry has arisen, dedicated to human smuggling, the production of false identity documents and the corruption of immigration officials. Most disturbingly for states, this industry is linked to (and has almost certainly fuelled) other illicit transnational activities: the trafficking of women and children for sexual purposes, narcotics and firearms smuggling, and possibly also terrorism.

Fourth and finally, it can be argued that the inability of states to come effectively to terms with the asylum issue has been politically and socially corrosive. Rather than showing real leadership in this area of public policy, governments and opposition parties in a number of countries have become locked into an unseemly competition to talk tough on asylum and (like their counterparts in the developing world) to scapegoat the asylum seeker. An inevitable effect of such negative political tactics will be to reinforce the marginalisation of those asylum seekers who are recognised as refugees, making it more difficult for them to find work and to contribute to the economy of their adopted country. In this way, the notion of the dependent refugee, relying on social welfare benefits, will become a self-fulfilling prophecy.

Alternative approaches to asylum

The primary response of governments to the asylum issue has thus been to deter or obstruct the arrival of people who intend to claim refugee status on their territory. At the same time, a variety of alternative approaches has been proposed or tested, all of them intended to make it unnecessary for people to move from one part of the world to another in order to seek asylum. These include:

- reducing 'migration pressures' in countries and regions of origin by means of development assistance, debt reduction, the promotion of human rights and good governance;
- opening up regular channels of labour migration, thereby also addressing the problems created by the ageing population profile of the industrialised states;
- launching 'migration information campaigns' to counter the unrealistic expectations of potential migrants living in low- and middle-income countries; and
- introducing 'humanitarian visa' programmes, which would enable people who consider themselves to be at risk to file an immigration application at a foreign embassy in their country of origin.

While such proposals have their merit, there is a general recognition that they also have their limitations and that they could produce unintended consequences. The evidence suggests, for example, that the successful promotion of economic development in countries of origin may initially lead to higher rather than lower levels of emigration, as people will have better access to the resources and information needed to leave their own country.

With regard to the proposal to open up channels of regular migration, experts generally agree that the industrialised states will never be able to satisfy the demand for migration opportunities in low- and middle-income countries of the world, and that such an initiative might, by facilitating the establishment of new transnational social networks, even lead to a growth in the level of irregular migration.

Finally, a humanitarian visa programme might indeed obviate the need for people to make their way around the world in an illegal, irregular and independent manner so as to seek asylum in one of the industrialised states. But can an individual or a family threatened with persecution by its own government really be expected to approach a foreign embassy for this purpose? And how many of the world's asylum seekers could realistically be expected to benefit from such arrangements?

Confronted with the failure of established asylum policies to meet their intended objectives, coupled with the limitations of the alternative arrangements on offer, certain countries have started to think in more radical terms about how they might address this issue. And, for what will become self-evident reasons, two island states—Australia and the United Kingdom—have taken a lead in this respect.

Australia's new approach to the issue of asylum migration was introduced in 2001, at a time when a small but growing number of boats from Indonesia, carrying asylum seekers originating in countries such as Afghanistan and Iraq, began to land on the country's territory. Significantly, it was also a time at which the government was facing re-election and needed a populist issue to generate public support. The country's asylum policy was already a determined one, involving the mandatory detention of all asylum seekers who arrived in Australia by 'unauthorised means'. But when in August 2001 the Norwegian-registered *Tampa* attempted to disembark a group of asylum seekers who had been rescued from a sinking Indonesian ferry, the authorities took an even firmer stand and refused to allow the supplicants ashore.

After a lengthy stand-off, during which Australian special forces boarded the *Tampa*, the asylum seekers were shipped to Nauru, a Pacific island state, where they were accommodated in detention centres managed by the International Organisation for Migration. Their applications for refugee status were subsequently processed by UNHCR. Those who were successful were resettled, both in Australia and in New Zealand, while some of those whose cases were rejected have been returned to Afghanistan. Subsequent arrivals in Australian territorial waters were sent to other Pacific island states, or in some cases sent back to sea.

Justifying this 'extraterritorial' approach to the refugee issue, the government argued that it had no obligation under international law to disembark the asylum seekers or to examine their claims on Australian territory. At the same time, the authorities pointed out that Australia has a substantial refugee resettlement programme, making it possible for people to seek entry to the country in a safe, orderly and legal manner. According to this argument, there was no reason why 'queue-jumpers', such as those who arrived on the *Tampa*, should be given precedence over refugees who were prepared to remain in countries of first asylum and await their turn for permission to settle in Australia.

In early 2003 Australia's extraterritorial approach to the asylum issue resurfaced in a more comprehensive and sophisticated form in Britain, in a joint report from the Cabinet Office and Home Office presented to Prime Minister Tony Blair. In future, the report suggested, the UK should not process any asylum applications on British territory, with the possible exception of some special groups, such as children, disabled people and high-profile political dissidents. All other asylum applicants should be automatically removed from the country. Some would be sent to a regional processing centre on the fringes of the European Union (Albania and Croatia apparently being two of the locations under consideration), where their applications for refugee status would be examined. Successful applicants would subsequently be admitted to the UK, or to another EU country, under the terms of a new resettlement programme. Those rejected would be returned to their country of origin.

According to the proposal, other asylum seekers would be removed to 'protection areas' in their regions of origin, where some of the money saved on the UK's domestic asylum procedures would be used to enhance the protection and assistance available to refugees. As a result, it was suggested, people who have been forced to leave their own country would no longer need to move halfway round the world, spending large amounts of money and taking huge risks in the process, in order to find a safe refuge.

Whether or not this radical proposal will be implemented is a matter of some doubt. On the one hand, the British government is under intense political pressure to bring the number of asylum applications down, and any system that prevents or deters asylum seekers from entering and remaining on British territory will undoubtedly be given serious considera-tion. At the same time, a number of commentators have cast doubts upon the practicality of the proposal. Will asylum seekers who have made their way to the UK quietly accept their removal to a regional processing centre or a protection area in their region of origin? Is it really possible to establish areas that are genuinely safe and secure in regions such as the Horn of Africa? Will the government really be able to transfer funds which are currently used for domestic asylum purposes to the country's overseas development and humanitarian assistance budget? Even if such funding is available, will states outside the EU agree to the establishment of regional processing centres and protection areas on their territory? And if such centres and areas are established, will it be possible to exclude human smugglers, seeking new clients among the mass of people whose dreams of moving to the West have been shattered?

While such questions remain to be answered, the significance of the Australian strategy and the British proposal cannot be disputed. For, rather than continuing to struggle with the spontaneous arrival of asylum seekers, the industrialised states are increasingly thinking in terms of 'migration management', whereby the movement of people—including refugees—from one part of the world to another takes place in a manner that is regulated by governments and other international actors.

The current UN High Commissioner for Refugees, Mr Ruud Lubbers, has recognised that this approach has some validity, and has acknowledged that a primary purpose for UNHCR is to be a partner for governments in the resolution of refugee problems. The organisation's role in resolving the stand-off between France and the United Kingdom in relation to the Sangatte reception centre has been cited as a successful example of this approach. Rather than relying solely on the provisions of the 1951 Refugee Convention, the High Commissioner has suggested that a complementary set of multi-lateral agreements are required (known as 'Convention Plus'), enabling states to address the many facets of the refugee issue—asylum, voluntary repatriation, resettlement, local integration, the secondary movement of refugees and international burden-sharing—in an agreed and concerted manner. The outcome of this initiative will undoubtedly have a great deal of significance for the future of the international refugee regime. There is now a growing recognition that the asylum systems of the industrialised states are in several respects dysfunctional. There is also a mounting sense that the refugee issue could be addressed in a more rational, predictable and organised manner.

But how realistic is this objective? Refugee movements are inherently chaotic and unpredictable, involving individuals and groups of people with strong emotions, intentions and aspirations. In seeking to regulate their movement, are states and international organisations trying to manage what is essentially unmanageable?

The Closing of the European Gates?
The New Populist Parties of Europe

JOHN LLOYD

THE rise of the populist parties of the right in Europe since the late 1990s has no single cause. Indeed, there has been no single 'rise': some of the groups have an active, if not a distinguished, past of some decades. The openly racist National Front of Jean Marie le Pen in France has occupied a significant slice of the vote since the 1970s: the anti-immigrant Northern League in Italy is in its second period of coalition government, having shared (and helped to destroy) Silvio Berlusconi's first brief administration in 1994; in Austria, the Freedom Party has already won and lost its period in power.

In some states, such as Italy, the number of immigrants is small; in France, it is relatively high. So it is in Germany and in the UK—but here, in spite of some local successes, there is no nationally powerful party of the far right. In two Scandinavian states with powerful social and Christian democratic traditions—Denmark and Norway—the populist parties are strong: in Sweden, the far right is weak, in spite of high immigration. The Netherlands had had a successful, liberally inclined and initially popular social democratic government—yet under its administration the Pim Fortuyn List (PFL) surged into second place in the 2002 general election, and into a coalition government of the right. The National Alliance in Italy has left behind at least some of its far right past—as the Italian Social Movement, it was proud heir to Mussolini's fascists—as its leadership seeks to position itself as a rightist radical party.

Nor is there a 'Populist International', with closely similar parties comparing notes and coordinating tactics across frontiers. Some of these parties can reasonably be called neo-fascist: some cannot. The violently expressed dislike of Jews and dark-skinned foreigners which has been Jean Marie Le Pen's stock-in-trade for decades was not matched by the socially liberal anti-immigrant stance of Pim Fortuyn—a gay former Marxist sociology professor, who opposed Muslim immigration because of what he saw as the religion's intolerance, and who once responded to a question on whether or not he objected to the Indonesian population in the Netherlands by responding that he had slept with most of them. The Danish People's Party refused to meet the Austrian Freedom Party because of the anti-semitism of the latter party's leader, Jörg Haider. The Northern League's main aim is not to oppose immigrants—though its leaders do so—but to win greater autonomy for Italy's wealthy north from the poorer south. The Belgian Vlaams Blok is at least as much opposed to the French in that deeply divided country as it is to immigrants.

© The Political Quarterly Publishing Co. Ltd. 2003
Published by Blackwell Publishing Ltd, 9600 Garsington Road, Oxford OX4 2DQ, UK and 350 Main Street, Malden, MA 02148, USA

But there are similarities, which transcend the particularities of states and of leaders. First, all these parties are populist: that is, they base their claim for support on having a direct, unmediated relationship with their base, and on opposing the political and other establishments of their countries on the grounds that they are remote from (or, at an extreme, have betrayed) 'the people'—and instead favour other peoples—whether immigrants, the bureaucrats in Brussels, Jews, Muslims or Americans.

Being populist, and accustomed to success based on giving simple and easily understood answers in largely single-issue campaigns, they tend to react badly to the compromises and zig-zags of democratic government. They have thus, for the most part, been unsuccessful when part of an administration, inevitably of the right. The Freedom Party's period of government ended when Haider opposed some of the compromises his ministers had made in the coalition government led by the People's Party chancellor Wolfgang Schüssel: the subsequent election handed such a decisive victory to Schüssel that he could dispense with the services of the Freedom Party. The PFL imploded after bitter infighting among its ministers in the coalition of the right, and its poll rating sank as quickly as it rose. Of the populist parties in government, only the Northern League has retained its role—and it is a very junior partner, after Berlusconi's own Forza Italia and the National Alliance, and with a shrunken electoral base.

Out of power, however, the populist parties continue to flourish—above all in Norway, Denmark, France and Belgium, where—especially in the first two—they have played a very large part in the tightening of immigration rules and the treatment of asylum seekers within the country. The French National Front could not, however, translate its nearly 20 per cent showing in the presidential race into any seats in parliament: it is thus difficult to judge how popular it remains, though it is unlikely to have slipped back much. In Britain and Germany, 2002–3 showed minor gains—in local elections—for the parties of the far right.

This is the electoral position of populism in early 2003 in western Europe. It is worth noting that parties of the far right have limited purchase elsewhere in the developed world. Neither the United States nor Canada has a significant party of the far right. In Australia, the sudden rise to popularity in the latter 1990s of Pauline Hanson's One Nation Party, perhaps the most classic populist party of the current wave—with a former fish-and-chip shop owner creating a party in her name because 'the little people weren't being heard'—has turned to collapse, with a trial for electoral fraud pending against Hanson. In central and eastern Europe, however, the right is tending to grow: right-wing populists have won elections at parliamentary level; and a mounting protest against the conditions of European Union membership, together with a stronger reassertion of nationalism than has been seen since the end of the Soviet bloc, is evident in different ways and strengths in Poland, the Baltic states, the Czech Republic and Hungary.

As has become obvious, the populist parties organise largely, sometimes exclusively, round the issues of race, immigration, citizenship and cultural assimilation. At one extreme, as in the British National Party, they are frankly racist, believing that the white, brown, yellow and black races—and Jews—should live apart, not intermarry; and that they should cease to pretend that they can be other than, at best, wary neighbours. At the other extreme (on this spectrum), the Pim Fortuyn List and the Danish People's Party concentrate on the inequalities and disruption caused to native Dutch or Danes by mass immigration (immigration in these countries has been, relative to their past and the size of their populations, relatively high and rapid in the last few years).

Nationalism

The political scientist Yves Meny, who has made a study of populism, believes that however different populist parties are from one another, 'the common glue is anti-elitism'—as well as hostility to institutions and regulatory intermediaries. Meny points out that since the 1960s checks and balances have grown greatly in number; most of them are designed to protect human rights, or allow appeals of various kinds, or to hold private and public powers to account, and all of them are open to being represented as standing between 'the people' and a direct expression of their will.[1]

The largest visible reason for the growth of intermediary institutions is the development of the European Union and its workings: the more the constitutional guarantees of Europe, and of the nation-states, are strengthened, the more distant the people are seen to become from those they elect to do their will. The public world is thus more easily represented as being a series of elites who respond only weakly, or not at all, to the general will: the elites who are in charge are held instead to be in thrall to foreigners, to the dictates of lawyers, or to distant and unelected, or unpopular, institutions. The renunciation of instruments which politicians or states had within their jurisdictions—whether central banks, courts, or regulatory instruments—lays them open to charges of indifference to the people's will. These developments, Meny believes, 'have gone very far from the sixties to the nineties—so that we have seen the popular side of the *demos* weaken. In the US you have a popular counterweight to federal constitutionalism—at the state level. But here we don't.'[2]

All populist parties are to a greater or lesser degree sceptical of, or hostile to, the EU. The nation-state is their necessary locus—whether the populists invoke its glories, or its victimhood. The cosmopolitanism of a union which can openly be a civic, rather than an ethnic, national, imperial or religious entity is necessarily inimical to the populist right. However, the populists have a strong ally in the remoteness and complexity of the Union's decision-making processes: and this weakness of the 'popular side of the *demos*' is and will remain a curb on further integration, from which the populist parties are well placed to profit. Even if they do not, other parties will: the remoteness of

Europe, evidenced by a turnout below 50 per cent (and falling) in nearly all of the member states in European elections, is a real, not a manufactured, problem.

The trends and effects of globalisation have produced a discourse which many find confusing: the pace of change which attends it disturbs, at times destroys, established patterns of life. Immigration is one of the most visible of these disturbances, and the increased movement of poor, even desperate, people to the richer parts of the world is a phenomenon about which many governing parties have been reluctant to speak, for fear of rousing public anger and losing political support. The discretion of political parties since the early 1990s, when relatively large numbers of refugees and asylum seekers were absorbed into west European societies, has opened up a fruitful line of political development for the populists, which they have exploited hungrily.

Populism, in Meny's view, can act as a corrective to excessive 'constitutionalism', and may have done so, or may still be doing so, in the EU states today. In the UK and in Germany, the moves taken by the left-of-centre Home Secretary and Interior Minister, respectively David Blunkett and Otto Schilly, have as their context the avoidance of the growth of populist parties: Schilly, in a rather downbeat interview in the summer of 2002, said that 'Europe is regulating immigration to combat the populist virus . . . fortunately we [in Germany] don't yet have figures like Haider or Le Pen. But I'm not sure we can carry on blocking the extremists.'[3]

Nationalism is also a reaction to what is commonly experienced as a malign globalisation, with the populists demanding that the nation-state protect people, especially the working class, from the ever more rapid technological changes which usually have a disproportionate effect on the lower paid. Le Pen played that card particularly strongly in the 2002 French presidential elections, sounding at times like a communist or Trotskyist candidate in his violent attacks on American-style capitalism.

Anti-semitism

There has been a sharp rise in anti-semitic incidents in most countries in western Europe—especially in France. As this was being written, a (liberal) rabbi was stabbed by an Arab assailant in Paris; while he was recovering from his wound, his car was set on fire. In the aftermath, French Jews interviewed by various media outlets expressed their despair at what they described as a rising tide of hatred directed, largely by Muslims, at them. Some said that they were safer in Israel than in France, and that they intended to emigrate: indeed, French emigration to Israel has doubled in the last few years.

There is a general—if not universal—view among European Jews, and a much more settled conviction among Jews living in the United States, that Europe is returning to its old anti-semitic ways. This owes much more to the frank and violent anti-Jewish prejudices, expressed as hatred of the oppression of the Israeli state, on the part of Muslims than to any other single cause;

but those who monitor anti-semitic incidents also point to the rise in support for Le Pen and Haider; to rhetoric by mainstream German politicians which has come nearer to anti-semitism than any has permitted himself for decades; to desecrations of Jewish graves in Rome; and to many other individual incidents. In a now-famous article (behind which there are many more pieces of protest), Charles Krauthammer wrote in the *Washington Post* in April 2002 that 'what we are seeing is pent-up anti-semitism, the release—with Israel as the trigger—of a millennium old urge that powerfully infected and shaped European history. What is odd is not the anti-semitism of today, but its relative absence in the past half century.' In the same month, the *New York Times* editorialised that 'the dark shadow of Europe's past seems to be reappearing', while the liberal Italian daily *La Stampa* depicted an Israeli baby looking up from the manger at an Israeli tank saying 'Don't tell me they want to kill me again.'

While some of these latter trends may be disquieting, it is a mistake to see them through the lenses of the 1920s and 1930s, far less those of biblical myth or medieval purges of Jews. Nazism, a pathological hatred of Jews, is confined to a tiny and reviled few, and there is no serious growth of the neo-Nazi groups. Popular and 'clubland' anti-semitism is smaller than it was, even in the decade immediately after the Second World War. Part of the 'entrance exam' which the applicant states of central and eastern Europe must pass before gaining entry into the EU is an explicit recognition of their own past and present anti-semitism—a pressure which has resulted in memorials, debate and publicly expressed regret by political leaders, where before there had been silence, anti-semitic outbreaks and covert sanctioning of these outbreaks at high political levels.

Again, while some anti-Israeli opinion may be disguised anti-semitism, much—even of the extreme expressions—is rooted in political disagreement rather than racial prejudice: political disagreement which is open and vivid within the democratic politics and civil society of Israel, as well as within the Jewish diaspora. In the UK, for example, where anti-semitism is an almost negligible force in politics, a ban on contacts with Israeli academics was proposed by the academics' trade union, following a campaign by some UK scholars among whom British Jews were prominent. Although (in my view) the ban was foolish, it proceeded from the reflexes and tactics of the intellectual left, not from those of the anti-semitic groups. Even those politicians for whom anti-semitism is part of their baggage—such as Le Pen and Haider—use it covertly, to bond with the hard core of their own movements who resonate to these strains: it is not the reason for their popularity. Indeed, Le Pen used it relatively little during his presidential campaign last year, because he wanted to concentrate on his main focus: north African immigration to France, and its effects.

The new virulence comes overwhelmingly from some of the Muslim immigrants and communities in the west European (and North American) states, and is intimately connected by them to the Israel–Palestine conflict. In making this connection, radical Muslims will, at times, use Nazi symbols and themes, and these have been visible in anti-war demonstrations, including in London. A report on an anti-war demonstration in Amsterdam in spring 2002 noted that 'never since 1945 have so many swastikas been shown in public: the procession counted some 75 . . . a photo of Hitler strangling Sharon. People chanting "Jews into the sea" . . . during the demonstration, participants shouted "Sieg heil" on at least two occasions.'[4] These conflations of Nazism with anti-Israeli militancy caused the centre-left parties in Italy to disengage themselves from anti-war demonstrations: the same has not always been true elsewhere, including in the UK.

How far Arab and Muslim feeling is or can be stirred by calls to hate Jews—and also Christians, as in Osama bin Laden's famous invocation to fellow Muslims to kill 'Jews and Crusaders'—will differ from country to country, community to community, individual to individual. It is certain that it has roused some, especially the young, to manifestations of hatred, from militant protest to murder. Jews are visible, at least at synagogues; often prominent in public life; but a small minority, and thus vulnerable. The laws in place in most Western states against the promotion of religious and racial hatreds sometimes appear to be unused in cases of blatant racial hatred; it is also true that much anti-Jewish and anti-Christian propaganda goes on in private and religious gatherings, and is spread by mullahs, who are implicitly at least accorded a kind of immunity for being men of the cloth.

These are issues with which the state has to deal: they fit into the present debates, current in most countries, on how to teach, or enforce, common norms of citizenship on increasingly heterogeneous national communities. If the 'new Nazi' panics, especially in the United States, are overdone, they gain basis from a reluctance to treat the Muslim citizens of west European states as responsible for their public speech and acts; and from the extremist habits of an intellectual left determined to demonstrate 'Israelo-fascism' and blind to the much more potent danger of 'Islamo-fascism'.

The Muslim communities

The growth of Muslim communities in the rich Western states has been largely recent, and relatively rapid. These communities are varied, both among countries and within them. In Germany, the overwhelming majority are Turkish 'guest workers'—and now their children and grandchildren—who were attracted to work in Germany for the higher wages and better social conditions on offer, and who have stayed. The social democratic coalition took a large step forward in its first term, by partly removing the bar on these 'guests' becoming citizens; at the same time, new Muslim communities appeared, from Bosnia and Kosovo, from Afghanistan and from the Indian subcontinent. In Britain, the older communities of mainly Pakistanis and Bangladeshis, recruited to work in the textile and other low-paid industries, have been joined not only by their extended families but also by Muslims from the former Yugoslavia, Turks from Cyprus and from Turkey, north Africans and Arabs. In France, the immigrant communities are very largely north African, with the largest part from Algeria.

Though there were many perceived problems within the European Muslim communities, and between them and the older native populations, these were rarely seen to be much more serious than those afflicting other minorities. There were and are more difficult issues surrounding the family—difficult both because they are in an area generally held to be private, and because they are often covered over—such as forced marriages. However, 9/11 has changed, and will further change, the nature of Muslims' relationship with the majority and other communities.

Many commentators have pointed up the nature of the European Muslim problem. Some young Western Muslims, according to the writer Yasmin Alibhai-Brown, live much of their lives in what she calls 'virtual Islam'—surfing websites which emphasise the militant rejection of Western values and secularism. The scholar Anshuman A. Mondal, underscoring the radicalising effect of the informatics age, writes that the effect of the global telecommunications revolution on the Muslim world will be to concentrate Muslim perceptions on the 'ideologically hot' issues at the expense of the more flexible, pragmatic modes of Muslim life: that is, to make the mindset of some young people revolve obsessively round themes of Muslim loss and defeat, and Western and Israeli/Jewish conquest and treachery. Foreign Secretary Jack Straw, whose Blackburn constituency contains 25,000 Muslims—the largest single concentration of any English constituency—has expressed the view that too many younger Muslims appear to show an unwillingness to integrate into mainstream British society.

This is mildly put, in the face of several instances of recruitment of British Muslims into terrorist gangs, and widespread scenes of rejoicing after the massacre at the World Trade Center. The men arrested in Wood Green for allegedly developing the poison ricin—two of whom were asylum seekers—were Algerian. Speculation has centred on whether their alleged activities are a sign that the radical Islamism in Algeria, a country in which terror is routinely used by radical groups against their government and Westerners, has now been exported to the UK. It has long been a problem in France. These arrests inevitably prompt the question: why is Britain giving harbour and succour to those who may prove to have been out to kill large numbers of its citizens? To have centres of enmity and hatred within Western societies, even if they never develop into full-scale terrorism, will continue to alienate all sections of society from the growing Muslim minority communities, a phenomenon which will demand much more proactive Muslim civic leadership in mediation than has been shown over the past year.

The invasion of Iraq may lead to increased instances of terror. It is worth noting, however, that foreign policy stances do not read off automatically into increased terrorism. France has suffered more from terrorist attack than the UK—and has been far more obviously reluctant to back a US-led invasion of Iraq. The United States suffers from fewer expressions of hatred for its values and its government from its resident Muslims than any European country. The argument, made especially by the America-based Lebanese scholar Fouad Ajami, is that the enmity expressed by many Muslims, both from within Western states and from Muslim countries, is a kind of displacement from the frustration felt, especially by a numerous, under-employed and rising generation, against their own corrupt and dictatorial regimes.

On this analysis, during the 1970s and 1980s the political and economic structures of the Arab world began to give way under pressure first from demographic trends and then from a radical Islamism that offered solace to the disaffected young along with the language of resentment and repudiation. For a time these pressures were confined to the Arab states themselves; but migration and transnational terror have provided conduits into the wider world.

If this analysis is right, then the position of the Muslim minorities, especially if they do not make clear their active wish to be good citizens of their adopted countries and their distance from the radical Islamists, will get worse; and there will be little that liberal politicians, comment-ators and civic of religious leaders can do about it. We on mainland Britain will learn something of the fear and hatred that have blighted Northern Ireland since the 1970s. Inevitably, the militant minority will make matters worse for the passive or even friendly majority—the more so, since the Pakistani and Bangladeshi communities in the UK have been and remain those most at risk from racist attacks. In such a situation, populist right parties will tend to flourish: a state of affairs where there are identifiable and active enemies within would lend itself to the growth of extreme groups.

Citizenship, culture and loyalty

The issues of identity within the rich and modern states have moved to the front of the political agenda since the early 1980s, and have tended to stay there. In the years after the Second World War, Europeans had seen the United States and Canada as countries of immigration forced to make a display of oaths of loyalty and of citizenship education which the older nations could take for granted. The growing realisation that these issues must now be made explicit and argued over in our countries too has, as Will Kymlicka explains in his essay below, been the largest feature underlying the debate and controversies now thrown up by the interlinked themes of culture and identity, citizenship and loyalty.

Among the major advanced countries—as represented in the Group of Seven—the United States and Canada occupy one pole, and Japan the opposing one. The latter remains largely and popularly hostile to immigration, and to the social links and cultural shifts which usually attend it, such as intermarriage and multiculturalism. Change, by European and certainly by North American standards, is slow; by Japanese standards, it is rapid—one example among many of how societies see themselves, and how they are viewed by others with wholly different experiences.

The two North American societies, though both operating active immigration programmes, differ quite markedly in their approach. Canada is the more planned: a figure of some 300,000 immigrants annually is currently a target to be attained—with government disappointment expressed when it is not. The criteria applied to the immigrants, however, means that with the exception of the 5–10 per cent who are refugees or asylum seekers, they must have substantial capital or be professional or highly skilled, and thus able to make an instant contribution to the economy. The United States is both more and less restrictive—more restrictive on those wishing to come to the country to work, less restrictive on allowing large numbers of hispanic immigrants, most of whom work in low-paid jobs in agriculture and service sectors, to come in over the southern borders.

In both cases, however, immigration has changed and is changing the social and political patterns of the state in profound ways. Canada's Asian immigration in the west and overwhelmingly non-white immigration in the east have together changed the demographic makeup of much of the country—with the original anglo and French settler communities now increasingly outnumbered not just by the various communities of central and east Europeans who moved before and after the Second World War, but by settlers from the Indian subcontinent, south-east Asia, Africa and the Caribbean. However, the two states differ again in their approach to loyalty. Though both demand an oath, Canada has taken multiculturalism at the official level to lengths further than any other state: when I asked in the course of an interview with the Prime Minister, Jean Chrétien, at the end of 2002 how he would define the national culture of Canada, he replied: 'It's multicultural: that's the essence.' The United States is much more concerned to instil a patriotism based on the constitution, and on the values the constitution represents: popular culture is consistently affirmative of diversity, but of diversity around a common morality and a common loyalty.

European states come relatively late to these issues of culture and citizenship, and some are better placed than others to cope with them. Germany had a concept of blood citizenship—which meant that the descendant of a Turkish guest worker with two generations of German-resident family behind him had no right of citizenship, while a family of German descent who had lived in the former Soviet Union for a century was given citizenship automatically. This has been modified: but it clearly reflected a widespread view of who did, and who did not, constitute a 'real' German which has not disappeared—even though, in the period after the Second World War, Germany accepted very large numbers of refugees as well as its resident guest workers.

France, like Britain, had a multinational empire and had given rights of citizenship and representation to the people of some of those countries. Its approach to the many nationalities was to extend French citizenship, and to inculcate the republican virtues coupled with strong central control—a control it finds it increasingly hard to exert. Italy, in spite of a late and disastrous stab at empire building, remained solidly Italian and Catholic: its divisions, which were deep, were between different regions and dialects, not between different nationalities. That experience has bequeathed a reluctance to adapt to different nationalities, and a low percentage of immigrants in the population.

Britain, the largest imperial power, which had scuttled out of empire leaving vast bloodshed behind it, was nevertheless best placed by history to deal with different nationalities. Its empire encompassed almost all the main racial groups. Moreover, its very formation, as a union of the Scots and English states with two other old nations added to it, meant an ethnic view of its own identity was impossible. As in Canada, where the state was formed on an (uneasy) compromise between the anglo and French communities, so the UK had national compromise built into its internal governance—a source of strength when the culture becomes more diverse.

These states, whatever their varied pasts and present state of popular feelings, must now adapt into societies that can give equal treatment to different races and faiths, as well as endeavouring to keep alive the humanitarian commitments most have made. That adaptation is made more difficult by the populist parties: indeed, that is what they are in business to do. However, it would be wrong to see them as the primary cause—any more than are those media which both reflect and promote resentment against immigrants and asylum seekers. The primary cause is the resentment and fears themselves, and they can be managed and calmed only by a range of responses: from the government and the mainstream political parties, from the immigrant and minority communities, and from the organisations of civil society such as churches, unions and charities.

Populism is not a serious problem in Europe—yet. In order to stop it becoming so, public policy must:

- ensure that the reasons for permitting immigration are clearly known: to enable the country to acquire needed skills, to fulfil its international obligations, to serve humanitarian ends;
- make clear linkages—between wars, famine and other disasters and migration; between increased productivity and increased immigration; between cultural vibrancy and new communities;
- seek to internationalise the problem—at the level of the European Union, but also at a global level—and explore new ideas, such as the mooted General Agreement on the Movement of People;
- within such a framework, consider new forms of agreement, such as payment to those developing countries whose skilled and professional

workers leave for the developed world; investment in projects in the developing world aimed at enabling them to retain their skilled and professional workforce; and more active intervention in avoiding refugee flows;

- examine good practice elsewhere, especially in the United States and Canada, the most successful countries of mass immigration;
- frame clear rules for would-be immigrants and insist on their observation; lay down clear guidelines for education on citizenship and in English; and make clear that cultural practices which are against the law have no immunity from it;
- set targets for immigration and keep to them.

In a recent report in the *New Yorker*, Jane Kramer gives a succinct commentary on the dual nature of immigration and asylum seekers. On the one hand, she suggests, the British believe—with reason—that they are being targeted by the poor and desperate. Writing of an Afghan woman who managed to obtain a permanent stay in Britain (most do not), she writes that

there was never a doubt in Afsana's mind that if she managed to leave Afghanistan she would try to get to England. Among refugees, England is the destination of choice in Europe. Its doors are ajar, if not entirely open; its pockets are deep, if not actually stuffed with cash; and its big cities are so polyglot that no one who survives the trauma of what is by all accounts a humiliating and very dangerous journey will find himself entirely alone.

This is the stuff on which anti-immigrant populism feeds—the themes of 'swamping', of 'taxpayers' money', of 'being taken for mugs', which are, at least in places, deeply believed and felt.

On the other hand, Kramer reminds us, most Afghans who fled the Taleban and came to Britain were highly educated, and many proved to be hugely resourceful and ambitious. She describes some of the (few) women:

Shakiba Habibula . . . today, a research fellow at the London School of Tropical Medicine; Najiba Kasraee . . . a producer and writer at the BBC World Service who broadcasts children's stories to the Farsi-speaking world; Seema Ghani, who came as a medical student and [now] . . . devotes herself to an orphanage and a health clinic for women and children she had founded with her first British pay check.

These two views—of the dislike of immigrants derived from bad experience, and of the benefits immigrants can bring to the societies in which they have come to live—coexist in our and other societies, producing parallel discourses which often do not touch. Politicians must attempt to bridge the chasm: a more than usually thankless task, which will be impossible if the chasm is forced more widely apart.

Notes

1 Yves Meny, interview with author, September 2002.
2 Ibid.
3 *La Repubblica*, 26 July 2002.
4 Open Democracy website (www.opendemocracy.net), 16 May 2002.

Muslims and the Politics of Difference

TARIQ MODOOD

THERE is an anti-Muslim wind blowing across the European continent. One factor is a perception that Muslims are making politically exceptional, culturally unreasonable or theologically alien demands upon European states. My contention is that the claims Muslims are making in fact parallel comparable arguments about gender or ethnic equality. Seeing the issue in that context shows how European and contemporary is the logic of mainstream Muslim identity politics.

Muslims in Europe

European anxieties and phobias in relation to immigration and cultural diversity focus on Muslims more than any other group. This does, however, beg the question: in what way are Muslims a group and to whom are they being compared? Here I can do no more than note that there is no satisfactory way of conceptualising people of non-European descent, what Canadians call 'visible minorities', and therefore also of conceptualising the constituent groups that make up this category. Nevertheless, it is clear that the estimated 15 million people in the EU who subjectively or objectively are Muslim, whatever additional identities they may have, form the single largest group of those who are the source of public anxieties.

Muslims are not, however, a homogeneous group. Some Muslims are devout but apolitical; some are political but do not see their politics as being 'Islamic' (indeed, may even be anti-Islamic). Some identify more with a nationality of origin, such as Turkish; others with the nationality of settlement and perhaps citizenship, such as French. Some prioritise fundraising for mosques, others campaigns against discrimination, unemployment or Zionism. For some, the Ayatollah Khomeini is a hero and Osama bin Laden an inspiration; for others, the same may be said of Kemal Ataturk or Margaret Thatcher, who created a swathe of Asian millionaires in Britain, brought in Arab capital and was one of the first to call for NATO action to protect Muslims in Kosovo. The category 'Muslim', then, is as internally diverse as 'Christian' or 'Belgian' or 'middle-class', or any other category helpful in ordering our understanding of contemporary Europe; but just as diversity does not lead to an abandonment of social concepts in general, so with that of 'Muslim'.

My contention, then, within the limitations of all social categories, is that Muslim is as useful a category for identifying 'visible minorities' as country of origin—the most typical basis for data collection and labelling. It points to

 © The Political Quarterly Publishing Co. Ltd. 2003
Published by Blackwell Publishing Ltd, 9600 Garsington Road, Oxford OX4 2DQ, UK and 350 Main Street, Malden, MA 02148, USA

people whose loyalties, enmities, networks, norms, debates, forms of authority, reactions to social circumstances and perception by others cannot all be explained without invoking some understanding of Muslims. Yet Muslims in Europe do not form a single political bloc or class formation, although they are disproportionately among the lowest-paid, unemployed and under-employed. Muslims do have the most extensive and developed discourses of unity, common circumstance and common victimhood among non-EU origin peoples in the EU. This sense of community may be partial, may depend upon context and crisis, may coexist with other overlapping or competing commitments or aspirations; but it is an actual or latent 'Us', partly dependent upon others seeing and partly causing others to see Muslims as a 'Them'.

For many years Muslims have been the principal victims of the bloodshed that has produced Europe's asylum seekers (think of Palestine, Somalia, Iraq, Bosnia, Kosovo, Chechnya, Afghanistan) and so are vulnerable to the anti-refugee mood and policies in the EU today. This, of course, also affects Muslim residents and citizens, and the situation has been thrown into sharp relief by September 11 and its aftermath, including the Iraq war. There are many reports of harassment and attacks against Muslims;[1] and Muslims, who have expressed both vulnerability and defiance, have become a focus of national concern and debate in many countries. They have found themselves bearing the brunt of a new wave of suspicion and hostility, and strongly voiced if imprecise doubts are being cast on their loyalty as citizens.

There has been widespread questioning about whether Muslims can be and are willing to be integrated into European society and its political values. In particular, whether Muslims are committed to what are taken to be the core European values of freedom, tolerance, democracy, sexual equality and secularism. Across Europe, multiculturalism—a policy suitable where communities want to maintain some level of distinction—is in retreat and 'integration' is once again the watchword. These questions and doubts have been raised across the political spectrum, voiced by individuals ranging from Berlusconi in Italy and the Dutch politician Pim Fortuyn to eminent *Guardian* intellectuals such as Hugo Young and Polly Toynbee. In the UK, many politicians, commentators, and letter-writers and phone-callers to the media, again from across the political spectrum, have blamed these concerns on the perceived cultural separatism and self-imposed segregation of Muslim migrants and on a 'politically correct' multiculturalism that has fostered fragmentation rather than integration and 'Britishness'.

National contexts

The same wind is blowing across the continent, yet the landscape is not uniform. Of the three most populous European countries, Germany, France and the UK, the former two have, in both absolute and relative terms, a larger foreign-born population and population of non-European origin than the UK.

Yet issues of racial discrimination, ethnic identity and multiculturalism have less salience in those two countries than in the UK. One aspect of this is that national debates on these topics have a lesser salience, and that such debates are less frequently led by non-whites or non-Europeans, who are more the *objects of*, rather than *participants in*, the debates. Another aspect is the relative lack of data about ethnicity and religious communities, and consequently of research and literature. Yet this is not a simple matter of scale. Each of the countries in the EU has a very different *conception* of what the issues are, depending upon its history, political culture and legal system.[2]

The German experience is dominated by the idea that Germany is not a country of immigration, and so those newcomers who can show German descent are automatically granted nationality while the others are temporary guest workers or refugees; none are immigrants. Hence, out of its population of 80 million, Germany has 5 million without German citizenship. This includes about 2 million Turks and Kurds, some of whom are now third-generation Germans but who until recently were excluded from citizenship by German self-conceptions of nationality as *descent*. In contrast, France has a history of immigration which it has proudly dealt with by a readiness to grant citizenship. But it has a republican conception of citizenship which does not allow, at least in theory, any body of citizens to be differentially identified, for example as Arab.

In Germany, the perception is that if you are of Turkish descent you cannot be German. In France, you can be of any descent but if you are a French citizen you cannot be an Arab. In each case, US-style—and now UK-style—composite identities like Turkish German, Arab French or British Indian are ideologically impossible. The giving up of pre-French identities and assimilation into French culture is thought to go hand in hand with the acceptance of French citizenship. If for some reason assimilation is not fully embraced—perhaps because some people want to retain pride in their Algerian ancestry, or want to maintain ethnic solidarity in the face of current stigmatisation and discrimination—then their claim to be French and equal citizens is jeopardised. The French conception of the republic, moreover, also has integral to it a certain radical secularism, *laïcité*, marking the political triumph over clericalism. The latter was defeated by pushing matters of faith and religion out of politics and policy into the private sphere. Islam, with its claim to regulate public as well as private life, is therefore seen as an ideological foe and the Muslim presence as alien and potentially both culturally and politically inassimilable.

The British experience of 'coloured immigration', in contrast, has been seen as an Atlantocentric legacy of the slave trade, and policy and legislation were formed in the 1960s in the shadow of the US Civil Rights Movement, black power discourse and the inner-city riots in Detroit, Watts and elsewhere. It was, therefore, dominated by the idea of 'race', more specifically by the idea of a black–white dualism. It was also shaped by the imperial legacy, one aspect of which was that all colonials and citizens of the Commonwealth were 'subjects of the Crown'. As such they had rights of entry into the UK and entitlement to all the benefits enjoyed by Britons, from NHS treatment to social security and the vote. (The right of entry was successively curtailed from 1962 so that, while in 1960 Britain was open to the Commonwealth but closed to Europe, twenty years later the position was fully reversed.)

Against the background of these distinctive national contexts and histories, it is quite mistaken to single out Muslims as a particularly intractable and uncooperative group characterised by extremist politics, religious obscurantism and an unwillingness to integrate. The case of Britain is the one I know in detail and can be illustrative.

The relation between Muslims and the wider British society and British state has to be seen in terms of the developing agendas of racial equality and multiculturalism. Muslims have become central to these agendas even while they have contested important aspects, especially the primacy of racial identities, narrow definitions of racism and equality, and the secular bias of the discourse and policies of multiculturalism. While there are now emergent Muslim discourses of equality, of difference and of, to use the title of the newsletter of the Muslim Council of Britain, 'the common good', they have to be understood as appropriations and modulations of contemporary discourses and initiatives whose provenance lies in anti-racism and feminism.

While one result of this is to throw advocates of multiculturalism into theoretical and practical disarray, another is to stimulate accusations of cultural separatism and revive a discourse of 'integration'. While we should not ignore the critics of Muslim activism, we need to recognise that at least some of the latter is a politics of 'catching up' with racial equality and feminism. In this way, religion in Britain is assuming a renewed political importance. After a long period of hegemony, political secularism can no longer be taken for granted but is having to answer its critics; there is a growing understanding that the incorporation of Muslims has become the most important challenge of egalitarian multiculturalism.

British equality movements

The presence of new population groups in Britain made manifest certain kinds of racism, and anti-discrimination laws and policies began to be put into place from the 1960s. These provisions, initially influenced by contemporary thinking and practice in relation to anti-black racism in the United States, assume that the grounds of discrimination are 'colour' and ethnicity. Muslim assertiveness became a feature of majority–minority relations only from around the early 1990s; and indeed, prior to this, racial equality discourse and politics were dominated by the idea that the dominant post-immigration issue was 'colour racism'. One consequence of this is that the legal and policy framework still reflects the conceptualisation and priorities of racial dualism.

To date, it is lawful to discriminate against Muslims *qua* Muslims because the courts do not accept that Muslims are an ethnic group (though oddly, Jews and Sikhs are recognised as ethnic groups within the meaning of the law). While initially unremarked upon, this exclusive focus on race and ethnicity, and the exclusion of Muslims but not Jews and Sikhs, has come to be a source of resentment. Muslims do enjoy some limited indirect legal protection *qua* members of ethnic groups such as Pakistanis or Arabs. Over time, groups like Pakistanis have become an active constituency within British 'race relations', whereas Middle Easterners tend to classify themselves as 'white', as in the 1991 Census, and on the whole have not been prominent in political activism of this sort, nor in domestic politics generally. One of the effects of this politics was to highlight race.

A key indicator of racial discrimination and inequality has been numerical under-representation, for instance in prestigious jobs and public office. Hence, people have had to be (self-)classified and counted; thus group labels, and arguments about which labels are authentic, have become a common feature of certain political discourses. Over the years, it has also become apparent through these inequality measures that it is Asian Muslims and not, as expected, Afro-Caribbeans, who have emerged as the most disadvantaged and poorest groups in the country.[3] To many Muslim activists, the misplacing of Muslims into 'race' categories and the belatedness with which the severe disadvantages of the Pakistanis and Bangladeshis have come to be recognised mean that race relations are perceived at best as an inappropriate policy niche for Muslims, and at worst as a conspiracy to prevent the emergence of a specifically Muslim sociopolitical formation. To see how such thinking has emerged we need briefly to consider the career of the concept of 'racial equality'.

The initial development of anti-racism in Britain followed the American pattern, and indeed was directly influenced by American personalities and events. Just as in the United States the colour-blind humanism of Martin Luther King Jr came to be mixed with an emphasis on black pride, black autonomy and black nationalism as typified by Malcolm X, so too the same process occurred in the UK (both these inspirational leaders visited Britain). Indeed, it is best to see this development of racial explicitness and positive blackness as part of a wider sociopolitical climate which is not confined to race and culture or non-white minorities. Feminism, gay pride, Québécois nationalism and the revival of a Scottish identity are some prominent examples of these new identity movements which have become an important feature in many countries, especially those in which class politics has declined in salience; the emphasis on non-territorial identities such as black, gay and women is particularly marked among anglophones.

In fact, it would be fair to say that what is often claimed today in the name of racial equality, again especially in the English-speaking world, goes beyond the claims that were made in the 1960s. Iris Young expresses well the new political climate when she describes the emergence of an ideal of equality based not just on allowing excluded groups to assimilate and live by

104

the norms of dominant groups, but on the view that 'a positive self-definition of group difference is in fact more liberatory.'[4]

Equality and the erosion of the public–private distinction

This significant shift takes us from an understanding of 'equality' in terms of individualism and cultural assimilation to a politics of recognition; to 'equality' as encompassing public ethnicity. This perception of equality means not having to hide or apologise for one's origins, family or community, and requires others to show respect for them. Public attitudes and arrangements must adapt so that this heritage is encouraged, not contemptuously expected to wither away.

These two conceptions of equality may be stated as follows:

- the right to assimilate to the majority/dominant culture in the public sphere, with toleration of 'difference' in the private sphere;
- the right to have one's 'difference' (minority ethnicity, etc.) recognised and supported in both the public and the private spheres.

While the former represents a liberal response to 'difference', the latter is the 'take' of the new identity politics. The two are not, however, alternative conceptions of equality in the sense that to hold one, the other must be rejected. Multiculturalism, properly construed, requires support for both conceptions. For the assumption behind the first is that participation in the public or national culture is necessary for the effective exercise of citizenship, the only obstacle to which are the exclusionary processes preventing gradual assimilation. The second conception, too, assumes that groups excluded from the national culture have their citizenship diminished as a result, and sees the remedy not in rejecting the right to assimilate, but in adding the right to widen and adapt the national culture, and the public and media symbols of national membership, to include the relevant minority ethnicities.

It can be seen, then, that the public–private distinction is crucial to the contemporary discussion of equal citizenship, and particularly to the challenge to an earlier liberal position. It is in this political and intellectual climate—namely, a climate in which what would earlier have been called 'private' matters had become sources of equality struggles—that Muslim assertiveness emerged as a domestic political phenomenon. In this respect, the advances achieved by anti-racism and feminism (with its slogan 'the personal is the political') acted as benchmarks for later political group entrants, such as Muslims. As I will show, while Muslims raise distinctive concerns, the logic of their demands often mirrors those of other equality-seeking groups.

Religious equality

So, one of the current conceptions of equality is a difference-affirming equality, with related notions of respect, recognition and identity—in short, what I understand by political multiculturalism. What kinds of specific policy demands, then, are being made by or on behalf of religious groups and Muslim identity politics in particular, when these terms are deployed?

I suggest that these demands have three dimensions, which get progressively 'thicker'.

No religious discrimination

One Muslim organisation concerned with these issues is the Forum Against Islamophobia and Racism (FAIR). Set up in 2000 'for the purpose of raising awareness of and combating Islamophobia and racism, monitoring specific incidents of Islamophobia and racism, working towards eliminating religious and racial discrimination, campaigning and lobbying on issues relevant to Muslim and other multi-ethnic communities in Britain', its mission statement sets out this first dimension of equality.

The very basic demand is that religious people, no less than people defined by 'race' or gender, should not suffer discrimination in job and other opportunities. So, for example, a person who is trying to dress in accordance with their religion or who projects a religious identity (such as a Muslim woman wearing a headscarf, a *hijab*), should not be discriminated against in employment. At the moment in Britain there is no legal ban on such discrimination, and the government said until recently that the case for it was not proven.

The legal system thus leaves Muslims particularly vulnerable because, while discrimination against *yarmulke*-wearing Jews and turban-wearing Sikhs is deemed to be unlawful *racial* discrimination, Muslims, unlike these other faith communities, are not deemed to be a racial or ethnic group. Nor are they protected by the legislation against religious discrimination that does exist in one part of the UK: being explicitly designed to protect Catholics, it covers only Northern Ireland. The best that Muslims are able to achieve is to prove that the discrimination against them was indirectly against their ethnic characteristics: that they suffered discrimination by virtue of being, say, a Pakistani or an Iraqi.

While it is indeed the case that the discrimination against Muslims is mixed up with forms of colour racism and cultural racism, the charge of race discrimination will provide no protection if it is clearly the individual's religion, not their race, that has led to the discrimination. Moreover, some Muslims are white and so do not enjoy this second-class protection; and many Muslim activists argue that religious freedom, being a fundamental right, should not be legally and politically dependent on dubious concepts of race and ethnicity. The same argument applies to the demand for a law in Britain (as already exists in Northern Ireland) making incitement to religious hatred unlawful, to parallel the law against incitement to racial hatred. (The latter extends protection to certain forms of anti-Jewish literature, but not anti-Muslim literature.)

After some years of arguing that there was insufficient evidence of religious discrimination, the British government has had its hand forced by Article 13 of the EU Amsterdam Treaty (1997), which includes religious discrimination in the list of the forms of discrimination that all member states are expected to eliminate. Accordingly, the government will implement a European Commission directive to outlaw religious discrimination in employment by December 2003. This is, however, only a partial 'catching-up' with the existing anti-discrimination provisions in relation to race and gender. The proposed legislation will be confined to employment and vocational training (not extended to discrimination in provision of goods and services), and will not create a duty upon employers to take steps to promote equality of opportunity.

Parity with native religions

Many minority faith advocates interpret equality to mean that minority religions should get at least some of the support from the state that longer-established religions do. Muslims have led the way on this argument, and have made two particular issues politically contentious: the state funding of schools and the law of blasphemy. After some political battle, the government has agreed in recent years to fund a few (so far, four) Muslim schools, as well as a Sikh and a Seventh Day Adventist school, on the same basis enjoyed by thousands of Anglican and Catholic schools and some Methodist and Jewish schools. (In England and Wales, over a third of state-maintained primary and a sixth of secondary schools are in fact run by a religious group—but all have to deliver a centrally determined national curriculum.)

Some secularists are unhappy about this. They accept the argument for parity but believe this should be achieved by the state withdrawing its funding from all religious schools. Most Muslims reject this form of equality in which the privileged lose something but the under-privileged gain nothing. More specifically, the issue between 'equalising upwards' and 'equalising downwards' here is about the legitimacy of religion as a public institutional presence.

Muslims have failed to get the courts to interpret the existing statute on blasphemy to cover offences beyond what Christians hold sacred, but some political support exists for an offence of incitement to religious hatred, mirroring the existing one of incitement to racial hatred. The government inserted such a clause in the post-September 11 security legislation, in order to conciliate Muslims who, among others, were opposed to the new powers of surveillance, arrest and detention. As it happened, most of the latter was made law, but the provision on incitement to religious hatred was defeated in

Parliament. It was reintroduced in a private member's bill from a Liberal Democrat, Lord Avebury, which also sought to abolish the laws governing blasphemy. Although unsuccessful, these provisions may yet return to Parliament in some form.

Positive inclusion of religious groups

The demand here is that religion in general, or at least the category of 'Muslim' in particular, should be a category by which the inclusiveness of social institutions may be judged, as they increasingly are in relation to race and gender. For example, employers should have to demonstrate that they do not discriminate against Muslims by explicit monitoring of Muslims' position within the workforce, backed up by appropriate policies, targets, managerial responsibilities, work environments, staff training, advertisements, outreach and so on.[5] Similarly, public bodies should provide appropriately sensitive policies and staff in relation to the services they provide, especially in relation to (non-Muslim) schools, social and health services; Muslim community centres or Muslim youth workers should be funded in addition to existing Asian and Caribbean community centres and Asian and black youth workers.

To take another case: the BBC currently believes it is of political importance to review and improve its personnel practices and its output of programmes, including its on-screen 'representation' of the British population, by making provision for and winning the confidence of, say, women, ethnic groups and young people. Why should it not also use religious groups as a criterion of inclusivity and have to demonstrate that it is doing the same for viewers and staff defined by religious community membership?

In short, Muslims should be treated as a legitimate group in their own right (not because they are, say, Asians), whose presence in British society has to be explicitly reflected in all walks of life and in all institutions; and whether they are so included should become one of the criteria for judging Britain as an egalitarian, inclusive, multicultural society. There is no prospect at present of religious equality catching up with the importance that employers and other organisations give to sex or race. A potentially significant victory, however, was made when the government agreed to include a religion question in the 2001 Census. This was the first time this question had been included since 1851 and was largely unpopular outside the politically active religionists, among whom Muslims were foremost. Nevertheless, it has the potential to pave the way for widespread 'religious monitoring' in the way that the inclusion of an ethnic question in 1991 had led to the more routine use of 'ethnic monitoring'.

These policy demands no doubt seem odd within the terms of, say, the French or US 'wall of separation' between the state and religion, and may make secularists uncomfortable in Britain too. But it is clear that they virtually mirror existing anti-discrimination policy provisions in the UK.

108

In an analysis of some Muslim policy statements in the early 1990s, following the activism stimulated by the Rushdie affair,[6] I argued that the main lines of arguments were captured by the following three positions:

- a 'colour-blind' human rights and human dignity approach;
- an approach based on extension of the concepts of racial discrimination and racial equality to include anti-Muslim racism;
- a 'Muslim power' approach.

I concluded that these 'reflect not so much obscurantist Islamic interventions into a modern secular discourse, but typical minority options in contemporary Anglo-American equality politics, and employ the rhetorical, conceptual and institutional resources available in that politics'.[7]

All three approaches are present today, though some high-profile radicals have made a Muslim power approach more prominent, in a manner not dissimilar to the rise of black power activism after the height of the civil rights period in the United States. This approach is mainly nourished by despair at the victimisation and humiliation of Muslims in places such as Palestine, Bosnia, Kashmir and Afghanistan. For many British Muslims, such military disasters and humanitarian horrors evoke a strong desire to express solidarity with oppressed Muslims through the political idea of the *Ummah*, the global community of Muslims, which must defend and restore itself as a global player. To take the analogy with US black power a bit further, one can say that as black nationalism and Afrocentrism developed as one ideological expression of black power, so, similarly, we can see political Islamism as a search for Muslim dignity and power.

Muslim assertiveness, then, though triggered and intensified by what are seen as attacks on Muslims, is primarily derived not from Islam or Islamism but from contemporary Western ideas about equality and multiculturalism. While simultaneously reacting to the latter in its failure to distinguish Muslims from the rest of the 'black' population and its uncritical secular bias, Muslims positively use, adapt and extend these contemporary Western ideas in order to join other equality-seeking movements. Political Muslims do, therefore, have an ambivalence in relation to multicultural discourses. On the one hand, as a result of previous misrecognition of their identity, and existing biases, there is distrust of 'the race relations industry' and of 'liberals'; on the other hand, the assertiveness is clearly a product of the positive climate created by liberals and egalitarians.

This ambivalence can tend towards antagonism as the assertiveness is increasingly being joined by Islamic discourses and Islamists. Especially, as has been said, there is a sense that Muslim populations across the world are repeatedly suffering at the hands of their neighbours, aided and abetted by the United States and its allies, and that Muslims must come together to defend themselves. Politically active Muslims in Britain, however, are likely to be part of domestic multicultural and equality currents—emphasising discrimination in educational and economic opportunities, political representation and the media, and 'Muslim-blindness' in the provision of health, care and social services; and arguing for remedies which mirror existing legislation and policies in relation to sexual and racial equality.

A panicky retreat to a liberal public–private distinction

If the emergence of a politics of difference out of and alongside a liberal assimilationist equality created a dissonance, as indeed it did, the emergence of a British Muslim identity out of and alongside ethno-racial identities has created an even greater dissonance. Philosophically speaking, it should create a lesser dissonance, for a move from the idea of equality as sameness to equality as difference is a more profound conceptual shift than the creation of a new identity in a field already crowded with minority identities. But to infer this is naïvely to ignore the hegemonic power of secularism in British political culture, especially on the centre-left. While black and related ethno-racial identities were welcomed by, indeed were intrinsic to, the rainbow coalition of identity politics, this coalition is deeply unhappy with Muslim consciousness.

While for some this rejection is specific to Islam, for many the ostensible reason is simply that it is a religious identity and in virtue of that should be confined to the private sphere. What is most interesting is that, if this latter objection is taken at face value, the difference theorists, activists and paid professionals are reverting to a public–private distinction that they have spent three decades demolishing. The unacceptability of Muslim identity is no doubt partly to do with the conservative views on gender and sexuality professed by some Muslim spokespersons, not to mention issues to do with freedom of expression as they arose in the Rushdie affair.[8] But these are objections to specific views. As such, they can be contested on a point-by-point basis; they are not objections to an identity. The fundamental objection of radical secularists to Muslim identity as a politicised religious identity is of course incompatible with the politics-of-difference perspective on the public–private distinction. It is therefore in contradiction with a thoroughgoing conception of multiculturalism, which should allow the political expression of religion to enter public discourse.

We thus have a mixed-up situation where secular multiculturalists argue that the sex lives of individuals—traditionally, a core area of liberal privacy—are a legitimate feature of political identities and public discourse, and seem generally to welcome the sexualisation of culture (if not the prurient interest in the sexual activity of public characters). Religion, on the other hand—a key source of communal identity in traditional, non-liberal societies—is to be regarded as a private matter, perhaps as a uniquely private matter. Most specifically, Muslim identity is seen as the illegitimate child of British multi-culturalism.

Indeed, the Rushdie affair made evident that the group in British society most politically opposed to Muslims, or at least to Muslim identity politics, was not Christians, nor even right-wing nationalists, but the secular, liberal intelligentsia. Muslims are frequently criticised in the comment pages of the respectable press in a way that few, if any, other minority groups are. Muslims often remark that if in such articles the words 'Jews' or 'blacks' were substituted for 'Muslims', the newspapers in question would be attacked as racist and indeed vulnerable to legal proceedings. Just as the hostility against Jews, in various times and places, has been a varying blend of anti-Judaism (hostility to a religion) and anti-semitism (hostility to a racialised group), so it is difficult to gauge to what extent contemporary British Islamophobia is 'religious' and to what extent 'racial'.

Even before September 11 and its aftermath, it was generally becoming acknowledged that of all groups, Asians face the greatest hostility, and many Asians themselves feel this is because of hostility directed specifically at Muslims. In the summer of 2001 the racist British National Party began explicitly to distinguish between good, law-abiding Asians and Asian Muslims (see BNP website). Much low-level harassment (abuse, spitting, name-calling, pulling off a headscarf and so on) goes unreported, but the number of reported attacks since September 11 was four times higher than usual (in the United States it has increased thirteenfold, including two deaths).

The confused retreat from multiculturalism has of course been given an enormous impetus by September 11. The events of that day led to widespread questioning, once again echoing the Rushdie affair, about whether Muslims can be and are willing to be integrated into British society and its political values, paralleling discourses in most of the EU. The New Labour government was at the forefront of this debate, as were many others who were prominent on the centre-left and had long-standing anti-racist credentials. For example, the Commission for Racial Equality published an article by the left-wing author Kenan Malik, arguing that 'multiculturalism has helped to segregate communities far more effectively than racism'. Hugo Young, the leading liberal columnist of the centre-left *Guardian* newspaper, went further and wrote that multiculturalism 'can now be seen as a useful bible for any Muslim who insists that his religio-cultural priorities, including the defence of jihad against America, override his civic duties of loyalty, tolerance, justice and respect for democracy'. More extreme again, Farrukh Dhondy, an Asian who had pioneered multicultural broadcasting on British television, writes of a 'multicultural fifth column' which must be rooted out, and argues that state funding of multiculturalism should be redirected into a defence of the values of freedom and democracy.[9]

'Faith schools'

One of the specific issues that, as I mentioned, has come to be a central element of this debate is that of 'faith schools'; that is to say, state-funded schools run by religious organisations. While they must teach the national curriculum and are inspected by a government agency, they can give some space to religious instruction, though not all do so. They are popular with parents for their ethos, discipline and academic achievements and so can select their pupils, often giving priority to children whose parents can demonstrate a degree of religious observance.

Yet the violent disturbances in some northern English cities in the summer of 2001, in which Asian Muslim men had been among the protagonists, were officially blamed in part on the fact of segregated communities and segregated schools. Some of these were church-run schools and were 90 per cent or more Christian and white. Others were among the most under-resourced and under-achieving in the country and had rolls of 90 per cent or more Muslims. They came to be called, including in official reports,[10] 'Muslim schools'. In fact, they were nothing of the sort. They were local, bottom-of-the-pile comprehensive schools which had suffered from decades of under-investment and 'white-flight' but were run by white teachers according to a secular national curriculum.

'Muslim schools' then came to be seen as the source of the problem of divided cities, cultural backwardness, riots and lack of Britishness, and a breeding ground for militant Islam. Muslim-run schools were lumped into this category of 'Muslim schools' even though all the evidence suggested that their pupils (mainly juniors and girls) did not engage in riots and terrorism and, despite limited resources, achieved better exam results than local authority 'secular' schools. On the basis of these 'Muslim schools' and 'faith schools' constructions, tirades by prominent columnists in the broadsheet newspapers were launched against allowing state funding to any more Muslim-run schools or even to a church-run school, and demands were made once again that the British state be entirely secular. For example, Polly Toynbee argued in the *Guardian* that a precondition of tackling racial segregation was that 'religion should be kept at home, in the private sphere.'

Reaffirming multiculturalism

The watchword has to be: Don't Panic. Perhaps we ought to brace ourselves for some excesses: I am reminded of the Marxist radicalism of my student days in the late 1960s and 1970s; as we know, that passed and many a radical now holds high office (and fulminates against young radicals!). But we must distinguish between criminal actions and militant rhetoric, between radical Islamists and the wider Muslim opinion; for the former, despite the bewitchment of the media, are as representative of Muslims as the SWP is of working-class politics. We must not give up on the moderate, egalitarian multiculturalism that has been evolving in Britain, and has proved susceptible to gradually accommodating Muslim demands.

Other than Muslims themselves, a leading actor in bringing Muslim concerns and racial equality thinking into contact has been the Runnymede Trust, recognising Islamophobia as one of the chief forms of racism today when it set up its Commission on Islamophobia. The demand for Muslim schools within the state sector was rejected by the Swann Report on multiculturalism in the 1980s and by the Commission for Racial Equality even in the 1990s, but it is now government policy. Adapting the Census to measure the extent of socio-economic disadvantage by religious groups has been achieved, and support has been built up for outlawing religious discrimination and incitement to religious hatred. Talk of Muslim identity used to be rejected by racial egalitarians as an irrelevance ('religious not political') and as divisive, but in the last few years Muslim organisations like the Muslim Council of Britain (MCB) and FAIR, mentioned earlier, have co-organised events and demonstrations with groups such as the National Assembly of Black People. The protests against the Anglo-American invasion of Iraq have brought Muslims into the political mainstream, with Muslims sharing the same analysis as many non-Muslims.

Certainly, there must be an emphasis not just on 'difference' but on commonality too. British anti-racists and multiculturalists have indeed been too prone to ignore this; but to do so is in fact less characteristic of Muslims than of the political left (see, for instance, the various statements of MCB from its inception, and its decision to entitle its newsletter *The Common Good*).[11]

To take up some recent issues, of course wanting to be part of British society means having a facility in the English language, and the state must be protective of the rights of those oppressed within their communities, as in the case of forced marriages. But blaming Muslims alone for segregation ignores how the phenomenon in the northern cities and elsewhere has been shaped by white people's preferences as individuals, and the decisions of local councillors, not least in relation to public housing.

It is foolish to disparage and dismantle the cohesiveness of Muslim communities. We ought to recognise that there is an incompatibility between radical secularism and any kind of moderate multiculturalism in which Muslims are an important constituent. Integration cannot be a matter of *laissez-faire*; we must be willing to redefine Britain in a more plural way. The French approach of ignoring racial, ethnic and religious identities does not mean that they, or the related problems of exclusion, alienation and fragmentation, vanish. They are likely, on the contrary, to become more radical; and so the French may actually be creating the unravelling of the republic that they fear.

The Future of Multi-Ethnic Britain, the report of the Commission on Multi-Ethnic Britain published in October 2000, is a high-water mark of thinking on these topics. It tried to answer the question: how is it possible to have a positive attitude to difference and yet have a sense of unity? Its answer was that a liberal notion of citizenship as an unemotional, cool membership was not sufficient; better was a sense of belonging to one's country or polity. The report insisted that this 'belonging' required two important conditions:

- the idea that one's polity should be recognised as a community of communities as well as a community of individuals;
- the challenging of all racisms and related structural inequalities.

Here we have a much more adequate concept of social cohesion than that which has emerged as a panicky reaction to the current Muslim assertiveness and which runs the risk of making many Muslims feel that they do not belong to Britain.

Conclusion

The emergence of Muslim political agency has thrown British multicultural-ism into theoretical and practical disarray. It has led to policy reversals in the Netherlands and elsewhere, and across Europe has strengthened intolerant, exclusive nationalism. We should in fact be moving the other way. We should be extending to Muslims existing levels of protection from discrimination and incitement to hatred, and the duties on organisations to ensure equality of opportunity, not the watered-down versions of legislation proposed by the European Union and the UK government. We should target more effectively, in consultation with religious and other representatives, the severe poverty and social exclusion of Muslims. And we should recognise Muslims as a legitimate social partner and include them in the institutional compromises of church and state, religion and politics, that characterise the evolving, mod-erate secularism of mainstream western Europe, resisting the wayward, radical example of France.

Ultimately, we must rethink 'Europe' and its changing nations so that Muslims are not a 'Them' but part of a plural 'Us', not mere sojourners but part of its future. A hundred years ago, the African American theorist W. E. B. Du Bois predicted that the twentieth century would be the century of the colour line; today, we seem to be set for a century of the Islam–West line. The political integration or incorporation of Muslims—remembering that there are more Muslims in the European Union than the combined populations of Finland, Ireland and Denmark—has not only become the most important goal of egalitarian multiculturalism but is now pivotal in shaping the security, indeed the destiny, of many peoples across the globe.

Notes

1 *Summary Report on Islamophobia in the EU after 11 September 2001*, Vienna, European Monitoring Centre on Racism and Xenophobia, 2002.
2 For the basis of at least medium-term pessimism about civic equality and multi-culturalism in France and Germany, see T. Modood, 'Ethnic Difference and Racial Equality: New Challenges for the Left', in D. Miliband, ed., *Reinventing the Left*, Cambridge, Polity, 1994, pp. 87–8. For a less anglocentric view, see R. Brubaker, *Citizenship and Nationhood in France and Germany*, Cambridge, Mass., Harvard

University Press, 1992; C. Bryant, 'Citizenship, National Identity and the Accommodation of Difference: Reflections on the German, French, Dutch, and British Cases', *New Community*, vol. 23, no. 2, 1997, pp. 157–72; A. Favell, *Philosophies of Integration*, London, Palgrave, 1998 (2nd edn, 2001); R. Koopmans and P. Statham, eds, *Challenging Immigration and Ethnic Relations Politics: Comparative European Perspectives*, Oxford, Oxford University Press, 2000; R. Kastoryano, *Negotiating Identities: States and Immigrants in France and Germany*, Princeton, Princeton University Press, 2002.

3 T. Modood, *Not Easy Being British: Colour, Culture and Citizenship*, London, Runnymede Trust/Trentham Books, 1992; T. Modood et al., *Ethnic Minorities in Britain: Diversity and Disadvantage*, London, Policy Studies Institute, 1997.

4 I. Young, *Justice and the Politics of Difference*, Princeton, Princeton University Press, 1990.

5 Forum Against Islamophobia and Racism (FAIR), *A Response to the Government Consultation Paper, 'Towards Equality and Diversity: Implementing the Employment and Race Directives'*, London, 2002; Commission on British Muslims and Islamophobia, *Response to the Commission for Racial Equality's Code of Practice*, London, 2002.

6 I refer to the protests against the offensive character of Salman Rushdie's *The Satanic Verses* as perceived by many Muslims, following its publication in 1988, and the reaction of the West to those protests.

7 T. Modood, 'Muslim Views on Religious Identity and Racial Equality', *New Community*, vol. 19, no. 3, April, 1993, p. 518.

8 Though it is noticeable that Muslim homophobia gets far more condemnation than say, black homophobia, and Muslim sensitivities against offensive literature get far less sympathetic treatment than those of radical feminists against pornography and Jews against Holocaust revisionism, not to mention legal restraints against incitements to racial hatred: T. Modood, 'Muslims, Incitement to Hatred and the Law', in J. Horton, ed., *Liberalism, Multiculturalism and Toleration*, Basingstoke, Macmillan, 1993.

9 F. Dhondy, 'Our Islamic Fifth Column', *City Limits*, vol. 11, no. 4, 2001. For a recantation of his Black Panther radicalism, see his 'A Black Panther Repents', *The Times*, 24 June 2002, T2, pp. 2–4.

10 H. Ouseley, *Community Pride, Not Prejudice: Making Diversity Work in Bradford*, Bradford, Bradford Vision, Bradford City Council, 2001.

11 Hence my plea that even at the time of Mrs Thatcher anti-racism must relate to a sense of Britishness, not just blackness, Muslimness etc.: Modood, *Not Easy Being British*.

itics of European Union
‿ation Policy

CLAUDE MORAES

WHILE the individual national migration policies of the fifteen member states of the European Union have remained as diverse as the history of those countries would suggest, a complex but steady process of EU cooperation has taken place from the 1980s: first on freedom of movement of EU citizens within the EU, then in relation to non-EU citizens on issues of immigration and asylum. Most recently, managed economic migration, integration and partnerships with countries of origin have reached the agenda.

The shaping of the migration policy of all EU countries is politically sensitive. It goes to the heart of their history (as in postwar colonial immigration to France and Commonwealth immigration to the UK), their economic development, and notions of national identity, sovereignty and autonomy. The outcomes of national migration policy and law-making have, in turn, had profound implications for the multicultural shape of many of the EU's cities and regions.

While the drivers for common policy-making have been building since the 1980s, that same political sensitivity over national decision-making in migration policy has been reflected at EU level. Progress on common EU policies has faced a range of obstacles, including tensions among the players within the European Union who make cooperation happen: the European Council (the member states acting together, and with the strongest powers of the three institutions); the European Commission (the collective name for the politically appointed executive Commissioners together with the EU civil service which, in the EU system, proposes legislation); and the directly elected European Parliament. The last of these bodies was given new powers in the Amsterdam Treaty (1997) and increased competence in justice and home affairs (JHA) policy, within which immigration policy lies.[1]

In this essay I set out the recent historical development of EU cooperation and the factors that have driven the view, broadly held by member states and the EU institutions, that national migration policies alone can no longer meet the migration challenges faced by EU states. Second, I identify the obstacles, pressures and tradeoffs faced by the EU institutions in reaching the goal of a 'joined-up policy', before exploring the current debate within the EU institutions on managed economic migration and integration. Finally, I look to future challenges, notably those presented by the most dramatic enlargement to date of the EU to twenty-five member states in 2004. I conclude that, if continued cooperation on migration among the member states of the 'new'

© The Political Quarterly Publishing Co. Ltd. 2003
116 Published by Blackwell Publishing Ltd, 9600 Garsington Road, Oxford OX4 2DQ, UK and 350 Main Street, Malden, MA 02148, USA

European Union is to work, a renewed drive to develop a comprehensive common migration policy will be essential.

Drivers of EU migration policy

The drive to achieve a common policy, begun in earnest in the late 1980s, has been both a response to the changed nature of migration to EU countries and a consequence of EU integration itself.[2]

Member states have travelled through 'traditional' patterns of postwar migration (primary and secondary immigration from former colonies, for example), managed at the national level, to experience new, in some cases dramatic, increases in asylum applications. The 'new' non-EU asylum seekers and migrants are often illegally trafficked to the EU. They regularly travel through more than one EU country; that is, within an EU area where most internal border checks have been abolished. The goal of free movement for Europe's citizens was set out in its founding treaties. That internal free movement has, in turn, implied a common approach by member states on whom they will admit at the external borders of their territory.

The roots of formal cooperation among EU member states in relation to non-EU migration lie in this process of cooperation on the free movement of EU citizens. The 1957 Treaty of Rome dedicated its signatories to the creation of an internal market with free movement of goods, services, persons and capital. In 1985 the Single European Act sought to make the internal market a reality. The UK (and Ireland, with which it enjoys open borders) insisted on stopping short of the free movement of people. It argued that, while EU citizens were free to cross its borders, it must be allowed to maintain its border controls to verify the rights of entry of non-EU nationals.

The UK's stance forced other member states to pursue their commitment to the free movement of people outside of the EU's formal legal framework. It perpetuated the frenetic period of intergovernmental activity within Europe but outside of the EU, which had begun with secretive meetings of interior ministers and senior civil servants in the early 1980s, discussing justice and home affairs matters in what was then knows as the 'Trevi Group'. In 1985 France, Germany, Belgium, the Netherlands and Luxembourg signed the Schengen Treaty to remove controls at their internal borders while introducing measures to tighten security at the common external border. These member states thus began the process of establishing common policies on asylum, immigration and visas, police cooperation and the exchange of information between national immigration and police authorities. Their commitment was implemented in a convention in 1990—but it was not until 1995 that internal border controls were finally abolished between these five original Schengen participants and Portugal and Spain. Only in 1997, under the Amsterdam Treaty, were the arrangements formally incorporated into the EU's legal framework.

Today all EU member states apart from the UK and Ireland have signed up to the Schengen free movement principle, in pursuit of the economic benefits of passport-free travel for EU citizens within properly enforced external borders—although some, like Greece, have continued to have difficulty in delivering it. Without collective EU efforts, for example on an EU border police (discussed by the Seville Council as late as 2002), the Schengen ideals remain only partly fulfilled. Member states' attempts to deliver on this agenda have been another key driver of EU cooperation.

Increase in asylum numbers

At the same time as the Schengen process was developing, all EU member states experienced relatively large historical increases in asylum numbers. The crucial impetus for action at the EU level was provided by the disproportionate numbers reaching particular member states, leading to calls for centrally determined 'burden sharing'. The call for common action came typically from those countries that were experiencing the greatest pressure, like Germany and Austria, rather than the UK or Ireland, which wanted to rely to a greater extent on national and bilateral actions.

As the Austrian government observed in the strategy document for its presidency of the EU in 1998,

immigration to Western Europe at the end of the 1980s and early 1990s has reached levels unprecedented since the Second World War. This has been in large part because of the collapse of the Soviet Union, the civil war in the former Yugoslavia, and through an increase in the level of organised illegal trafficking of people from developing countries facing war, political upheaval or increasing levels of poverty.[3]

The Austrians estimated that during this period around 4 million asylum seekers had entered western Europe; between 1990 and 1996 nearly 1.5 million people applied for asylum in Germany alone. At this point the Austrian presidency said that Germany, Austria, the Netherlands and Sweden had received a 'disproportionately large number', while Spain, Portugal and Italy had received 'relatively few' of those fleeing from the wars in Bosnia and Kosovo.

The call for joint action was also an admission that the national policies of member states could not alone deal effectively with a situation where asylum seekers and trafficked migrants may enter at either the weakest or the closest point on the EU's external border. It also acknowledged that, while UNHCR figures showed that the vast majority of the world's refugees were pouring not into the EU but into other developing countries, the increasing sophistication of organised traffickers of people was a factor leading to greater numbers of asylum applicants reaching Europe.[4]

Public pressure for action

A key driver for a common policy has been the pressure of public opinion on EU governments to find national or EU solutions, particularly to the problems of those asylum or illegal immigration flashpoints constantly in the news. This could be said of media coverage of the 'Sangatte' crisis between the UK and France, where asylum seekers held at a Red Cross camp close to the French end of the Channel Tunnel made repeated and dangerous attempts to reach the UK. Their aim was to enter and remain illegally, or to make an application for asylum in the UK rather than in France—so-called 'asylum shopping'. Similar media coverage of the dangerous migration route from North Africa to southern Spain, and the migration route through the so-called 'Sarajevo Corridor', the Adriatic route to Italy which has claimed the lives of many migrants, has equally inflamed public opinion.

Both those unsympathetic and those sympathetic to the plight of these migrants have come to realise that existing bilateral and intergovernmental action by member states has often failed, and that more formal EU-wide action may provide better solutions. Of course, public fear of greater EU involvement has, on the other hand, also been an obstacle to progress, as I discuss below.

Solutions to 'asylum shopping' and 'burden sharing' have often been seen as achievable only through cooperation—although the proposed joint solutions have not always been sound. Some politicians have argued, for instance, that similar reception and social assistance conditions across member states would deter 'asylum shopping', ignoring the many stronger reasons why a choice of destination is made, including asylum seekers' desire to join established refugee communities. A positive example of managed 'burden sharing' was, however, seen after the intervention by NATO in Kosovo, where refugees were dispersed by the UNHCR and the EU throughout the EU, with subsequent levels of return to Kosovo being relatively high.

From the 1980s, then, asylum began to register as a key priority in most member states and, especially for those close to the instability in eastern Europe, it fostered a period of intergovernmental cooperation continuing into the 1990s.

Tampere: towards a comprehensive approach

As cooperation has developed, it has gradually but increasingly done so within more formal EU structures. It has also moved towards consideration of more comprehensive policies looking at the causes or 'push factors' of migration to the EU, and at the immigration needs of the EU itself. The formal phase of EU cooperation began as early as the Edinburgh European Council in 1992,[5] but the most important recent staging point was the Tampere European Council meeting in October 1999. Wholly devoted to

JHA issues, it agreed 'that the separate but closely related issues of asylum and migration call for a common EU policy'.[6]

Tampere was important because it was the first time the Council had been explicit both in calling for the EU to work formally towards a binding common EU policy and in setting out a blueprint for a common policy which could be described as comprehensive. It contained all the headings for such a strategy: common entry and post-entry standards for asylum seekers; the management of immigration policy, as well as the integration of third country nationals; and the need to address the causes and push factors of migration, leading to partnerships with source countries.

I was elected to the European Parliament in the same year as the Tampere discussions, and it was undoubtedly the view inside that institution that this was the most significant attempt to date to 'join up' EU migration policy. Over the years, the EU had been perceived as following a path of intergovernmental (rather than EU) agreement, often reacting to situations rather than planning ahead. The EU—particularly the Council—was also gaining a reputation for secrecy, and the controversial packaging of migration issues with the other JHA issues of cross-border crime and policing had the political effect of associating migration with negative security issues, while excluding discussion of its positive economic and cultural benefits.

There was a genuine feeling at Tampere, emerging from all three EU institutions, that a common policy should be balanced and comprehensive. The Council's conclusions undoubtedly built on the progressive work done by the European Commission in its 1994 communication on immigration, but this time there was agreement to take action. The Tampere commitment was reaffirmed at the Laeken Council in December 2001; and the subsequent Council meetings in Seville in 2002 and during the Greek presidency in 2003 continued to make progress on some of the positive elements of the Tampere agenda, such as family reunion policy. But there was also a clear political change in tone at the Seville Council, which was dominated by the issue of 'illegal immigration', prompting a fear that this shift would be an obstacle to faster progress towards the comprehensive goals of Tampere.

Obstacles in the path of a comprehensive EU strategy

Political progress towards achieving a common asylum and immigration policy has often been frustrated. As an MEP observing and taking part in the debate from within the institutions, I have been able to see a number of obstacles and tensions that have slowed the progress of the Tampere agenda and continue to create barriers to the realisation of a more comprehensive policy. Five areas are worth highlighting:

- problems with the way in which the EU forms JHA policy;
- political tensions between the Council, Commission and Parliament;
- distinctions among member states' views on cooperation;

- governments' fears of public resistance to EU involvement in migration issues, and the way in which public and media pressure at national level has been played out at EU level;
- the impact of September 11.

JHA decision-making

A continuing barrier to progress is the way in which the EU has historically made decisions on migration. As part of the JHA policy field, which accounts for 40 per cent of the EU's new legislation, migration is now an element of the EU's most active policy area.

EU citizens are ambivalent about the potential benefits of JHA cooperation. Many, increasingly exercising their right to free movement, may see the benefit of EU police cooperation in tackling cross-border crime or improvements in the way they can access justice in an EU country that is not their own. Others perceive JHA cooperation as inadequate in addressing increases in drug trafficking or miscarriages of justice in EU criminal justice systems other than their own.

The great political sensitivity of JHA issues has contributed to cumbersome decision-making processes, often as the result of member states' reluctance to hand over greater powers to the European Commission or the European Parliament. When the process of decision-making on migration issues first began it was, as noted above, entirely an intergovernmental process, widely criticised for its secrecy and for its exclusion of the Commission, the Parliament and European Court of Justice.

Acknowledging that cooperation on JHA was necessary at *some* level, in the 1992 Maastricht Treaty the EU created its structure of three pillars: JHA was given its own pillar, the third; the common foreign and security policy made up the second and the traditional Community business the first. At Amsterdam in 1997 member states agreed to move most of JHA, including asylum, migration and external border controls, into the first pillar (judicial cooperation in criminal matters and policing remained in the third). This was a hugely significant move, placing JHA matters at the centre of EU decision-making and regulation alongside employment relations, the environment and internal market policy. Crucially, however, for those resisting EU control of JHA policy, the member states have maintained a strong intergovernmental element to that process. The role of the Parliament has been limited and decisions will be taken by unanimous vote at least until 2004, rather than by qualified majority vote (QMV).

The key to faster decision-making in JHA is to extend QMV to migration policy. There is some member state resistance to this because it is seen as a loss of control on an issue which is too close to national sovereignty. Interestingly, the main objections are coming not from the UK, which wants to extend QMV, but from Germany which, despite being integrationist, wants to protect the control that it can exercise on this issue through its veto.

Another obstacle to faster and better-quality decision-making is that the Commission and member states (through the Council) share the right to initiate legislation on migration matters until 2004. The Commission has the sole right of initiative on other first pillar issues. The tension here is that member state initiatives have sometimes overlapped with, or prevented discussion of, Commission proposals. If the Council were to continue to set the overall direction of EU migration policy and the Commission left to work out the detail, as happens in other areas of EU policy-making, a clear tension would be removed. EU decision-making on JHA also suffers from lack of transparency because, for example, it does not use the same legal instruments as apply in the rest of the first pillar: rather than 'directives' and 'regulations' it uses other means with different and confusing terminology like 'framework decisions'.[7]

In the European Parliament, cooperation is often seen as a solution by political parties across the political spectrum, all of which believe it will deliver their own priorities. Put simply, for those towards the right of the political spectrum cooperation holds out the possibility of stronger policing of external borders through sharing of police intelligence or the creation of an EU border police; or of a driving down of common standards of reception and social assistance as a way of deterring potential asylum seekers. Towards the left of the spectrum, cooperation holds out the possibility of 'burden sharing', *improved* social assistance and *higher* common standards, as well as new EU cooperation on integration issues like family reunification. Within the European Parliament problems in reaching agreement thus include the fact that common policies are seen as all things to all people, with both right and left arguing that cooperation, in itself, fits their agenda.

Tensions between the institutions

There are also tensions between member states and the Commission on JHA policy in general and on migration policy in particular. The Commission believes—with justification, in my view—that it has taken a longer-term view, been stronger in advocating a comprehensive approach that embraces integration, insisted on retaining human rights standards in asylum policy, and been proactive on the question of managed migration. Senior Commission officials privately believe that, because migration policy is politically charged, member states will say little about potential long-term EU coordination issues like managed migration even if they are persuaded by the economic case for such collective planning or coordination. The Council, in turn, will hit back and say that the Commission is too far removed from the day-to-day reality of political pressures over asylum and illegal immigration.

An interesting illustration of how the Commission perceives the actions of the Council arose recently when I questioned the JHA Commissioner, Antonio Vittorino, about priorities within the migration agenda. I asked him whether the Commission was still committed to the Tampere agenda, despite what seemed to be a change in focus at the Seville summit. His answer was that the Council had been strong on the political rhetoric of tackling illegal immigration, making it appear that there was a greater shift since the earlier Council than there was in reality; and that the Commission was steady in its pursuit of a balanced agenda.

Impact of public opinion

A major site of tension in EU cooperation is the way in which public opinion and media coverage influence national government attitudes, which are then played out at EU level. This could be seen in the way some member states prepared for the Seville summit. There was a perception that the Council at Seville took the political initiative away from the Commission, which had seemed to have the upper hand in Tampere. Key member states, notably the UK and Spain, took the opportunity to put 'illegal immigration' at the very top of the EU's agenda. The change in gear was typified by proposals which, until that time, had not been seriously discussed at the highest levels—like the proposal to make development aid an integral part of the negotiation of future asylum and immigration accords, promising 'unspecified political reactions' for failure to cooperate. Illegal immigration was nothing new in the EU context; so why the shift against Tampere's more balanced political tone?

My argument here is that particular member states were reacting, in the build-up to the Seville summit, to public concerns over illegal immigration flashpoints like Sangatte, and equally intense media coverage over illegal migrants and their supposed link to crime in southern Spain. Also feeding into the Seville agenda were broader concerns that public perceptions of the failure of the EU to act on illegal immigration were a major cause of the sharp rise of populist anti-immigration parties across the EU, including Le Pen's entry into the second round of the French presidential election, the trajectory of support for the Austrian Freedom Party (FPÖ), the Pim Fortuyn List in the Netherlands and the MSI in Italy, and the local electoral success of the Vlaams Blok in Belgium.

At Seville, member states set out the stall proclaiming that 'illegal immigration' and asylum pressure were fuelling support for the far right. At a deeper level, what seemed to be happening—in some member states at least—was a 'mainstreaming' of some far-right directions and ideas, based on a concern was that a 'Dutch auction' on migration at national level could break out if action were not seen to be taken at EU level. In Denmark, the ruling Liberal–Conservative coalition had already shifted towards the hard-line stance on migration taken by the far-right Danish People's Party. Legislation was passed which prevented any Dane under the age of 24 from living in Denmark with a non-EU spouse. It also stopped asylum seekers from marrying while their applications were being processed. The law's unspoken rationale was to deter arranged marriages between members of Denmark's Muslim community and people in major Islamic countries.

Meanwhile, Italy's proposed compulsory fingerprinting of all new entrants and Austria's proposed compulsory learning of German were seen as representing the hardening of national policies that would be inevitable across member states if EU-wide policies on illegal immigration were not made more transparent. This is a judgement with which I disagree, but which was I believe held by more than one EU government going into Seville.

September 11

A final obstacle to pursuit of the Tampere agenda at Seville came with the association made between asylum seeking and terrorism after September 11. Shortly after the attacks, the EU's then Belgian presidency tried to ensure that the momentum to forge a common policy was maintained. But the attacks' effect on the Tampere agenda has been profound. It is arguable that the mindset in the Council and in the European Parliament shifted to those parts of the JHA agenda emphasising anti-terrorism and common security measures. Legislative progress in tackling cross-border crime, for example, has been remarkably rapid since September 11.[8] While it is certainly the case that 9/11 has led to calls from the right in the European Parliament to toughen asylum policy and to make connections between asylum and terrorism, nevertheless, on the left it has led to calls to deal with Islamophobia and integration problems like race discrimination which, since 9/11, are perceived to have increased.

I now turn to the drivers and political barriers to newer elements of EU cooperation: the managed migration agenda and integration.

The new debate on economic migration and integration

While the asylum and illegal immigration aspects of the EU migration debate continue to be politically charged, and dominate the EU's migration agenda, there is the beginning of a political debate within the EU on labour migration and the related and important issue of integration.

The Commission has issued a communication on immigration, social policies and integration in 2003. While not legislative, it is an important development for a number of reasons.

Labour migration

Member states at present continue to make their own national choices about whether to open up to the demand for skilled and low-skilled labour, coming to different conclusions. Progress in changing national rules to meet current and projected labour needs has been made in certain member states, such as the UK (where eligibility criteria for temporary workers have been relaxed and numbers of work permits granted have soared) and Germany (where in 2000 controversial special immigration programmes to attract non-EU workers for areas suffering shortages, like computing, have been attempted), but there is currently little coordination.

The view from the Commission and Parliament is that this is an issue which would benefit greatly from some coordination, particularly in view of the growing, if controversial, view that the EU as a whole will need more immigration as its population ages. The Commission and many in the Parliament believe that, if EU member states worked towards comparable rules, more transparency would result in the way in which member states compete for the 'brightest and best' workers from non-EU countries. There is also a need to take into account the concern of developing countries that EU member states will 'cherry-pick' their best people.

It was at the Tampere Council that the deeper debate on the whole nature of immigration to the EU and the immigration needs of the Union as a whole was made explicit. In its conclusions, the European Commission said:

It is clear from an analysis of the economic and demographic context of the Union and of the countries of origin, that there is a growing recognition that the zero immigration policies of the last thirty years are no longer appropriate. On the one hand large numbers of third country nationals have entered the Union in recent years and these migratory pressures are continuing, with an accompanying increase in illegal immigration, and people trafficking. On the other hand, as result of growing shortages of labour at both skilled and unskilled levels, a number of member states have already begun to actively recruit third country nationals from outside the Union.

In this situation a choice must be made between maintaining the view that the Union can continue to resist migratory pressures and accepting that immigration will continue and should be properly regulated, and working together to try to maximise its positive effects on the Union of the migrants themselves and for the countries of origin.[9]

Romano Prodi, President of the European Commission, underlined the thinking within the Commission at Tampere when, at the Council's meeting in Stockholm in March 2001, he identified a growing skills gap as a challenge facing the EU. The Union, he argued, urgently needs to ease restrictions on labour mobility, particularly in the technology sector, and to coordinate policies on labour migration where appropriate.

There are also some structural reasons behind the Commission's and Parliament's desire to coordinate policy on skilled labour. It is significant that the recent Commission communication emanates from the Employment Directorate and is the responsibility of the Employment and Social Affairs Committee in the Parliament, rather than the Justice and Home Affairs Committee. This reflects an acknowledgement that immigration is an issue for the EU-wide economy, not just one of border control. One of the EU's current priorities is to fulfil the 'Lisbon agenda', which set targets for the EU to improve its employment levels, productivity and take-up of technology, and pursue a range of other goals to ensure that the EU would be able to compete with the 'knowledge-based' economic blocs of the US and the Far East. It is here that the EU sees immigration policy and its connection to employment as a strategic matter for the Union as a whole, as well as a matter for individual national policies.

Current national problems which, in this context, are seen as necessarily part of an EU-wide agenda, include education and training policies that are struggling to adapt to the needs of a changing economy (for example, Germany's demanding and lengthy training courses mean that only a limited number of qualified workers emerge each year) and lack of mobility of workers in most EU countries even within their own member states, let alone in exercising their free movement rights to take up jobs across the EU (for example, in Italy there is persistent high unemployment in the south and a labour squeeze in the north, but southern workers are reluctant to relocate).

There are obstacles to EU coordination of primary immigration even when it is clear that it would benefit local companies and not threaten communities. Political sensitivity, particularly with current levels of unemployment in the larger member states of France (2 million unemployed) and Germany (4 million unemployed), is acute. Moreover, policies on immigration have implications for integration and race relations. The European Commission understands how politically sensitive it is to suggest that immigration is the answer to labour shortages, and is therefore keen to set out the objective facts about the demographic needs of EU economies, and that this be discussed openly within the Parliament. The Commission hopes that in this way the debate on immigration, which has historically been linked with negative aspects of race and ethnic relations, can be focused on the economic needs of EU member states as well as the needs of new immigrants, for example in family reunion policy.

Integration

Closely related, then, to the new Commission interest in managed immigration, is the growing debate over the coordination of integration policies— economic, social, cultural and political. While integration issues, dealing as they do with issues of race and religious discrimination and other forms of social exclusion, have often been seen as country-specific and necessarily addressed at national and local level, there have been a number of factors applying pressure for the issue to be dealt with at EU level, leading to its inclusion in the Tampere Council conclusions as an essential element in a comprehensive policy.

The political drivers for EU-level action include recognition that migration will be a permanent feature of Europe—particularly after enlargement, and given the perceived failure of member states to deal adequately with the issue. Enlargement will, it is perceived in the Commission and Parliament, bring new integration problems with, for example, the movement of the Roma who already face high levels of ethnic discrimination.[10]

The Commission in particular, but joined by the Parliament and Council, threw its weight behind the Amsterdam Treaty's Article 13 anti-discrimination directive on race equality and the employment directive which includes a provision on religious discrimination. These measures should provide protection in the labour market and beyond for new migrants of ethnic minority background, and for settled ethnic minorities who continue to suffer race or religious discrimination.

At the time of writing the available evidence shows that member states have, with some exceptions, been slow to incorporate the directives into national legislation before the 2003 deadlines. Collective action is now required both to ensure that the provisions are effected, using the Commission's powers of enforcement, and to ensure by the exertion of general political pressure that anti-racism legislation is then implemented properly, not only in existing member states but also, eventually, in the ten new members. Other important drivers include the need for a collective approach to tackle Islamophobia and racism in the aftermath of 9/11.

The significant barriers which arise in the EU's drive to create common policies on managed migration and integration are similar to those described above. But additional problems arise from tension between the JHA and the employment and social affairs parts of the Commission, and similarly of the Parliament, on who will take the lead.

Progress on integration issues like family reunion was made both during the Greek presidency in the first six months of 2003, and at the same time in the European Parliament. In April 2003 an encouraging sign of political consensus on integration matters came with the voting through of the Cerdeira and Santini Reports on Family Reunion, which go further than some member states' family unity immigration policy. Political sensitivity in coordinating immigration and integration policy is, however, likely to ensure that the 'open method of coordination' is used—a light-touch device giving member states the freedom to adapt EU guidelines to their national positions, rather than imposing directives.

The future of migration policy for the EU

Having looked at the drivers for cooperation and the obstacles and tensions over making progress towards an EU strategy, we may ask: what does the immediate future hold? Are there real political prospects for a comprehensive, common EU asylum and immigration policy, and what will be the effect of EU enlargement?

In the recent stream of common EU proposals and initiatives from the Council and the Commission there are mixed political messages. On the Council side, France proposed, for instance, to coordinate a pilot project to set up special charter flights to deport illegal entrants from the EU; while Greece offered to run a training scheme for members of the EU's as yet non-existent border police force. According to the European Council on Refugees and Exiles, the European umbrella body for asylum NGOs, seventeen separate border control projects were launched during the Danish presidency of the EU in the second half of 2002.

It is difficult to see this emphasis on illegal immigration ebbing. Its continued salience was confirmed in March 2003 at the Greek informal Council in Veria, a meeting devoted to assessing the Seville agenda on combating illegal immigration, which welcomed a highly controversial UK proposal for non-EU transit centres for asylum seekers. A joint draft operational policy document submitted jointly by the Greek and Italian governments to their EU partners in December 2002 contains a shopping list of Union-wide border control measures that the two states want to see in place by the beginning of 2004.

At the same time, it must be acknowledged that the 'other side' of the Tampere agenda has by no means disappeared. The Greek presidency strongly pushed the managed migration agenda and agreement on the key integration issue of family reunion, and has a genuine interest in making progress on the coordination of integration policy. It is possible that this is reflective of the centre-left position of the Greek government (notwithstanding that the Greeks have found it difficult to resist the control-focused proposals of other member states), while the earlier, more control-focused Spanish presidency reflected the priorities of its centre-right government.

The mixed messages emanating from the EU suggest that the issue of illegal immigration will continue to be the 'top note', and most publicised aspect, of future EU cooperation, but at the same time there is evidence of progress on proposals from the other elements of the Tampere agenda—managed migration, integration and partnership with source countries. A comprehensive approach is still the acknowledged goal.

The Italian and Irish presidencies, running respectively through the second half of 2003 and the first half of 2004, may return to the political emphasis of the Seville agenda, reflecting their right/centre-right national positions. But they will also be under pressure to take up those issues of managed migration and integration that are already on the table. Moreover, they will certainly have to address the migration implications of EU enlargement, as pressure is building to get further agreement before enlargement becomes a reality in June 2004.

Enlargement

All ten new member states will be entitled to the freedoms enshrined in the EU treaties, including free movement within the Union. But lengthy transition periods have been imposed on the movement of new EU citizens from Poland, Hungary and the Czech Republic into their nearest neighbours Germany and Austria. In contrast, other member states, including the UK and Ireland, decided that immediate free movement rights for candidate countries were acceptable. This debate was played out at the Copenhagen Council, which set the ground rules for enlargement.

It is highly likely that there will be further discussion at EU level on three key propositions that are still causing tensions within the EU and are likely to be played out in the run-up to 2004. The first is that there is a wave of potential migrants waiting to 'flood' into west European labour markets, increasing unemployment, displacing local labour and depressing wages. The second is that, even if labour mobility can be shown to be good for receiving regions, it must be bad for the source region. And the third is that, after enlargement, a potentially much larger source of migrants from outside the enlarged EU will necessitate further cooperation to strengthen the EU's vastly lengthened external border.

Most of the accession countries have relatively open borders—such as that between Poland and Ukraine—which will have to be policed more strongly on entry to the EU. This curbing of traditional flows across often artificial, post-1945 borders is likely to stimulate the greatest collective EU action in the run-up to enlargement, given that differences of opinion on the first two propositions have to some extent been resolved in the short term through the adoption of transition periods. The senior Commission voices I hear in the EU suggest that pressure to grant financial and other assistance to accession countries to enable them to close their new external borders will steadily and markedly increase over the coming months.

In conclusion, I would suggest that the way forward for the EU in relation to migration policy is to renew its commitment to the Tampere agenda. That agenda has provided the clearest blueprint to date for a common EU migration policy, balancing the focus on illegal immigration control set out at Seville with all the essential elements of a comprehensive approach. In the immediate future, then, the following elements will be important in making progress.[11]

First, the EU needs to develop further common rules on asylum, including the reception of asylum applicants. A directive proposed by the European Commission in 2001 would lay down minimum standards for the humane treatment of asylum seekers, covering aspects from rights to information on immigration procedures to access to healthcare. That would not in itself eliminate secondary movements between countries, but it would remove one of the differentials that encourage migrants to 'asylum shop'.

Second, EU governments need to establish a uniform refugee status and a common procedure for deciding who qualifies. Member states currently frame their national rules in line with the 1951 Geneva Convention, but they or their courts interpret the convention's provisions differently. Thus Britain recognises as refugees people fleeing non-state persecution—such as women escaping forced marriages—while Germany does not. The Commission proposed draft rules in September 2001. But agreement could be years away. Some member states are now trying to reinterpret the Geneva

Convention in a way that appears to water down the guarantee that those fleeing persecution will be granted refuge. The Commission rightly insists that the convention should be applied in full. Recent attempts in the UK to open up an unprecedented discussion on opting out from Article 3 of the European Convention on Human Rights, and suggestions that the UK should even leave the Geneva Convention altogether, have been widely criticised. The 1951 convention has already been eroded substantially by member states in their use of deterrent policies like carrier liability fines and arbitrary immigration detention.

Third, once the EU has established common standards it should devise a system for sharing the burden of refugees. One way would be to distribute people among EU countries. But far easier, and more humane, would be a system of financial compensation. Countries that receive disproportionate numbers would receive money from a central EU fund.

Fourth, the EU should adopt a more comprehensive immigration policy, including a move towards coordination of managed labour migration, to meet the requirements of those member states that may need more skilled and unskilled workers from outside the EU. Coordination at EU level (even on the open coordination method) could increase transparency and check the possibility of member states competing for the 'brightest and best' from the developing world.

Fifth, the EU should ensure that constructive coordinated partnerships are made with source countries.

Sixth, new discussions on EU coordination of integration policy should be encouraged and progressed, including ensuring implementation of the directives addressing racial and religious discrimination.

Finally, EU justice and home affairs policy has suffered from lack of speed and transparency and from over-complexity. The Council should set the overall aims of JHA policy and the Commission should work out the measures necessary. The current joint right of initiative creates overlap and unnecessary tensions between the Council and the Commission. The imperative of unanimity has baulked progress where it is needed. In my view, qualified majority voting is necessary if progress is to be made towards a comprehensive migration policy for the EU.

An EU blueprint for a comprehensive strategy exists. It should be developed; but it will require political leadership to join it up, and make it a reality.

Acknowledgement

I should like to thank in particular Ben Hall for discussing with me his original insights, which have contributed to my thinking in writing this essay.

Notes

1 See Richard Corbett, Francis Jacobs and Michael Shackleton, *The European Parliament*, 4th edn, John Harper Publishing, 2003.

2 Throughout the early part of this article I draw on Stephen Castles, Heaven Crawley and Sean Loughna, *States of Conflict: Causes and Patterns of Forced Migration*, London, Refugee Studies Centre/Institute for Public Policy Research/University of Oxford, 2003.

3 Austrian Presidency Strategy Paper on Immigration and Asylum, July 1998.

4 Annual UNHCR statistics, quoted in Michael Mann, 'Uproar over Asylum Policy May Fail to Add Up', *Financial Times*, 11 June 2002.

5 Edinburgh European Council Conclusions, 1992.

6 Tampere Council Conclusions, 15–16 October 1999, SN 200/99.

7 Heather Grabbe, *Justice and Home Affairs—Faster Decisions, Secure Rights*, London, Centre for European Reform, Oct. 2002.

8 Charles Grant, 'The Eleventh of September and beyond: The Impact on the European Union', in Lawrence Freedman, ed., *Superterrorism: Policy Responses*, Oxford, Blackwell/The Political Quarterly, 2002.

9 Tampere Council Conclusions, 15–16 Oct. 1999, SN 200/99.

10 European Parliament, 'Opinion on Combating Racism and Anti-semitism in the Candidate Countries', Rapporteur Claude Moraes, Dec. 1999.

11 See Ben Hall, 'Europe Must Tackle Asylum', *Centre for European Reform Bulletin*, no. 20, October/November 2001.

The Politics of US Immigration Reform

SUSAN MARTIN

THE United States has long been ambivalent about immigration. Proud of being a nation of immigrants, Americans tend to look at earlier waves of migrants through rose-coloured glasses while exhibiting concerns about the absorption of current and future immigrants. Public opinion polls often show the public to favour reductions in levels of immigration, but these same polls also show considerable support for the admission of close family members, skilled workers and refugees: the three groups that constitute the bulk of US immigration. The strongest opposition is to illegal migration. The public believes, however, that a large majority of foreigners in the United States are there illegally, whereas the reverse is the case.

Until very recently, one element of the founding principles of the United States remained in force, despite the ups and downs of immigration policy itself: the view of immigrants as presumptive citizens. Immigration levels rose and fell in successive waves of expansion and restriction, but legal immigrants continued throughout to be accorded full social, economic and legal rights. This conception is now under considerable strain.

September 11 unleashed grave concerns about the capacity of the country to separate bona fide foreign visitors and immigrants who benefit the country from terrorists and criminals who pose security risks. The changes documented in this essay, however, began well before September 11 and, I shall argue, provided the environment in which some of the excesses of the post-September 11 period have been allowed to flourish. A combination of factors—high levels of illegal migration, what were perceived to be excessive welfare costs attributed to immigrants, and the 1993 World Trade Center bombing carried out by foreign terrorists—led to legislative changes enacted in 1996 that significantly changed the social, economic and legal rights of foreign nationals, including legal immigrants.

My intention here is to explore, in the context of historical trends on immigration and immigrant integration, the current politics of immigration reform in the United States (including some unlikely and shifting alliances between interest groups), considering the implications for admissions policies as well as for the social and legal rights of immigrants. While expressing concern about the erosion in traditional US commitments to the inclusion of immigrants, I conclude that the framework for immigrant integration remains strong and likely to reassert itself.

© The Political Quarterly Publishing Co. Ltd. 2003

132 Published by Blackwell Publishing Ltd, 9600 Garsington Road, Oxford OX4 2DQ, UK and 350 Main Street, Malden, MA 02148, USA

The roots of American immigration policy

The roots of American ambivalence about immigration go deep, as do conflicting views about its role and the likelihood of immigrants integrating into US society. Lawrence Fuchs, in his seminal work *The American Kaleidoscope*, described three ideas that developed during the colonial period that influenced thinking about immigrants and their membership in US society:

To oversimplify: Pennsylvania sought immigrants who would be good citizens regardless of their religious background; Massachusetts wanted as members only those who were religiously pure; and Virginia, with its increasing reliance on a plantation economy, wanted workers as cheaply as it could get them, without necessarily welcoming them to membership in the community.[1]

Fuchs argues that the Pennsylvania ideal—that immigrants (specifically, white European settlers) would be welcomed on terms of equal rights—prevailed, although competition from the other two ideas continued. The Massachusetts model 'became influential in the development of a national ideology of Americanism, but it was too restrictive to form a dominant immigration and naturalization policy',[2] while the Virginia ideal reoccurs as a model of labour migration, but, having found its most extreme form in slavery, remains suspect. In Fuchs' view, the Pennsylvania ideal 'emphasizing inclusion of immigrants' triumphed over the exclusionary views promulgated in Massachusetts and Virginia precisely because it reflects the basic civic values—equal protection and justice under the law, freedom of speech and religion, and representative government—that have come to govern the civic culture of the United States.

Although immigration had its detractors even during colonial times (most notably Benjamin Franklin, who feared that the German migrants would never adopt the English language and customs), Americans generally came to view immigration as essential to the growth of the new nation. Indeed, the Declaration of Independence faults King George III for curtailing immigration into the colonies, citing as justification for independence that 'he has endeavored to prevent the Population of these States; for that purpose obstructing the Laws for Naturalization of Foreigners; refusing to pass others to encourage their migrations hither, and raising the conditions of new Appropriations of Lands.' Immigration made eminent sense for a country with a small population, large expanses of unsettled land, a growing economy and a belief in its manifest destiny to be a beacon of democracy for the rest of the world.

The founding fathers were not, however, totally sanguine about the potential effects of immigration on the new nation. For example, Jefferson questioned whether immigrants would attach themselves to the democratic principles and constitutional bases of the American form of government: 'May not our government be more homogeneous, more peaceful, more durable' without large-scale immigration?[3] Along with other founders, he was particularly concerned that the subjects of European despots, monarchs and aristocrats would undermine the republican form of government if they were not required to renounce prior allegiances.

Despite such concerns, the founders recognised that immigration was necessary to the growth of the republic and that immigrants, at least from Europe, should be incorporated into their membership. By 1802 the basic framework for naturalisation that would last for two centuries was established: after fulfilling a short residency requirement (five years), immigrants who took the oath of allegiance, hence repudiating former allegiances, would be welcomed into full membership. Hence, in setting out the laws governing naturalisation, Americans set aside the worst of their fears and assumed that immigrants could and would acclimatise rapidly to the civic values of the new country.

In effect, immigrants were conceived of as presumptive citizens who would quickly become Americans and hence should enjoy the same rights and privileges of other Americans. By this view, immigration was good for the country and immigrants would be its future. This founding ideal, given voice by George Washington, adhered to the basic principles of inclusion set out in Pennsylvania: 'The bosom of America is open to receive not only the Opulent and respectable Stranger, but the oppressed and persecuted of all Nations and Religions; whom we shall welcome to a participation of all our rights and privileges, if by decency and propriety of conduct they appear to merit the enjoyment.'[4]

Similar sentiments echo throughout US history. The novelist Herman Melville gave voice to the confidence of a new nation built on immigration: 'We are the heirs of all time, and with all nations, we divide our inheritance. On this Western Hemisphere all tribes and people are forming into one federal whole; and there is a future which shall see the estranged children of Adam restored as to the old hearthstone in Eden.'[5] And as recently as 1996 former Congresswoman Barbara Jordan, as Chair of the US Commission on Immigration Reform, also lauded the process by which the US has grown:

The United States is the most successful multiethnic nation in history. It has united immigrants and their descendants from all the world around a commitment to democratic ideals and constitutional principles. Those ideals and principles have been embraced by persons from an extraordinary variety of religious and ethnic backgrounds, partly because they permit and protect religious and cultural diversity within a framework of national political unity.[6]

This is not to say that the US welcomed all newcomers equally, even while adopting the Pennsylvania ideal. There has also been a strong nativist, racist side of US immigration policy which has seen repeated changes from relatively open standards to ones reflecting the country's exclusionary impulses. The restrictionist tendency had its saddest impact during the 1930s, when the United States refused entry to many refugees fleeing Nazi oppression. Certainly, distinctions as to who could enter and exercise full rights continued to be made on the basis of race and national origin well into the twentieth century. Ambivalence about immigrants remained, with concerns heightened into nativism when mass migration and economic and/or political instability collided.

Repeatedly, too, elements of the Massachusetts and Virginia models have triumphed. Exclusions based on ideological beliefs, along with affirmative policies for admission of refugees from communist regimes, formed a twentieth-century counterpart to the Massachusetts requirement of religious conformity. The importation of Chinese labourers to build the railroads and perform other unskilled jobs, followed by the Chinese Exclusion Act of 1882, reflected the Virginia idea of immigrants as expendable workers rather than members of the society. The Bracero programme, under which Mexican workers were admitted on a temporary basis to fill wartime labour shortages, also followed the Virginia pattern.

In recent years, US policies regarding legal immigrants, particularly as defined by their social and legal rights, are increasingly coming to reflect the previously discarded models of exclusion. Yet, as the final section of this essay will explain, the principal elements for effective integration continue to operate. The absorptive capacity of the country remains strong. As long as these factors work, the pendulum should shift back towards the Pennsylvania model of immigrant integration.

The politics of US immigration reform

To understand how immigration policy has become more exclusionary in recent years, it is necessary to understand the politics behind these changes. The politics of immigration reform is today, as it has been throughout US history, highly complex. The actors interested in US immigration policy fall into four broad groupings, each group forming alliances with others when specific interests bring them together. The four groups can be characterised by their attitudes towards *immigration*, on one dimension, and their attitudes about the rights of *immigrants*, on the other. Echoes of the Pennsylvania, Virginia and Massachusetts conceptions can be seen in their approaches.

Advocates

The members of this group favour generous levels of immigration and the full inclusion of immigrants. Broadening the Pennsylvania model to include non-European immigrants, they support current US policies that define family reunification broadly, include provisions for admission of both skilled and unskilled workers, and maintain a substantial refugee admissions effort. They would also bestow full rights and access to public services and benefits on legal immigrants. This group has an abiding conviction in the capacity of the

United States to absorb large numbers of new immigrants and in the capacity of immigrants to contribute to their new society. They make distinctions, however, between legal immigration and illegal migration, believing the latter undermines the former. Nevertheless, this group generally supports policies that permit illegal aliens to become legal immigrants with few barriers if the aliens otherwise meet criteria for admission. They also oppose restrictions on due process rights for aliens in deportation proceedings.

Free-marketeers

The members of this group favour generous levels of immigration, but restricted rights for immigrants. Sharing many of the elements of the Virginia model, they invite immigrants to come to the United States but offer the newcomers no safety net and little compassion if they find they cannot support themselves or are in trouble with the law. The slogan used by representatives of this group during the 1996 debates on immigration policy was: 'Immigration Yes, Welfare No'. The free-marketeers are particularly comfortable with admitting foreigners as temporary workers who can be sent home if they are not needed or no longer benefit the US economy. Their views are well represented on the editorial boards of such newspapers as the *Wall Street Journal*, in such think tanks as the Cato Institute, and among many of the Republican congressional leadership. In this view, business should be able to recruit from a global workforce in order to obtain the best labour at the lowest cost. Seeing immigration as a key ingredient in economic growth, they tend to dismiss the concerns of labour, environmentalists and others about negative effects on US workers and communities. Although the free-marketeers do not support illegal migration, they come close to believing that business should have unlimited access to foreign workers, making illegal migration a *non sequitur*.

Restrictionists

The members of this group support numerical restrictions on legal immigration as well as restrictions on access of immigrants to benefits and legal rights. They tend to see immigration as a problem for society rather than a benefit to it. They favour strong measures to combat illegal migration, including restrictions on the rights of those apprehended in the United States to due process in deportation proceedings. Their reasons for supporting restrictions vary. Some are concerned about the labour market and the economic effects of immigration, particularly the impact of both legal and illegal immigrants on the native-born unskilled population. They also point to the fiscal costs of immigration. Others support immigration restrictions because of demographic factors, pointing to immigration as a major contributor to population growth that will prove harmful to the environment. Still others, often in language reflecting the Massachusetts model, argue that immigration, particularly of ethnic, religious or racial minorities, threatens what they perceive to be the white, Anglo-Saxon cultural foundation of the nation. Peter Brimelow gave voice to this point of view in his book *Alien Nation*.[7] A less hostile variant questions whether the United States has the absorptive capacity to integrate a continuing stream of immigrants, arguing that earlier immigrants adapted well because of periodic lulls in migration that provided a breathing space. While some or all of these concerns about immigration policy may be shared by the integration-oriented group (see next subsection), the major distinguishing characteristic of traditional restrictionists is their willingness to restrict the rights of the immigrants already in the United States.

Integrationists

The members of this group believe that the test of the US commitment to immigration is in the country's immigrant policies (that is, how the United States treats immigrants already admitted, including the rights granted to them), rather than the levels of immigration in any given year. They support full rights for those who are admitted legally, and they tend to prefer permanent admissions, which permit full economic, social and political integration, over temporary admissions. Members of this group generally recognise that immigration has costs as well as benefits. If it appears that the costs are borne by those least able to afford them (for example, already resident low-skilled workers or heavily impacted local communities), the integrationists will consider a variety of solutions, including reductions in the levels of immigration, shifts in the criteria for admission to offset the negative impacts, and/or support for impact aid programmes or other mechanisms to assist immigrants and resident populations. This group strongly opposes illegal migration as a serious violation of the rule of law, a process that undermines legal immigration, and a particularly egregious form of unfair competition for unskilled residents, including legal immigrants. They measure strategies to combat illegal migration against due process considerations, opposing those that pose a danger to these principles.

Complicating the politics of immigration reform in the United States are the alliances that form to propound certain positions. These alliances defy traditional political party divisions, with bipartisan coalitions developing over specific issues. During the 1996 debate on immigration legislation, for example, conservative libertarian free-marketeers, immigration attorneys, and liberal ethnic and civil rights groups (sometimes called the left–right coalition) joined together to block proposed changes that would have both reduced legal admission numbers and shifted priorities towards nuclear families and high-skilled immigrants.[8] A similar coalition then pressed successfully for expansion of the H-1B visa category for admission of professional and specialist workers; for continued permission for unauthorised aliens already in the

United States to transfer to permanent resident status if they otherwise met admission criteria; and for mechanisms to regularise the status of Nicaraguans, Salvadorans, Guatemalans and Haitians.

At the same time, some members of this coalition (for example, free-marketeers and conservative libertarians) joined with restrictionists in a successful effort to reduce the access of legal immigrants to public benefits, much to the chagrin of the ethnic, religious and generally socially liberal members of the original coalition. They also successfully pressed for increases in the income levels that family sponsors of immigrants must have to demonstrate that the newcomers will not become charges on the public purse. In addition, the same coalition urged some relaxation of the rules for deporting legal immigrants who commit crimes, regardless of when they entered the United States or how long ago the crime was committed. The new rules reduced due process rights available to legal immigrants, particularly by curtailing judicial review and administrative discretion to waive removal. Although retroactive application of some of the new welfare rules was reversed in 1997, the 1996 changes continue to apply to immigrants who entered after 22 August 1996.

In effect, what emerged from the legislative battles of 1996–8 was expansion in the potential number of immigrants to be admitted into legal status, albeit with increased financial barriers to their actual admission, with simultaneous serious erosion in the social and legal rights of immigrants who have not yet naturalised. These policies then provided the backdrop to the US response to the terrorist attacks of 2001, which led to further erosion of the legal rights of non-citizens (and even of some citizens).

The following sections describe these policies in greater detail.

Immigration admissions policies

The United States is now experiencing one of the largest and longest waves of immigration in its history. There are three principal routes for those seeking entry and work in the United States: a front door, a side door and a back door. These are respectively, admission for legal permanent residence (immigrants); temporary admission as a foreign student or worker (non-immigrants); and unauthorised migration.

The total *net* flow of foreign nationals (those entering minus those departing) into the United States each year, excluding visitors, is estimated, by the National Research Council (NRC), to be about 820,000.[9] Not since the earliest years of the twentieth century has the United States seen such high levels of annual immigration. The peak then, which occurred in 1907, was almost 1.3 million (gross levels) with an estimated return migration rate of 30 per cent.

The total stock of foreign-born residents in the United States is more than 30 million. Of these, about 30 per cent are naturalised citizens. According to estimates by Jeffrey Passel,[10] the remainder includes about 9 million legal immigrants (including those who obtained amnesty during the 1980s), 2.3 million humanitarian immigrants, 9 million unauthorised aliens, and at least 1 million non-immigrants. The absolute number of foreign-born nationally is at record levels, although the current proportion of foreign-born residents (about 11 per cent) is lower than the previous high (almost 15 per cent at the turn of the last century).

About 800,000 to 1 million legal immigrants become Legal Permanent Residents (LPRs) each year, which is the category that permits eventual citizenship. Legal immigrants are admitted as family members of US citizens and LPRs (about 450,000–600,000 per year); skilled workers and professionals (about 100,000 per year); refugees, asylum seekers and others admitted for humanitarian reasons (about 100,000–150,000 per year); and diversity immigrants admitted through a lottery system for countries with relatively low levels of immigration to the United States (about 50,000 per year).

As a result of various ceilings on admission, large backlogs develop in popular categories. In some cases, applicants must wait more than a decade before they are able to obtain admission. Efforts to reform this system by specifying priorities for admission and eliminating some of the most egregious backlogs failed in 1996. Under one proposal, submitted by the bipartisan Commission on Immigration Reform, the admission numbers available to siblings and adult children of US citizens would have been transferred to the admission of the more than 1 million spouses and minor children of legal immigrants in this category's backlog. After a five- to seven-year period of enhanced numbers in order to accomplish backlog clearance, all priority groups (in this case, nuclear family members) could have been admitted with lower overall levels of immigration than under current law.[11]

Proposals such as the Commission's to reform legal admissions brought criticisms from several different perspectives. Some opposed the eventual decline in overall admissions; others argued that all groups now admitted should continue to have access to the US programme and opposed the transfer of numbers from one category to another. Support for admission of siblings ran particularly high within the Asian American community, whose leaders argued that limiting admission to nuclear families was culturally insensitive to Asian views of family relationships. Perhaps the most effective argument against reforming the legal system was the need to concentrate legislative efforts on mechanisms to curtail unauthorised migration. By placing changes to legal immigration in legislation that focused primarily on illegal movements, the argument went, Congress would blur an already fuzzy distinction between legal and illegal migration.

Unauthorised and temporary migration

Having said this, reform efforts after 1996 did focus primarily on access to legal permanent residence for individuals who were already in the United States, mostly in illegal status. The most contentious issue has been regularisation of the status of Mexicans. When Presidents George Bush and Vicente Fox took office, they pledged cooperation in solving the problem of unauthorised migration from Mexico to the United States. A series of high-level meetings, including presidential summits, began to outline a set of policies to be adopted by both countries. Mexico would enhance border controls to dissuade its nationals from exiting the country illegally, while the United States would provide a mechanism through which Mexicans could enter as temporary workers and/or regularise their status within the United States. Termed 'earned legalisation', the idea was that Mexicans who were working in the United States had proven themselves worthy of regularisation.

What was referred to as a 'Grand Bargain' soon ran into problems when members of Congress questioned whether the components of the agreement would reduce illegal movements, or just reward persons who had entered or worked illegally. They pointed to the amnesty adopted in 1986 that had legalised more than 3 million unauthorised migrants, only to see the numbers of illegal aliens grow even higher in subsequent years. In addition, other governments questioned why Mexicans should get special treatment when their nationals were also contributing to the US economy. The negotiations between the United States and Mexico came to an almost complete halt after September 11. Although some security experts argued that it would be beneficial to bring the very large—some 8–9 million—illegal population into the open, most political observers believed it impossible to sell a legalisation programme or an expanded temporary worker programme in the aftermath of the terrorist attacks by foreign nationals.

In fact, temporary work programmes have attracted considerable political interest during the past few years, reflecting the re-emergence of the Virginia model of labour migration. The trend has been towards expansion in these categories. In 1998 and again in 2000, for example, Congress accepted industry claims of a shortage of professionals in information technology fields and passed legislation (the American Competitiveness and Work Force Improvement Act of 1998, and American Competitiveness in the Twenty-First Century Act of 2000) to increase the number of professionals and specialist workers admitted under the H1-B temporary visa programme. The increases established under the 1998 and 2000 legislation were temporary, and with the downturn in the US economy, particularly in information technology, it is likely that the numbers will revert to the original level.

The most striking example of return to the Virginia model of labour migration without membership has been the tacit acceptance of high levels of unauthorised migration, as long as the newcomers are gainfully employed. As the economy boomed in the late 1990s, Immigration and Naturalization Service (INS) officials indicated that they would not conduct workplace raids. In part, the shift in focus reflected frustration with the overall inadequacy of sanctions on employers as a mechanism for enforcing immigration laws. However, the hands-off policy also reflected recognition that aggressive workplace enforcement brought attacks from powerful constituencies when the unemployment rate was the lowest in decades. The INS undertook some publicised raids on farms growing Vidalia onions in south-eastern Georgia at the height of the harvest, for example, that led to protests even from members of Congress who voted for tough controls on illegal immigration. Although the INS takes pains to emphasise that shifting enforcement activities away from workplace raids should not be taken as a green light by employers to hire unauthorised workers, the message nevertheless gets through that its focus will be elsewhere.

In a surprising move that reflects the changing coalitions on immigration matters, the trade union federation AFL-CIO also backed off from its traditional support for tough workplace measures against unauthorised migration, recommending an end to employer sanctions as well as a new amnesty programme for the migrants already in the United States. The ostensible reason for this policy change was the twin failure of sanctions on employers: they were not curbing illegal work but they were putting foreign workers at risk of discrimination. The interest of a number of unions in organising industries heavily dependent on unauthorised immigrant labour is widely believed to have precipitated the policy change.

The repercussions of September 11

After September 11, the focus of attention shifted from the number of migrants to be admitted to the United States to the tracking of those coming in. All of the hijackers had entered the United States as temporary visitors or foreign students; some had overstayed their visas but others remained in legal status throughout their stay. Two problems became apparent. First, immigration authorities did not have sufficient access to intelligence data on the identity of suspected terrorists, making it highly likely that these persons could be granted visas. Second, even with good intelligence, it was difficult, in not impossible, to find suspected terrorists who had already entered the country. Consequently, the government has sought to improve the intelligence used in issuing visas and when inspecting foreign nationals at ports of entry.

Efforts have also been made to develop various systems to track the entry, exit and whereabouts of non-immigrants. The most controversial of these systems is the National Security Entry–Exit Registration System (NSEER), which applies to male non-immigrants who are 16 years or older from about twenty-five mostly Arab and Muslim countries. Under the NSEER, these foreign nationals must register with immigration authorities at a port of entry on arrival in the United States. If they are already in the country, they must register at an immigration office (now incorporated into the Department of Homeland Security). Every year they must re-register, with additional interviews in person at an immigration office, and they must give timely notifications to immigration authorities of changes of address, employment or school. These nationals also have to use specially designated ports when they leave the country and report in person to an immigration officer at the port on their departure date.

The special registration procedure, along with special interviews conducted with foreign nationals from these countries in the weeks after September 11, has been criticised as ethnic and religious profiling. Profiling is not in and of itself problematic as a mechanism to identify potential terrorists. If based on solid information encompassing a wide range of indicators and used in conjunction with other law enforcement tools, profiling becomes one among an arsenal of techniques to give greater scrutiny to certain individuals than to others. However, when profiling is based on crude characteristics, such as race, ethnicity and religion, it can be a counterproductive tool for law enforcement that places an excessive burden on innocent persons.[12]

Interestingly, one part of admission policy that has not been seriously affected by September 11 has been the asylum system.[13] In consultation with advocates for greater refugee protection, the United States introduced significant changes in asylum processing in 1990 and again in 1995 that succeeded in making decision-making more professional while curbing some of the major abuses in the system. The 1990 reforms created a corps of asylum officers who were specially trained to adjudicate applications for refugee status, established a documentation centre with a multiplicity of materials from different sources that could be used to check the validity and credibility of claims, and reduced the linkages between US foreign policy interests and asylum decisions. The 1995 reforms streamlined the asylum adjudication process to ensure that all cases were heard (first instance and appeal) within six months of application, made asylum applicants ineligible for work authorisation during the six-month application process (to deter those without valid claims from applying merely to obtain work permits), and applied the new processes on a 'last in, first out' basis. These changes resulted in a sizeable reduction in the number of new applicants, along with a significant increase in the proportion of new cases that were approved.

Legal rights of immigrants

The legislation that emerged from the intense debates in 1996 represented a clear diminution of the legal rights of immigrants, leaving current policies at odds with the founding principle that immigrants were to be full members of the citizenry. Two pieces of legislation are at issue: the Antiterrorism and Effective Death Penalty Act and the Illegal Immigration Reform and Immigrant Responsibility Act. Although most of the provisions of these two laws focus on control of illegal aliens, both made significant changes in the rights of legal immigrants as well. Of most concern is the curtailment of due process in removal hearings involving aliens, whether they entered legally or illegally. Additional restrictions on the legal rights of immigrants were made after September 11, particularly in the USA Patriot Act.

The most substantial changes affect persons defined as aggravated felons in

US immigration law. Certainly, the founding ideal did not expect that immigrants who commit serious crimes would be welcomed with open arms. The Washington statement quoted in the introduction clearly welcomes only those who 'by decency and propriety of conduct . . . appear to merit the enjoyment' of the rights to be bestowed. Yet there is ample evidence of an expectation that even criminals could find second chances in America, as witnessed by the pride Georgians hold in their earliest founders, many of whom had been released from English gaols.

Perhaps the best measure of a society's willingness to admit newcomers to full membership is its attitudes towards those who stray. It is relatively easy to be generous towards those who play by all the rules; it is far more difficult to embrace strangers who violate them. For much of America's history, removing an immigrant because of criminal activity was not an easy process, despite concerns, many valid, about crime rates in immigrant neighbour-hoods. During the 1990s, however, the law changed several times to facilitate such deportations. In the Immigration Act of 1990, provisions were adopted to ease removal of 'aggravated felons', defined as persons who committed such serious crimes as murder and rape. Immigration judges could, however, waive deportation if removal would pose an extreme hardship. Various factors would be taken into account, including the seriousness of the crime, when it was committed, at what age the immigrant came to the United States, whether subsequent behaviour showed a change, and whether the immigrant had family in the United States.

The 1996 legislation made additional changes that put legal immigrants who committed crimes at greater risk of removal. Most important, the definition of an aggravated felony was revised to include far less serious crimes. Just about any offence resulting in a potential—not necessarily actual—custodial sentence of one year or more could render the alien deportable. The new rule was applied retroactively so that crimes committed many years ago, even if there were evidence of no subsequent criminality, qualified as grounds for removal. The 'one strike and you're out' policies carried over even to those who had come to the United States as young children and were likely to have learned their criminal craft in their new country. The discretion that immigration judges had to weigh factors in ordering deportation was eliminated. Also curtailed was the right to appeal decisions to the federal judiciary. Mandatory detention was required until removal took place. If the government claimed certain national security interests, the evidence upon which the removal decision was made could be kept from the immigrant.

The principal architect of the 1996 aggravated felony provisions was Senator Spencer Abraham, who sponsored a number of the bills that led to expanded legal immigration and admission of temporary workers. As with the welfare debate, the new removal rules made clear that the welcome given would be a guarded one. Immigrants would not be full members, and could remain only to the extent that they violated no laws.

The anti-terrorism provisions of the 1996 legislation, combined with the USA Patriot Act, affected legal immigrants as well as non-immigrants and unauthorised migrants. The provisions pertain not only to those convicted of terrorist acts but also those who espouse or support what may be construed to be terrorist organisations. Perhaps the most controversial provision allows the removal of an alien who is a member of a foreign terrorist organisation, as designated by the Secretary of State, which the alien knows to be or *should have known to be* a terrorist organisation. The USA Patriot Act, passed after September 11, expanded the definition of terrorist activity, for example, to include persons who have used positions 'of prominence within any country to endorse or espouse terrorist activity, or to persuade others to support terrorist activity or a terrorist organisation, in a way that the Secretary of State has determined undermines United States efforts to reduce or eliminate terrorist activities'.

Social rights of immigrants

Some of the most profound changes to occur in immigration policy found their way into law through the welfare reform legislation also passed in 1996. The Personal Responsibility and Work Opportunity Reconciliation Act (Welfare Reform Act), in combination with the 1996 Illegal Immigration Reform and Immigrant Responsibility Act (Immigration Reform Act), reduced substantially the access of legal immigrants to public benefit programmes available to citizens. Although parts of these laws have since been amended, all of the reversals pertain to retroactive application of the new standards to immigrants in the United States at the time of passage. The significant derogation from the social rights of legal immigrants entering now and in the future has not changed.

Until 1996, no federal benefit programme denied eligibility to permanent resident aliens solely on the basis of alien status. During the course of the 1970s and 1980s, however, the courts held that Congress (but not individual states) could make distinctions among different immigration statuses and between aliens and citizens, paving the way for the 1996 changes. The Supreme Court held that as long as distinctions between citizens and aliens are not wholly irrational, Congress may draw them. Through legislative and regulatory actions, distinctions were then made between aliens residing permanently and legally in this country and undocumented aliens. The former were generally determined eligible for federal assistance while the latter were generally barred from these programmes.

In the early 1980s, in part because of concern about costs, legislation had been passed to restrict legal immigrants' access to benefits, though not to deny eligibility. In determining eligibility for three programmes—Aid to Families with Dependent Children (AFDC), Supplementary Security Income (SSI) for aged and disabled persons, and Food Stamps—the income of sponsors was to be 'deemed' during the first three to five years after entry, depending on the specific programme. Under 'deeming' provisions, the income and resources of an alien's 'sponsor' are considered to be available to the sponsored alien when he or she applies for the applicable public benefits. Deeming was seen to have several advantages: it reinforced the responsibility of sponsors for family members whom they brought into the country; it allowed access to public programmes, however, if changed circumstances made the sponsor unable to provide the support; and because the deeming requirement was for a limited period of time, it did not construct a permanent second class of resident who paid taxes but would not realise any benefits.

Beginning in 1994, Congress began to explore more basic changes restricting eligibility of immigrants for public assistance programmes as it began consideration of fundamental welfare reform. The impetus for the restrictions on eligibility stemmed from a number of different concerns, as did the opposition to them. Budget pressures may have been the most important in stimulating discussion of such restrictions. In an era where funding for any new programmes at both the federal and state levels had to come from cuts in existing ones, restricting coverage of immigrants was seen as a possible source of revenue. There were also concerns about what appeared to be the erosion of sponsor responsibility for new arrivals. The foreign-born component of some federal public assistance caseloads had risen dramatically during the 1980s. Of particular concern was the SSI programme. A large proportion of the immigrants who applied for this programme did so soon after their sponsor's income ceased to be 'deemed' when determining whether they met the income eligibility requirements. This practice was not illegal but appeared to many members of Congress to be a violation of the spirit of the immigration law.

Proponents of welfare restrictions included many supporters of high levels of immigration. Senator Spencer Abraham, who successfully fought restrictions on the number of immigrants to be admitted, was a staunch supporter of the welfare changes and one of the proponents of the 'Immigration Yes, Welfare No' campaign. Rick Santorum, one of the senators responsible for managing the debate on the Senate floor, countered proposals to retain eligibility for immigrants already in the country with the following words:

I am pro-immigration. I am the son of an immigrant. I am not one of those people who says 'I'm in. OK. Close the door.' I believe immigration is important to the future of this country . . . If we clean up [the abuse of welfare programmes] I think we improve the image of immigration and there is less pressure on lowering those caps and doing other things that I think could be harmful with respect to the area of immigration and, I think, save the taxpayers a whole bundle of money in the process.[14]

This sentiment was countered by arguments that linking eligibility, particularly for safety net services, to citizenship would debase citizenship as well as shift the traditional notions that immigrants should be included in, not excluded from, membership. As early as August 1994, Barbara Jordan, Chair of the US Commission on Immigration Reform, raised concerns about the debasement of citizenship before the Ways and Means Committee of the US House of Representatives:

I believe firmly that citizenship in this country is something to be cherished and protected. I want all immigrants to become citizens. I want them to seek citizenship because it is the key to full participation in our political community, to know first hand and understand the American form of democracy. I want unnecessary barriers to naturalization—and there are many of them—to be removed. *However, I do not want immigrants to seek citizenship because it is the only route to our safety nets. To me, that would be a debasement of our notions of citizenship.*[15]

The Commission also emphasised that responsible immigration policy meant a system of mutual obligations that the welfare reform changes would undermine: 'Immigrants must accept the obligations we impose—to obey our laws, to pay taxes, to respect other cultures and ethnic groups. At the same time, citizens incur obligations to provide an environment in which newcomers can become fully participating members of our society.'[16] Opponents of the restrictions further pointed out that immigrants were taxpayers and, through their labour, contributed billions of dollars to the US economy each year. As contributors to the US economy, they should be eligible for the same safety nets as other Americans.

For the most part, Congress ignored the arguments against denying legal immigrants eligibility for public benefits. The 1996 reforms in the welfare system reduced their eligibility significantly; the Welfare Reform Act made legal immigrants ineligible for SSI and Food Stamps until granted citizenship or having worked for forty qualifying quarters. The Act also made legal immigrants ineligible for other means-tested benefits during their first five years after entry. Unlike SSI and Food Stamps, many of these other programmes involve matching federal and state funds.

In a further departure from earlier policy, the Act authorised states to determine whether they will permit legal immigrants (except those granted citizenship or having worked for forty qualifying quarters) to receive temporary assistance for needy families (the amended AFDC), certain social services and Medicaid. Until 1996, the sole authority for determining policies related to immigrants rested with the federal government. The 1996 Act now gives states wide discretion, including the authority to limit eligibility of legal immigrants and non-immigrants for their own programmes, and to deem sponsor income and assets.

The full effects of the welfare reforms on immigrants are not yet known. Budget surpluses stemming from the thriving US economy permitted changes in federal law, as well as generous responses from states, that blunted the effects on individual immigrants. Questions remain, however, about the capacity of states to continue benefits not covered by the federal government in the event of economic recession. At least one state, Colorado, has introduced legislation to reduce the access of legal immigrants to medical assistance as a way to address deficits building up in 2003.

The effects on US notions about immigration are clearer. At a time when the United States is admitting record numbers of immigrants, and a sizeable proportion live and work in poverty, restricting eligibility for safety net programmes sends the message that immigrants are welcomed as workers, but not as full members of the community. Another sign of the re-emergence of the Virginia model of immigration, the welfare reforms adopted in 1996 say, in effect, that all obligations are one-sided: immigrants must continue to pay taxes, benefit our economy, obey our laws and otherwise contribute, but the broader society has no reciprocal obligations towards them.

Conclusion

This survey of legislative reforms during the past decade raises many questions about the future direction of US immigration policy. Still a country that values immigration, it is not at all clear that the United States is still a country that protects its immigrants. Perhaps never before has the Pennsylvania model been under so much pressure, with the impulse towards limited membership for immigrants coming increasingly from the supporters of large-scale immigration, and not just from its opponents.

Of course, there are signs that run counter to this bleak picture (bleak, at least, to someone steeped in the Pennsylvania model of inclusion). As immigrants naturalise they are exercising political power in a number of our most populous states. This political power, combined with the growing economy in the late 1990s, permitted the reversal of many of the most egregious violations of the rights of immigrants in terms of their access to public programmes.

Ultimately, the fate of the Pennsylvania model will be determined by the extent to which new immigrants integrate into the United States despite the restrictions placed on their rights. Here, the picture is very positive, because integration is facilitated by a broad set of factors that go deeper than the legislative changes of the past decade. Unlike the other major immigration countries (Canada and Australia), the United States has no explicit immigrant integration policies or programmes supported by government. Rather, integration largely occurs within the private sector. Almost all immigrants to the United States are sponsored by family members or employers who take principal responsibility for ensuring their successful adaptation to the new country.[17] Their work is facilitated by a flexible labour market that makes it relatively easy for immigrants to find employment. Although many positions are low paid, upward mobility is possible and immigrants can own their own businesses. For more highly skilled immigrants, economic rewards can be particularly attractive. Given the high levels of employment, immigrants often tend to be characterised as hard-working individuals who contribute to the nation's economy—a reputation that also eases the integration process.

Although the federal government tends not to provide direct support for immigrant integration programmes, integration is aided by several broad government policies. Perhaps most important is birthright citizenship. By definition, being a 'foreigner' lasts for only one generation. The children of immigrants are automatically citizens if they are born on US territory. This provision applies even to the children of unauthorised migrants. Also important are the policies that protect both citizens and immigrants from discrimination on the basis of race, religion, nationality and, in some cases, citizenship. There are even laws that protect persons from 'immigration-related unfair employment practices'. Should an employer refuse to hire a foreign-sounding or foreign-looking person because s/he fears the applicant is working illegally, or require an applicant to show additional or different documents to verify work authorisation, the employer may be penalised for inappropriate discriminatory practices. Further, the federal government provides funds to school systems to help them teach English to children with limited proficiency in the language.

Finally, immigrant integration is facilitated by the very history that makes the United States a nation of immigrants. Having weathered cycles of pro- and anti-immigration sentiments and policies, the United States remains indebted to the contributions of the millions of immigrants who have settled the country. So, too, will it weather this latest assault on its best traditions.

Notes

1 Lawrence H. Fuchs, *The American Kaleidoscope*, Hanover, New Hampshire, Wesleyan University Press, 1990, p. 8.
2 Ibid.
3 Ibid., p. 13.
4 Ibid., p. 1.
5 Lawrence H. Fuchs and Susan Forbes (Martin), 'Immigration and US History: The Evolution of the Open Door', in Thomas Alexander Aleinikoff, David A. Martin and Hiroshi Motomura, eds, *Immigration and Citizenship: Process and Policy*, St Paul, Minnesota, West Group, 1998.
6 US Commission on Immigration Reform, 'Americanization and Integration of Immigrants', appendix to *Becoming an American*, Washington DC, US Commission on Immigration Reform, 1997.
7 Peter Brimelow, *Alien Nation: Common Sense about America's Immigration Disaster*, New York, Random House, 1995.
8 James G. Gimpel and James R. Edwards, Jr, *The Congressional Politics of Immigration Reform*, Boston, Allyn & Bacon, 1999.
9 James P. Smith and Barry Edmonston, *The New Americans: Economic, Demographic and Fiscal Impacts of Immigration*, Washington DC, National Research Council, 1997.
10 Jeffrey S. Passel and Michael Fix, 'US Immigration at the Beginning of the 21st Century', testimony prepared for the Subcommittee on Immigration and Claims, Hearing on 'The US Population and Immigration', Committee on the Judiciary, US House of Representatives, 2 August 2001, available at http://www.house.gov/judiciary/passel_080201.htm.
11 US Commission on Immigration Reform, *Legal Immigration: Setting Priorities*, Washington DC, US Government Printing Office, 1995.

12 Profiles tend to be based on the last threat rather than an analysis of future threats. To give an example, just as the US government began to interview 5,000 young men from Arab and Muslim nations, two Palestinian women suicide bombers committed serious terrorist acts.

13 The same cannot be said of refugee resettlement admissions, many of which came from such countries as Somalia, Sudan, Iraq, Iran and Afghanistan. Immediately after September 11, refugee admissions from abroad were suspended pending a security review. Although new procedures were put into place to increase security, the resettlement programme is still not functioning at pre-September 11 levels and efficiency.

14 Congressional Record, *Proceedings and Debates of the 104th Congress, Second Session*, Washington DC, US Government Printing Office, 18 July 1996, S.8146.

15 US Commission on Immigration Reform, 'Americanization and Integration of Immigrants'.

16 US Commission on Immigration Reform, *Becoming an American*.

17 The exception proves the rule. The only major groups without such sponsorship are resettled refugees and those granted asylum. The federal government provides grants to private agencies and state and local governments to receive these individuals, place them in local communities, and provide language training and job counselling and placement services. Similar federal assistance is not available to any other immigrants.

Migration and the Welfare State in Europe

ANDREW GEDDES

DEBATES about immigration in Europe have become intensely focused on welfare and social rights. They relate both to migration defined by European states as 'wanted' (such as high-skilled labour migration) and to that defined as 'unwanted' (such as asylum seekers). Arguments for openness or closure then centre on the implications of migration for 'national resources', for it is important to note that even in this era of European economic and political integration these welfare states remain decidedly national.

This essay explores the boundary issues and tensions that international migration in its various forms raises for national welfare states. Migration is shown to highlight some key organisational and ideological pressures on these welfare states: in particular, pressures to demarcate more tightly a community of legitimate receivers of welfare state benefits, along with heightened pressure to place outside of this community those forms of migration deemed bogus or abusive while including those seen as making a welfare state contribution. There is a broader point here, too, which touches upon more general issues of welfare state integration and social cohesion. Debates about migration and welfare are not solely about the treatment of newcomers—although this is the point at which debates can be at their most intense—but also about social rights, cohesion and solidarity, and how these notions can be sustained in relation to pressures deriving from economic change and population movement.

Border tensions

Lydia Morris has captured the core dynamics underpinning relations between migration and welfare by observing that European states have sought to 'manage the contradiction' between the pressures to expand migration (the continuing demand for migrant workers, the assertion of human rights and the right to protection) and the countervailing pressure for closure exerted by limits on national resources.[1] These contradictory forces are made manifest as tensions between national welfare states, open markets, regional integration within the EU and the resultant 'negotiated pragmatism' at the borders of European welfare states. At the local level they can be evident in tensions between residents and newcomers over access to scarce welfare resources.

Negotiated pragmatism exposes some policy concerns. Is migration a drain on national welfare state resources such that it poses a 'threat'? Or can

© The Political Quarterly Publishing Co. Ltd. 2003

150 Published by Blackwell Publishing Ltd, 9600 Garsington Road, Oxford OX4 2DQ, UK and 350 Main Street, Malden, MA 02148, USA

immigration actually help 'rescue' these welfare states because demographic and labour market changes require new immigrants to plug gaps in the labour market and in retirement income? Both arguments in this simple form are overblown because international migration at current levels, and with current national and international approaches towards it, possesses the capacity neither to save nor to destroy these welfare states. To construct arguments in such bombastic terms is to neglect the subtler relations between the various forms of migration and different types of welfare state. Migration scholars would presage any such discussion by highlighting important distinctions between forms of migration that differ according to the purposes of movement, the duration of stay and so on. Scholars of European welfare states would similarly highlight distinctions between types of welfare state. The analytical terrain I shall explore is thus not that of ethical arguments about the legitimacy of the regulation of migration, but the ways in which various forms of international migration encounter a political universe of semi-sovereign European states and interact with a key organisational and ideological component of these countries—namely, their welfare states—and the consequences of this encounter.

Policy dilemmas

Relations between migration and welfare raise some troubling policy dilemmas. If we look back to the postwar period of large-scale guest-worker and postcolonial migration, then access to social rights was granted to immigrant newcomers who did not hold the citizenship of the country to which they were moving on the basis of legal residence. Immigrants were thus ushered into the antechamber of 'denizenship', within which they were accorded legal and social rights short of full citizenship. Since the 1990s, economic and political pressures have meant that some migrants continue to be made welcome—usually on the basis of a perceived economic contribution—while others are viewed as a potential drain on welfare state resources. The denizenship status has come under pressure from those forms of migration deemed abusive or undeserving.

If arguments for or against immigration were centred entirely on demographic or economic factors, then the outcomes would be far from clear-cut because future labour market, population, welfare and migration trends are well-nigh impossible to predict with any degree of certainty. Yet it is clear that demographic and economic arguments have underpinned the opening of the door to new immigrants that has occurred in countries such as Britain (the dramatic increase in work permits issued since Labour came to power in 1997, the launch of the High Skilled Workers Programme in 2002 and new legal channels for low-skilled migrants) and Germany (the so-called 'green card' scheme for IT workers, although the more accurate transatlantic comparator is the US H1-B visa). Before these innovations, both Britain and Germany had virtually closed the door to labour migration more than thirty years ago.

A key point here is the ways in which arguments for such positive policies have found more fertile ground since the late 1990s and the subtle shift in arguments about 'needs' and 'resources' that these approaches symbolise. The other side of the migration policy coin has been a renewed determination to keep out those would-be migrants defined by state policies as unwanted, because they are seen as in some ways bogus or abusive, such as asylum seekers. There is nothing new in this connection between openness and closure at the heart of European immigration politics. It does, in fact, highlight a classic dilemma of immigration policy and politics: namely, accounting for the walls that states build and the small doors that they then open within them.[2]

These policy tensions are difficult to resolve, and will remain all the more so if attention is not paid to the variety of types of migration and to the different types of welfare state that can be observed in European countries. The relationship between migration and welfare needs to be broken down into more specific consideration of forms of migration and types of welfare state. Such disaggregation reveals the subtle reconfiguring of both the organisational and the conceptual borders of these welfare states—broader tensions between openness and closure, and the political constellations at national and supranational level that develop around them. What is more, migration provides a fascinating lens through which these broader changes in European welfare states can be viewed. It would be to get the issues precisely the wrong way around to argue that migration in some ways *drives* changes in European welfare states. Rather, it is more useful to explore the organisational and ideological changes within European welfare states and the effects that these in turn have on understandings of migration.

Forms of welfare state and types of migration

The different forms of welfare state organisation and the diversity of forms of international migration mean that sweeping statements about immigration and welfare are unlikely to be very helpful when trying to understand the political and social dilemmas that arise. This section explores pressures to demarcate more tightly a community of legitimate receivers of welfare state benefits while identifying the ways in which welfare states have also played a role as internal mechanisms for immigration control and deterrence.

European welfare states are more than the sum total of social policies. They are powerful institutional forces embodying ideas and practices associated with inclusion, exclusion, membership, belonging, entitlement and identity; that is, the classic boundary issues that concern migration scholars and policy-makers. Migration is a fascinating boundary issue precisely because the treatment of various types of migrants can highlight structural characteristics of these welfare states, expose core tensions within them, and illustrate the pressures that have existed particularly since the 1990s to demarcate more tightly the 'community of legitimate receivers of welfare state benefits'.[3]

The definition and redefinition of this 'community' across Europe has included the making of distinctions between 'wanted' and 'unwanted' migrants, derived from perceptions of the implications for national resources in general and welfare states in particular. Note the use of the word 'perceptions', because these are central to the politics of migration. Analysis of the politics of migration becomes less a set of arguments about why migration *occurs* and more a series of arguments about how it is *understood* and *interpreted*, because perceptions underpin arguments about migration, welfare, resources, integration, social cohesion, security and so on. As a consequence, no debate on these issues can be resolved simply by appealing to 'the facts', because they are closely connected with values and beliefs.

As well as being important symbols of membership, entitlement, identity and belonging, European welfare states have become an 'internal' method for the regulation of migration. By providing access to, or exclusion from, welfare support, European states have sought to welcome some forms of migration while deterring others. This more coercive side of the welfare state (pursuing social inclusion while simultaneously endorsing certain norms of social acceptability and deterring forms of population movement deemed damaging) has long been a feature of welfare systems. Recently, asylum seekers have found themselves strongly exposed to this more coercive and disciplinary side of European welfare states. In Britain, for instance, legislation enacted in 2002 has made asylum seekers subject to a system of reception and accommodation in detention centres. The suspicion that underpinned this policy was that many of these asylum seekers were 'bogus' and as such undeserving of welfare state benefits. The system put in place by the 2002 legislation has three effects. First, it minimises chances for social inclusion by separating asylum seekers from mainstream society. Second, it enhances the ability of the state to monitor, observe and control the lives of these asylum seekers while they are on the territory of the state. Third, the combined effect of separation and observation is that these migrants do not put down roots and can be removed. Thus, the intention is that this form of migration (unlike earlier waves of labour and family migration) should be reversible.

In these terms, the connections between migration and welfare present a set of thorny boundary issues while also providing a lens through which more general debates about the future of European welfare states can be viewed. International migration tends to be viewed as something that 'happens' to these states. If this view is taken for granted then the task becomes one of charting the responses of these nation-states to migration in its various forms. This is an unsatisfying approach because some prior sociological questions linger. It is abundantly clear that a key feature of immigration politics is the categories into which migrants are placed, which largely determine whether these migrants are welcome or not. These categories relate not to the personal character or quality of individuals (although media representations of migrants as 'bogus' or 'abusive' assume that they do), but to the ways in which the implications of their migration are evaluated; that is, whether it is construed as potentially harmful or beneficial. Since the 1960s there had, until recently, been a progressive narrowing of the channels for legal migration into European countries. A corollary of this has been the growth in forms of migration defined by state policies as illegal because new restrictions produce new evasions (of which human trafficking and people smuggling are troubling examples).

Processes of categorisation play a central role in the politics of migration and welfare. Migration is not something 'out there' that 'happens' to these welfare states, because welfare states and perceptions of needs, requirements and resources structure perceptions of migration as wanted or unwanted. In such circumstances it is not international migration that 'challenges' the welfare state but, rather, changes within these welfare states that can 'challenge' understandings of international migration. If we follow this approach, and focus on migration as a subset of broader debates about welfare and social rights, then this brings into view organisational, ideological and institutional processes within these welfare states relating to the definition (and redefinition) of welfare state boundaries; processes that play a key role in shaping understandings of 'wanted' and 'unwanted' forms of international migration.

This is more than an arcane point of method. If migration in its various forms is taken in such terms as a *dependent* variable—and if this point of departure is followed by examination of the institutional and organisational arenas from which understandings of it as 'wanted' or 'unwanted' emerge— then it can be demonstrated that these are not solely immigration questions. Rather, the debate about migration and welfare relates strongly to internal pressures within these welfare states (responding to the pressures of economic internationalisation and social individualisation, for example). Moreover, the questions of 'integration' and social cohesion with which welfare states are centrally concerned are matters for all members of society, not just immigrant newcomers. Immigration is not the driving force for these general welfare state debates, but arguments can be at their most intense when immigrant newcomers are the subjects of discussion. Moreover, the consequences of excluding some newcomers from welfare state protection can have particularly negative implications for their economic and social integration while questioning longer-term stability and social cohesion.

Analysing migration and welfare

The discussion so far has focused on broad characteristics of debates about migration and welfare. The organisational boundaries of these welfare states (the basis for entitlement) and their conceptual boundaries (the notion of who 'belongs', is 'entitled' and 'deserves') are strongly grounded in national political processes. Immigration policy too has been largely the preserve of the nation-state. Indeed, controlling access to the state territory is a hallmark of national sovereign authority.

A core puzzle for students of European immigration politics is that, while European migration policies have since the 1970s been restrictive, it is also apparent that migration continued into European countries even after the 'immigration stop' of the early 1970s. Cornelius, Martin and Hollifield formulate what they call a 'gap hypothesis' to account for the disparity between the rhetoric of control and the reality of continued immigration.[4] Moves towards restriction and exclusion encounter countervailing trends towards openness and inclusion because of labour market needs, humanitarian concerns and the imperative of refugee protection. This raises two further points. The first relates to the relationship between welfare states and migration flows, the second to the relationship between welfare states and the social rights of immigrant newcomers.

To take the first point, does continued openness to some forms of migration have corrosive effects on welfare states? The US political scientist Gary Freeman saw the openness signified by international migration as inducing pressures for restrictions, as new migration could be seen as potentially corrosive of welfare standards.[5] There clearly have been welfare-state-related arguments behind restrictive policies. However, the view that national welfare states *necessarily* incline towards closure and restriction has been contested by those who identify some welfare-state-related openness as due to the continued need for forms of migration that contribute to these welfare states. This openness can currently be seen across the EU in sectors such as information and communications technologies (ICT), healthcare and education, while longer-term demographic pressures also underpin arguments for more 'positive' migration policies.

The second point centres on the relationship between welfare states and social rights for migrants. It then becomes important to identify the institutional venues within which decisions about migration are made. Immigration is typically an issue for the executive, although judicial interventions have moderated executive impulses to closure. Virginie Guiraudon's comparative analysis of France, Germany and the Netherlands showed how decisions taken behind 'gilded doors' by courts and officials have been more accommodating of the rights of migrants than those exposed to the fuller glare of public debate.[6] The outcome, Guiraudon contends, has been the extension of some social rights to migrants despite the political rhetoric of exclusion.

This is not to say that national policies have been open and expansive to all forms of migration. Rather, it serves to counter the overblown rhetoric of 'fortress Europe' and to prompt analysis of the ways in which European states have been open, but at the margins. It is these margins that analysts of migration and welfare necessarily explore.

To embark on such an exploration requires that attention be paid to welfare state types and their relation to various forms of migration. This can help circumvent discussion of 'openness' and 'closure' when neither applies in its absolute form. Instead, analysis can be directed towards the ways in which a community of legitimate receivers of welfare state benefits has been defined and redefined. These processes encapsulate openness towards some forms of migration and closure towards others. Moreover, while there are some cross-European similarities, there are also some national particularities that relate to the type of welfare state organisation.

European welfare state models

Gøsta Esping-Andersen, who distinguished liberal, conservative and social democratic types, developed the best-known typology of European welfare states.[7] The effects of immigration were peripheral to these attempts to classify European welfare state types, just as they were to classic works on the institution of modern citizenship, such as that by T. H. Marshall.

According to Esping-Andersen's schema, liberal welfare states such as that in Britain emphasise individual self-reliance and the primacy of the market (either subsidised or actively encouraged by the state). Lower levels of state welfare support are accompanied by patterns of social stratification that see a minority of low-income dependants, and a majority of the public with more capacity to provide for themselves. Migrants and their descendants in the UK are more likely to be found in lower-income and lower-status occupations, while controversial measures have sought to place 'unwanted' asylum-seeking migrants entirely outside the community of legitimate receivers of welfare state benefits.

The conservative–corporatist type of welfare state, such as that in Germany, combines moderate levels of welfare support with the historical legacies of corporatism (that is, bargaining between the social partners on levels of support) and a system of income maintenance linked to occupational status. In Germany too there have nevertheless been pressures to demarcate more sharply the community of legitimate receivers of welfare state benefits. Interestingly, this led to the ethnic German *Aussiedler* (entitled to 'return' to Germany from former Soviet republics on the basis of their ethnicity, even though most had never been to Germany) being treated less as co-Germans and more as an immigrant group, as I shall explain below. Germany also experienced controversy about intra-EU migration arising from 'posted workers' moving from one EU member state to another, again casting into stark relief the German model of consensus capitalism.

The social democratic welfare state typically found in Scandinavia was seen to combine higher levels of welfare support with a social democratic principle of social stratification that seeks to apply universal and redistributive benefits and to prompt universal solidarity in favour of the welfare state. Access to welfare state entitlements by immigrants has, here too, become a key political issue. The principle of welfare state egalitarianism has been compromised by attempts—most notably in Denmark—to close the door of the social democratic welfare state to new immigrants.

The southern European type of welfare state was not included within Esping-Andersen's schema, but has been seen as a distinct form of provision based on a mixture of employment-related protection with universalism (for instance, of healthcare provision), in combinations that are not seen elsewhere in Europe. The migration context is also rather different in southern Europe, with higher levels of economic informality and a relationship between citizens and the state that, as we shall see, differs in important respects from those in 'older' west European destination countries.

Migration and the national welfare state

Britain

Two main strands running through British debates about migration and welfare have exemplified the tension between openness and closure. Immigration had almost disappeared from the British political landscape in the early 1990s, but returned with a vengeance in the late 1990s as asylum-seeking migration became intensely politicised. Responses to asylum have had a strong welfare state component. Legislation in 1993, 1996, 1999 and 2002 was driven by the idea that there was some kind of welfare state 'pull effect' for asylum-seeking migrants that brought them to the UK. The legislation included measures that established an ever more tenuous relationship between asylum seekers and welfare support in the belief that this would serve as a deterrent and enable the growth in this form of migration to be reversed. On all criteria there are grounds for doubting the efficacy of this policy. The number of asylum applicants rose steeply at the end of the 1990s from 41,000 and 58,000 in 1997 and 1998 respectively to 91,000 and 97,000 in 1999 and 2000.

The UK government has also encountered the constraining effects of the courts. The 1993 measure introduced by the Conservative government, removing welfare rights from 'in country' applicants (all those who did not make a claim at their point of entry into the UK) was ruled invalid by the Court of Appeal on the grounds that the likely destitution of asylum applicants contravened the provisions of the 1948 National Assistance Act. The fact that the costs of support for asylum seekers then fell on a small number of places (London and some coastal towns) motivated the introduction of a dispersal scheme and the replacement of welfare state benefits paid in cash with vouchers. The failings of this system, as marked by continued increases in asylum applications and social tensions in the towns to which asylum seekers were dispersed, prompted the measures in the 2002 legislation. Here again the core logic was strongly focused on welfare with a further attempt, this time by a Labour government, to remove welfare rights from those who did not make an asylum application at the earliest opportunity. Once again the courts intervened with a February 2003 ruling, on the basis of human rights legislation, that the measures would lead to destitution and that such an outcome could not have been the intention of law-makers.

These kinds of judicial intervention have elicited the rage of the executive. They are redolent of the arguments advanced by James Hollifield that domestic institutions have had constraining effects on immigration controls in European countries and that social and political spaces have thus been opened for migrants.[8] Hollifield goes on to argue that this can motivate states to pursue European cooperation to 'externalise' immigration controls, to avoid these legal and social checks on executive power. This in turn can help explain the quite recent conversion of the UK government to the merits of a common EU approach that would keep refugees closer to their countries of origin (see the essay by Jeff Crisp in this volume) without the ability to make claims on either the legal or the welfare system in Britain.

Attempts to close the door to asylum-seeking migrants have been accompanied by new openings to skilled migrants (as Mark Kleinman describes in this volume). Here the relationship to the welfare state is different in the sense that skilled economic migration has been viewed in some influential quarters as potentially beneficial in labour market sectors where there are skill shortages. The subtle recasting of perceptions of needs and resources that has opened the door to new migration is an interesting feature of debates in Britain. For the first time in more than thirty years the UK has even allowed labour migrants to enter the UK without a job, on the basis of a Canadian-style points system, and has vastly expanded the reach of the mechanism which allows employers to attract skilled migrants to fill vacancies in sectors such as IT and engineering (in total, 104,000 entered in 2001 alone) on renewable permits with permanent residence possible after four years.

Germany

Debates about migration in the conservative–corporatist German welfare state have had rather different components from those in the UK, but fundamentally revolve around similar basic issues: the definition of the community of legitimate receivers of welfare state benefits and the negotiated pragmatism at the borders of the welfare state. German immigration politics was characterised as distinct by the denial that Germany was an immigration country and the absence of an immigration policy. This changed in the late 1990s when the new red–green coalition introduced provision for the recruitment of IT workers. The government also introduced Germany's first acknowledged immigration law, with measures relating both to the regulation of migration flows and to the integration of immigrant newcomers, although the legislation floundered following objections on procedural matters by the opposition Christian Democrats, sustained by the Constitutional Court.

There is an interesting point of comparison between the UK and Germany with regard to asylum. The German government maintained the state's constitutional commitment to asylum, but it became more symbolic than substantive as the explosive issue was defused through externalisation via European cooperation and bilateral agreements with surrounding states. Germany thus retained the constitutional right to asylum, but made it more difficult for asylum seekers to access the state territory. Numbers declined and the asylum issue was thus defused.

During the 1990s the organisational and conceptual borders of the German welfare state were also redrawn to exclude the ethnic German *Aussiedler* (ethnic Germans mainly from former Soviet republics) whose status shifted during the 1990s from ethnic co-belongers with full welfare state entitlements to one more akin to that of other immigrant groups. Even though geographically distant, the *Aussiedler* had been seen as part of the German 'community of fate' (*Schicksalsgemeinschaft*). As Michael Bommes has shown, the *Aussiedler* were thus initially given welfare state biographies that matched those of other Germans, and which generated entitlements as though they had spent their whole lives in Germany. This began to change when around 2 million moved to Germany between 1988 and 1992, in which year quotas were introduced. In the newly reunified Federal Republic, notions of 'special obligations' were weakening. German immigration politics was 'normalised' in the sense of containing core components that were more akin to those in other European countries—dispersal of asylum seekers and more limited access to welfare state benefits.

A more specific debate within Germany arose because of the effects on the status-oriented, conservative type of welfare state of intra-EU migration: so-called 'posted workers' taking advantage of EU laws to work in other EU member states. This was particularly evident in the construction sector, where workers moved from EU member states where both wages and social costs were lower, such as Britain, Ireland and Portugal, to take jobs in Germany.[9] The deeper significance of this debate was that it exposed core, structural features of the German welfare state such as the emphasis on training and skills. These can guarantee high workplace standards, but can also protect the labour market from outsiders without the necessary certification of their skills. High standards of training in the German construction sector contrast with the more deregulated UK sector, where possession of a mobile phone, a van and a Yellow Pages listing could suffice. In such terms, 'posted workers' evoke Freeman's arguments in the sense that this kind of immigration could potentially erode the German system of consensus capitalism. Some left-leaning academics shifted from a defence of immigration and the immigrant to a defence of the German social model in the face of these unwelcome 'Anglo-Saxon' deregulatory pressures.

Scandinavia

Developments in Scandinavia bear strong relation to Freeman's arguments about pressures for welfare state closure in the face of 'unwanted' immigration. Tomas Hammar also detects a strong welfare state component in the drive to tighten controls on immigration in Scandinavian countries, as these states seek to close the migration door to their welfare states.[10] Relative economic decline, Europeanisation, the weakening of corporatist structures and individualisation have all affected the perception of the capacity of the social democratic welfare states to include all their citizens. Immigration had been accepted on the basis that immigrant workers would be provided with immediate access to welfare state membership on the same basis as citizens of these welfare states because otherwise core principles of universal egalitarianism would be undermined.

The welfare state pressures experienced by Scandinavian countries have not induced a wholesale abandonment of core welfare state principles, not least because these remain dear to sizeable numbers of voters in these countries. The pressures have actually been more specific and focused on the redrawing of the community of legitimate receivers of welfare state benefits to place 'unwanted' migrants in a more marginal position. This has been most noticeable in Denmark with the introduction of a seven-year qualification period for immigrant newcomers before full access to welfare state entitlements can be gained. This has fundamentally recast the relationship between migrants and the welfare state, because migrants previously attained the status of 'denizenship' upon arrival, with legal and social rights short of full citizenship. They could then wait in the antechamber of national citizenship. The 'denizens' have now become 'margizens'.

Southern Europe

In southern Europe the situation is rather different, both because these are newer destination countries for immigrants and because they have different, less extensive forms of welfare state. Moreover, the debates about immigration have become strongly focused on control of external frontiers, while a key 'internal' feature of these countries is the size of the informal economy and the spaces within it for irregular migration. Irregular migrants will often do jobs that native workers are no longer prepared to do. In Italy, for instance, a reserve army of southern Italian workers moved north in the 1950s and 1960s to help fuel Italian economic growth. Since the late 1980s, however, southern Italians have been less willing to move north to take low-status and low-paid jobs, and have been more able to rely on a welfare state and family 'safety net'; thus immigrant workers have been needed to fill many of those jobs. The result is that high levels of unemployment in parts of Italy coexist with a continued need for migrant workers.

Similar patterns exist in other southern European countries, alongside an increased diversity among migrant populations. In Portugal, for instance, large number of migrants from east European countries such as the Ukraine and Moldova have filled labour market gaps in sectors such as construction. This migration lacks the political–historical structuring based on colonial ties or the formal recruitment agreements of much of the migration into 'older' west European destination countries. Traditional ties to particular source countries have weakened, as verified by the fact that 30 per cent of the 90,000 migrants who had taken advantage (by August 2000) of a Portuguese regularisation programme were from the Ukraine. These countries have no strong connections to the source countries, but have become the basis for migrant networks based on the availability of employment in Portugal and the ease of entry to the country.

The persistence of informality in the labour market has important implications for migration and welfare because, as I have argued, welfare states are more than the sum total of social policies. They also amount to an institutional repertoire of inclusion and belonging, with important implications for state–society relations and ideas about citizenship and membership. If our point of comparison were only with more highly organised west European welfare states then some of the nuances of debates in southern Europe would be missed. The expectation that the state will care and that it will seek to deliver social inclusion, and the norms of social acceptability that accompany this quest, are features of debates about welfare in the more highly organised west European welfare states (particularly the social democratic and conservative–corporatist variants). The fear that these states can no longer perform such roles underlies some of the anxiety about the future of welfare, an anxiety that can focus on newcomers whose entitlement to a share of the threatened resources is questioned.

Debates in southern Europe are cast in rather different terms because here distrust of the state, pervasive informality and state avoidance are all but ubiquitous. As Maria Baganha has pointed out, if citizens have not fully internalised their own rights of social citizenship then it is unlikely that there will be any great clamour for such rights to be extended to immigrant newcomers.[11] Yet, to tackle this 'internal' dimension is to take a political risk, because external controls at state borders affect foreigners who cannot vote, while attempts to impose internal controls, such as clamping down on the informal economy, will affect citizens who can, and who may bitterly resent the state's encroachment into the 'private' sphere.

Conclusion

Welfare is central to debates about migration in contemporary Europe, but unless distinctions are made between types of migration and forms of welfare state organisation, meaningful understanding of core policy dilemmas will be elusive. Relations between migration and welfare pan out rather differently in various European countries, but this should not cloud scope for comparison in the fog of national particularities. Rather, similar pan-European dilemmas centre on the role played by national welfare states in mediating relations between openness and closure, between inclusion and exclusion and, fundamentally, in defining the boundaries of the community of legitimate receivers of welfare state benefits.

Welfare-state-related arguments have been used to support some forms of migration while arguments about 'resources' have been deployed to justify closing the door to 'unwanted' forms of migration. But, as I have argued above, it would be to get the issues precisely the wrong way around to argue that migration drives these changes. Rather, a set of more general economic and social changes underpins debates about welfare and social rights in Europe. It is these general changes in the role of these welfare states (and public expectations of this role) that are at the core of the debate. If there are diminished expectations about the capacity of welfare states to deliver integration, then we should expect to see this reflected with passionate intensity when immigrant newcomers and their welfare claims are the subject of discussion. To erode provision for immigrant newcomers is, however, to raise serious questions about longer-term stability and social cohesion as they affect not just those newcomers but all members of society.

Acknowledgement

Research for this essay was supported by the Economic and Social Research Council through the project 'The Contentious Politics of Asylum in Britain' (grant no. R000239221).

Notes

1 L. Morris, 'Britain's Asylum and Immigration Regime: The Shifting Contours of Rights', *Journal of Ethnic and Migration Studies*, vol. 28, no. 3, 2002, pp. 409–25.

2 A. Zolberg, 'The Next Waves: Migration Theory for a Changing World', *International Migration Review*, vol. 23, no. 3, 1989, 403–30.

3 M. Bommes and A. Geddes, eds, *Immigration and Welfare: Challenging the Borders of the Welfare State*, London, Routledge, 2001.

4 W. Cornelius, P. Martin and J. Hollifield, *Controlling Immigration: A Global Perspective*, Stanford, Stanford University Press, 1994.

5 G. Freeman, 'Migration and the Political Economy of Welfare', *Annals of the American Academy of Social and Political Sciences*, vol. 485, 1986, pp. 51–63.

6 V. Guiraudon, 'The Marshallian Triptych Re-ordered', in Bommes and Geddes, eds, *Immigration and Welfare*, pp. 53–76.

7 G. Esping-Andersen, *The Three Worlds of Welfare Capitalism*, Cambridge, Polity Press, 1990.

8 J. Hollifield, 'Migration and the Politics of Rights', in Bommes and Geddes, eds, *Immigration and Welfare*, 109-33

9 U. Hunger, 'Temporary Transnational Labour Migration in an Integrating Europe and the Challenge to the German Welfare State', in Bommes and Geddes, eds, *Immigration and Welfare*, pp. 191–213.

10 T. Hammar, *European Immigration Policy*, Cambridge, Cambridge University Press, 1986.

11 M. Baganha in Bommes and Geddes, eds, *Immigration and Welfare*, pp. 213–29.

Understanding Anti-Asylum Rhetoric: Restrictive Politics or Racist Publics?

PAUL STATHAM

THIS essay investigates the nature of political debates and public perceptions about asylum. It begins by giving a general overview of the European and British approaches to asylum and examining the nature of the conflicts within domestic national politics. I then discuss the British case, in the light of original empirical research on public debates and public understandings. Findings are presented on the structure of the public discourse on immigration and asylum, showing which type of actors enter the debate and the extent to which they hold either pro- or anti-migrant positions. These findings are interpreted with reference to two main theoretical interpretations of immigration and asylum politics: Freeman's interest group approach, and the 'racist public' thesis which sees restrictive politics as a response to mobilised anti-migrant sentiments.

I then move from the macro, national level to the micro level, exploring the way in which individuals, among their peers, form opinions on these contentious political issues. The central idea of the research was to investigate the values and meanings that people give to asylum and immigration, drawing on their local experiences. We selected one geographical area where people had little objective experience of asylum seekers, and one area where they did, to draw out the way in which opinions varied in relation to local experiences.

A reason for taking this approach was that, although public opinion polls show aggregate opinion in response to specific questions, they tell us little about the values of individuals on which such opinions are based; nor whether their opinions would be strong enough to provoke political action, such as voting or protest. Moreover, as well as knowing that people are 'against immigration', it is important to know what specifically they are against, because views on immigration and asylum can in fact be an outlet for real or perceived grievances about other problems, such as urban decline.

In the conclusion, an attempt is made to draw the strands together, and some speculative remarks are made on how the British government could act differently on asylum in the public domain. The position is advanced that continued anti-asylum rhetoric could store up problems for the future. If recent reforms to liberalise immigration for certain groups of economic migrants produce a new and sizeable 'guest-worker' population, without the same rights as citizens, the guests may, in a period of economic downturn, no longer be considered welcome. They could become the objects of the same ethnic competition arguments, advanced by political issue entrepreneurs,

© The Political Quarterly Publishing Co. Ltd. 2003
Published by Blackwell Publishing Ltd, 9600 Garsington Road, Oxford OX4 2DQ, UK and 350 Main Street, Malden, MA 02148, USA

about scarce social welfare which the government currently legitimates against asylum seekers.

Northern Europe's asylum politics

From the early 1990s the wealthy countries of northern Europe witnessed the development of mass asylum seeking, although it should be said that the size of the inflows (for example, in 2001 an estimated 80,000 to the UK, which has a population of 60 million) do not in fact justify the image of 'alien swamping' often portrayed by the mass media. Official figures indicate that, from the peak of 675,500 applications to the EU in 1992, there are signs of a levelling off in the number of applicants to about half that figure, with a total of 385,000 in 2001. Nevertheless, it is clear that the context of political asylum has changed dramatically over the last decade to the point where claiming asylum has become a major form of primary migration from the world's periphery to the European core.

Traditionally, west European states had small-scale systems for granting asylum on an individual basis to people fleeing persecution. Embodied in the Geneva Convention of 1951, the rationale for such a system was a moral response to the collective failure of countries to provide refuge for Jews fleeing Nazi persecution before and during the Second World War. At the same time it was a convenient way of keeping the door open to political refugees fleeing the Cold War communist states.

The collapse of state communism in 1989, and the associated unleashing of a large number of potential new applicants, served to underline that this approach to asylum had become an historical anachronism. The asylum provisions were not designed to cope with large groups of refugees. Moreover, as European countries had implemented 'zero immigration' policies since the 1970s, asylum seeking had become, in effect, a path for economic migration from developing countries.

Such a situation was not sustainable. There were policy and procedural problems. The administrations of receiving countries were not capable of processing large numbers of applications for political asylum, and over-burdened systems soon experienced bureaucratic meltdown. In addition, the suspicion by political elites that claiming asylum had become a form of economic immigration led to a politicisation of the status of asylum seekers, with the result that they have to a large extent become categorised as 'unwanted economic migrants'. In mass media discourses, this has led to the almost automatic stigmatisation of people claiming refugee status as 'bogus' (in the United Kingdom) or *Scheinasylanten* (in Germany), unjustly making demands on the scarce resources of domestic populations.

It is worth looking in more detail at the dynamics within domestic national politics through which asylum has become a contentious political issue, as well at the policy outcomes.

Populist nationalism versus human rights obligations

Asylum is highly prone to becoming an arena of conflict within domestic politics, not least because it is the field for disputing the criteria for entry to and membership rights in (that is, citizenship of) a national community. The issue of asylum opens up a particular contradiction within liberal nation-states: it puts the universal principle that they should respect and protect human rights by offering asylum to aliens fleeing persecution in direct competition with the principle that they should primarily serve the interests of the national community of people from whom sovereignty derives—a group with a self-image of common descent and ethnicity enshrined in a shared nationhood.

Domestic politics in west European countries has come down firmly on the side of legitimating anti-asylum policies, through the logic of defending the national interests of the state's existing citizens. Politicians and groups from the native domestic population mobilise concerns about the legitimacy of asylum seekers, questioning whether they are deserving of humanitarian protection or are really economic migrants, and the level of rights to entry and scarce social resources that should be extended to these 'outsiders'. In this situation, the process of political deliberation about the factual nature of problems, such as the scale of immigration or the efficacy of administrative and judicial procedures, can be transformed through competition among political actors in the public domain into highly normative conflicts about national values.

Publics and politicians who already see national identity and sovereignty under challenge from the combined forces of 'Europeanisation' and globalisation have found a convenient outlet for expressing these grievances in a populist reassertion of the national community, united against these 'bogus' intruders. As a consequence, conflicts over asylum have increasingly come to focus on perceptions of the ethnic differences between the native population and migrants. In many countries, anti-asylum sentiments have become a topic for party competition between mainstream political parties, as well as a source of potential popular support for the radical right.

At times this tendency has led to increasing levels of xenophobic violence directed against asylum seekers. After 11 September 2001, a further twist was added in that the perceived cultural threat from immigration became specifically focused on Muslim migrants, their assumed 'unassimilability' and the 'terrorist risk' they posed to Western democracies. The electoral successes of the Pim Fortuyn List in the Netherlands and of Jean Marie Le Pen in the first round of the French presidential election, the growth of the People's Party in Denmark and even the gains of local seats by the BNP in Britain have been achieved on a platform designed to appeal to the anti-Islamic and anti-immigrant sentiments of the native population. This assault by the radical right on what it sees as the failures of multiculturalism has effectively linked the anti-immigration debate to questions about the loyalty of groups of migrants who are in many cases already citizens, but ones of Muslim faith.

Although it is tempting to view today's immigrants to Europe as hapless victims of repressive receiving states, the fact that asylum politics is highly contentious across Europe shows also that there are self-limiting factors within the sovereignty and core values of liberal democratic states which provide sustenance, resources and rights to the pro-migrant case. For example, when political conflicts over asylum have entered the legal domain, the courts have sometimes made rulings upholding a nation-state's human rights obligations towards migrants, thus clipping the restrictive measures of government policies. In February 2003, for instance, the UK Court of Appeal upheld a ruling by the High Court that the Labour government's attempt to remove welfare benefits of food and shelter from certain in-country applicants was 'inhumane' and in breach of the European Convention on Human Rights.

The pro-asylum case has thus found some levels of support from national judiciaries keen to uphold human rights principles, as well as from solidarity movements backed by churches and naturalised ethnic minorities. In addition, violence against asylum seekers, for example in Germany, where issues of racial intolerance are always highly sensitive, has mobilised large gatherings of anti-racist protesters. Here it should be noted, however, that the mass candle-lit demonstrations and human chains across West Germany in the early 1990s were in stark contrast to the applause from bystander publics for the burning of asylum hostels in the East.

Overall, immigration policies have for the most part been shaped by domestic politics, and in ways that restrict rights of entry and access to social rights for new migrants. It is also clear that within a domestic politics in which parties compete for the votes of national citizens it is going to be difficult to defend the attribution of rights to a constituency of non-citizens. This is especially the case when debates become framed in a language of national, cultural and ethnic difference. As a consequence, in the majority of leading European countries, national politics has promoted and implemented a series of restrictive policy responses, erecting stronger external borders and more resistant internal rights regimes against potential asylum applicants.

The view from the island: contemporary Britain

The UK's 2002 asylum legislation, the fourth new measure in nine years, specified so-called 'white lists' of states from which all applications would be rejected as 'clearly unfounded', and the withdrawal of the right to state provision of food, accommodation and clothing from some applicants. When the bill was published, the Labour Home Secretary, David Blunkett, wrote in *The Times* that 'We can only defeat the right if we tackle issues of public concern.' Since then, in the light of public fears that asylum may be a route for terrorists to enter the country, the Prime Minister, Tony Blair, has stated that

Britain might have to re-examine its commitment to the European Convention on Human Rights (which prevents the UK returning asylum seekers to countries where they could face torture). Around the same time, a British National Party candidate won a council seat in Halifax, having focused his campaign on asylum seekers.

In the British case, this sounds like a victory for the values of national popular sovereignty over human rights protection for asylum seekers. A media-conscious Labour government has pre-empted the policies of the right and introduced a set of draconian measures which appear to want to deter claims of asylum by making the lives of the applicants so nearly unbearable that only the most desperate and reckless would apply. Providing legalised sanctuary from persecution appears no longer to be the rationale of British policies. Conservatives would go even further, however, and lock up all asylum seekers on ships, requiring their security screening before admission.

Against this backcloth, there have been racial attacks on, even murders of, asylum seekers in Southampton, Norwich, Sighthill (near Glasgow) and Sunderland, and mobilisations of local people against plans to build asylum centres on rural sites in villages such as Throckmorton in Worcestershire. A few years ago this type of event was largely confined to metropolitan London and the port towns of Dover and Folkestone; but the dispersal policies for asylum seekers have distributed not only the local burden of paying for the support of asylum seekers but also the experience of living with asylum seekers to a greater number of localities across the kingdom.

Politicians in Britain appear to believe in the 'racist public thesis', namely, that there are untapped resources of public grievances against asylum seekers, verging in many cases on racism or outright xenophobia, and that their policy proposals must compete for this political territory. In order to address the actual nature of public discourses and perceptions of asylum and immigration, I briefly review some research findings in the light of relevant theories in the academic literature.[1] I look first at the macro, national level of British public discourse and the positions of the political parties, and then at the private understandings of the public on asylum, before drawing some overall conclusions.

Public debates: some empirical evidence

In the literature on whether immigration politics is liberal or restrictive, an important explanatory factor is whether policies are seen as the outcome of political elite decisions or, alternatively, as an outcome of populist politics.

One position on the role of public debates is presented by those authors who argue that immigration politics is conducted by political elites and organised interest groups in the policy domain, who work discreetly in institutional arenas away from the noise and distortions of public discourse.[2] Here the leading argument is that, in spite of facing an apparently universal anti-migrant and xenophobic national public opinion, political elites and organised pro-migrant lobbies have been surprisingly successful in continuing to uphold the liberal principles of 'open' immigration regimes.

According to the 'client politics' thesis of American academic Gary Freeman, the primary defenders of migrants' rights within national domestic politics are employers seeking cheap labour, and strong ethnic groups standing up for their kith and kin. These groups, who are the main beneficiaries of immigration, are seen as a concentrated constituency who are resource-rich and well able to defend their interests. In contrast, the diffuse and disadvantaged groups from the native population, who have to compete with migrants for jobs and houses, are the cost bearers of immigration, but these are much less well organised as a public constituency. As a consequence the pro-immigration interest lobby is far more capable of mobilising political resources than its anti-immigration opponent, with the outcome that political power is exerted over the executive to keep the approach to immigration 'liberal'.

In this view, the anti-populism of elites means that whatever noise may be made about the issue of migration during elections, the real business of migration policy takes place behind closed doors in the arena of organised politics. Politics thus keeps the door open for migrants regardless of how unpopular their presence may be with the native public. Obviously, it needs stating here that Freeman's interest group 'client politics' approach has principally economic migrants in mind, not people seeking asylum. Nonetheless, it provides insight on how sensitive political issues can be managed by political elites away from the public domain, by building up a strong civil society of interest groups—in the asylum politics field, for example, churches, trade unions and organisations that distribute welfare services to asylum seekers. Their interest-based involvement would present a buffer in civil society against their xenophobic competitors who would possess resources only to the extent that they could mobilise anti-asylum sentiments in the public domain.

A second strand in the literature places much more emphasis on the public participatory and cultural dimension of politics as the explanatory factor for what the authors see as the continuing shift towards restrictive immigration politics.[3] In contrast to Freeman's 'client politics', we may label this the 'racist public thesis'. These authors emphasise the importance of the social construction of immigration as a problem in public discourse, arguing that this cultural framing and politicisation of the issue shapes and influences the decisions taken by the executive in policy arenas. Thomas Faist calls immigration 'symbolic politics', by which he means that it is a form of political expression that is devoid of substantive meaning, but operates as a cultural symbol in the public discourse. In this view, political entrepreneurs are able, cynically, to bring immigration politics into the public domain. They do this to trigger hot public debates about the cultural basis of membership and belonging, which lead to a reassertion of the ethnocultural nation against the 'cultural threat' of foreign aliens. In this view, it is national political discourse that makes immigration and immigrants the scapegoats for social problems such as unemployment and the crisis of the welfare state.

It is not possible to test these theses fully here. However, a first empirical look at the structure of the political discourse on immigration and asylum in Britain can yield some instructive insights.[4]

Table 1 shows data gathered on political demands that were made by collective actors in the field of immigration and asylum politics in Britain. The data-set is derived from a content analysis of instances of 'political claims-making' from 1990 to 1999 which were reported in the national media.[5] Acts of political claims-making may range from demonstrations and protest actions to speech acts and conventional forms of public statements and political decisions.

For each intervention by a collective actor into the public discourse up to five political demands were coded in detail for each act. This gives an overall sample of 1,291 political demands relating to immigration and asylum politics that were made in 714 coded claims-making acts (on average 1.8 demands were raised per act). In addition, each political demand was coded with a valence score of −1 if it was anti-migrant, 0 if it was neutral or technocratic and +1 if it was pro-migrant. This average valence position gives a first indicator for the ideological position of an actor, ranging on a scale of −1 anti-migrant/immigration to +1 pro-migrant/migration.

By looking at the visible patterns of a contentious issue-field, it is possible to gain a first overview of where different types of institutional and civil society actors position themselves, through their political demands—in this case, within the conflict lines of the public debate on immigration and asylum politics. In Table 1, the first column of figures shows the share of political demands voiced by each of seven different types of collective actors. The

Table 1: Share and position of political demands by collective actors in the immigration and asylum issue-field in Britain (sample 1990–1999)

Type of collective actor	Share of political demands (%)	Average valence of political demands
Nation-state actors	57.9	−0.07
Supranational and foreign state actors	5.1	+0.38
Other civil society actors	8.0	+0.30
British ethnic minorities	3.1	+0.75
Human rights and welfare NGOs	4.7	+0.90
Specific pro-migrant NGOs	16.7	+0.97
Migrants, refugees and asylum seekers	4.5	+0.90
All demands	100.0	+0.27
No. and (%) of all demands	1,291	(100)

Average valence position: from +1 pro-migrant/immigration to −1 anti-migrant/immigration.

second column shows the average valence position of these actors relative to each other in immigration politics.

A first observation to make is that the public debate is strongly dominated by the national state and executive actors, who account for about six-tenths of demands (57.9 per cent) and hold a position that is strongly defined against the interests of migrants (–0.07 valence compared to the overall +0.27). This demonstrates that the British government and state actors have a strong role in shaping the public debate about immigration and asylum, and do so in a way that promotes an anti-migrant/anti-immigration position. This finding contradicts Freeman's 'client politics' thesis, which sees immigration politics as tightly controlled by political elites and interest groups that favour migration, away from public debates.

Another finding that goes against the 'client politics' thesis is that there were very few interventions by 'other civil society actors', such as trade unions (1.1 per cent), churches (1.6 per cent) and employers' associations (1.8 per cent). The 'client politics' thesis would predict a prominent role for employers' associations (with their vested interests in cheap labour) on one side, and for British minorities (3.1 per cent), defending the interests of their foreign national kin, on the other. Of course, the 'client politics' position might claim that such deals occur outside of the visible public domain, as insider deals between elites and interest groups. But it is hard to see how, if this were the definitive feature of immigration politics, it could be rendered invisible from the public domain. Instead, it is more likely to be the case that British immigration politics does not fit Freeman's American interest group model, and instead remains largely in the control of strong executive decision-making with a restrictionist orientation.

A second point to make, however, is that our findings also seem to contradict those authors who see anti-migrant, organised publics expressing xenophobic sentiments as the driving force behind political elites taking restrictive stances on immigration. Counter to the 'racist public' thesis, our findings show that, to the extent that they do get involved in these debates, civil society actors do so with a pro-migrant stance. The main challenge to the British state's anti-migrant stance comes from the pro-migrant NGOs (16.7 per cent; +0.97) and human rights and welfare NGOs (4.7 per cent; +0.90). Taken together, these NGOs account for six-tenths of all civil society demands (57.9 per cent) and have a strongly pro-migrant position.

Of course, our data exist only at an empirical level descriptive of reality, and are not able to indicate to what extent the elite's perception of 'public racism' is a motivation for anti-migrant/immigration positions. Nonetheless, there are clearly limits on the extent to which anti-migrant sentiments are expressed in the British public domain by civil society actors. Even if one limiting factor may be that they are unnecessary because of the strong anti-migrant/immigration position of the state, it does not seem plausible from our findings to see the state's anti-immigration politics as a direct result of mobilised public pressure. At the national level, there is even very little mobilisation in civil society by the extreme right and anti-migrant groups (0.3 per cent). On the contrary, it appears that nation-state actors definitively shape the public discourse on immigration and asylum; and that actors in civil society, to the extent that they mobilise at all, mobilise against this expressed position. In this view, restrictionist public debates come top-down and from governments.

A last observation to add is that it is possible from our data to aggregate the positions of actors on the basis of their party political identities. In the period of our sample, Labour had a much more pro-migrant stance in opposition (January 1990–May 1997: 32.1 per cent share of political party claims; +0.80 valence) than in government (May 1997–December 1999: 80 per cent share; valence –0.02). This provides evidence of a clear shift towards a restrictionist stance since entering government.

Public understandings

After looking at the contested field of immigration and asylum politics in the public domain, we now turn to the localised level of peer group discourses in private. Here we review some findings on how ordinary groups of people from the 'native' population form political understandings of immigration and asylum issues.[6] Much literature on political socialisation has emphasised the importance of peer group interaction as the environment in which political norms are internalised.[7] Given that official mediated political discourse is filtered through an interpretative screen of personal and cultural experiences, it is important to look at the private discourses through which people understand issues of immigration and asylum. In order to analyse public perceptions, we used an original experimental method for peer group discussions that was inspired largely by the classical tradition for the focused interview and subsequent advances.[8] Here I present an account of initial findings that are relevant to the current discussion.[9]

As we have seen, the dispersal of asylum seekers around Britain has led to hostile reactions in several localities. At the same time, public opinion surveys regularly tell us that Britons are against asylum seekers. Thus we have considerable scientific knowledge about the 'end product' of British public opinion, namely its aggregate anti-asylum stance; but we have far less knowledge of what these issues mean to people and the values on which their understandings are based. Public opinion is significant not only quantitatively, in an aggregate sense, but also qualitatively, in the range of opinions that are available for interpreting specific problems. We aimed, first, to examine the normative limits of expressed opinions about refugees and asylum seekers in peer group settings, by comparing them to those about British ethnic minorities. Second, we wanted to understand the values that were underpinning this expressed stance, namely, the basis of the groups' concerns about asylum seekers.

Our first finding was that the position of our 'white' groups on asylum seekers used significantly more motivated arguments, and was significantly more anti-migrant, than their stance on British ethnic minorities. Asylum seekers were depicted as 'outsiders' to the British community, who saw 'England' as an easy country to come to, and became a burden on limited social resources. In some cases, highly stigmatising language was used. At first glance this appears to be grist to the mill of the 'racist public' thesis. However, when discussions among peers were allowed to proceed further, other features emerged about the basis of this anti-asylum stance.

Three of our peer group discussions were conducted in Catford, in south-east London, and three in Bradford, a northern town, working on the general assumption that people from the metropolitan London locality would have been more likely to have personal experience of coming into contact with asylum seekers. In the Bradford groups, people's ability to talk about personal experiences of contact with asylum seekers was indeed much lower than in the London groups. After their initial hostile reaction, when they were asked to talk in detail about asylum seekers the Bradfordians in fact started talking about how *Asians* had taken over their town, the ways in which the town had changed since their youth, and how Asians were treated better than white people.

Moderator: 'What about the position of refugees, do you have any kind of sympathy with them?'

'You can have sympathy with their position but you wonder why they come five or six thousand miles for refuge when there are other countries all around them.'

'I think a lot of the problem is contraception as well. If an Asian chap is out of work it doesn't stop him having kids, does it? Not many English families have more than three or four children yet Asians just seem to breed. It's the same as these African countries, they have all these kids and then as soon as things start getting tough they come over to Britain.'

Moderator: 'So you think it's a burden on the taxpayer?'

'I think so, yes. The trouble is, there's no one to say no, you can't do that, whereas in Australia it's not like that.'

'Everybody in this room must have heard somebody say that they went down to the Post Office last week and there were two Asians stood in front of them and they come out of there with £300 or £400.'

White male group, Bradford, age 25–45

As this extract shows, the Bradford groups' discussion of asylum soon shifted to stigmatising British Asians. When talking about Asians in relation to immigration issues, they felt able to use much more openly racist language than they did when talking about Asians in relation to race relations issues, earlier in the session. This indicates that people learn the normative limits of what it is acceptable to say within an issue-related context. Race relations politics makes it difficult to criticise local Asians, but government-sanctioned anti-immigration norms make this a possibility when discussing asylum. Such a finding indicates that official policy positions are important in shaping the limits of how people talk about these issues, and suggests that they take their lessons on political issues from cues set by political elites and embedded in politics.

In contrast to their London counterparts, however, who were able to recount their personal experiences of what they saw as the negative aspects of asylum seekers, such as begging on the streets and wastefulness of resources, the Bradford group were using the asylum-seekers as a vehicle for complaints about something else. What this implies is that, for people who live remote from the actual consequences of having asylum seekers on their doorstep, the asylum issue is really being used to express values that are related to other perceived grievances. Our Bradford groups were talking about urban decline and the loss of local prestige, which they attributed to the presence of British Asians.

It is still a problematic finding for race relations that in areas where people are distant from the intensity of problems associated with hosting asylum seekers, asylum becomes a language for airing grievances against British minorities. What it does show, however, is the importance of local conditions in shaping people's understanding of asylum and immigration issues. Thus there is not a uniform, unidimensional opposition to asylum seekers across the British nation. The values behind anti-immigration sentiments are different, relating to personal experiences in different localities. From this, we can expect that, in the few localities that bear the social costs of hosting asylum seekers, such as ports and the towns targeted for dispersal, there will be articulated political grievances against asylum policies. In many other cases, however, opposition to asylum seekers is not formulated into a political stance about asylum, but serves as a way to express grievances and disillusion about other social issues. Accordingly, one would predict that xenophobic politics may gain some support within localities where there are problems associated with hosting asylum seekers, but that it would be unlikely to be successful at galvanising political support at the national level.

A final point about public perceptions of asylum refers precisely to those localities where the public has become politicised about asylum issues because of the local presence of an asylum centre. It is not a foregone conclusion that British public values will swing in the direction of ever more anti-asylum positions. When we interviewed a campaigner from a protest against a detention centre in Oxfordshire, the Campaign to Free Campsfield, and asked where their public constituencies of support came from, the response indicated that the values of popular sovereignty, British-style, do not necessarily translate automatically into ever more anti-asylum positions:

People who would have been very doubtful about Britain accepting immigrants and very . . . quite racist basically . . . have been transformed by the idea that people lose their liberty on the basis of nothing; and particularly it's extraordinary in Oxford to meet lots of . . . how do I put this lightly . . . little old ladies who are completely radicalised by the experience of visiting detainees . . . they come out much more political and active about the whole issue.

Here it seems that, when faced by real dilemmas rather than ticking boxes on opinion surveys, the British public can after all in some cases see the detention of non-criminals as against the national values of upholding human rights. This suggests that the outcomes of debates about asylum are not necessarily restrictionist. Instead, political arguments that address objective problems in a non-stigmatising and technocratic way, or even those that make defending human rights protection a national cause, may have the potential for gaining pro-asylum support from public constituencies.

Concluding remarks

Our findings show that British governments dominate and shape public discourse on asylum. This supports the view that the nature of the asylum debate—at present restrictive and stigmatising—to a large extent comes politically from the top down, rather than in response to mobilised public pressure. In addition, our focus group research on public perceptions seems to indicate that the perceived government policy position sets the normative limits of public understandings of asylum and immigration issues. If this assumption is correct then a Labour government, with a massive electoral majority, which decided to take a more pro-migrant position and emphasised Britain's international obligations to asylum seekers, would not automatically lose public support to the sponsors of anti-asylum sentiments in the public domain. On the contrary, it is possible that, if it gave more official legitimacy to pro-asylum norms, for example by supporting subsistence-level social welfare for asylum seekers, it would become harder for the public to oppose such a position.

This argument is not just a moral plea, but is based on an understanding of the workings of organisations within civil society. Even a limited pro-asylum public policy stance from the government would have an effect on civil society. Where the stance taken by the government offers material resources of grants, for example, for supplying welfare services, and symbolic resources of legitimacy, that would stimulate pro-asylum civil society organisations and bring other organisations, such as churches and trade unions, into active and compliant positions. Receiving legitimacy and support from government, organised pro-asylum actors would be able to occupy the political space in civil society on asylum, thus creating a buffer zone against any potential xenophobic political entrepreneurs. In a sense, the pro-migrant interest-group-based politics envisaged by Freeman could work—albeit to a more limited extent—for the asylum issue too.

To achieve such a situation, the government could remain publicly quieter on asylum, and try to clear up and manage the objective problems associated with it away from the public domain. Over time it could even be that a more pro-asylum government stance would bring a recoupling of asylum seeker rights within notions of national popular sovereignty. And then, echoing our 'old ladies' from Campsfield, it would become patriotic to treat asylum seekers with civility. At present, when the government prefers to shrink welfare rights and stigmatise asylum seekers, this seems no more than a pipe dream.

Turning to our focus group research, our preliminary findings suggest that public opinion on immigration is not uniform, nor are British values necessarily uni-dimensional in their opposition to asylum. Asylum and immigration politics stand for different things for publics in different localities, depending on their personal experiences of the objective problems relating to the issue. Anti-asylum politics is therefore unlikely to be much of a vote winner at the national level, although there may be some electoral gains in specific localities which bear the disproportionate social costs of hosting asylum seekers. The policy answer here, though, is to spread the—actually small—social costs of asylum more evenly, through sensible policies, and not to become publicly hostile to asylum seekers in the hope of pre-empting a perceived—and actually weak—political opposition.

Government public hostility to asylum seekers simply legitimates xenophobic sentiments. It encourages anti-asylum mobilisation and provides the public with cues for seeing problems in a distorted and exaggerated way. Such entrenched political pathologies become difficult to reverse, with the result that it becomes hard for governments to legitimate even subsistence levels of welfare rights for asylum seekers; that decision in turn leads to more asylum seekers begging or looking dishevelled on street corners, further aggrieving local populations. In the final analysis, much depends on the political will of the elite. In Britain governments have sufficient executive power to exercise such will on asylum, if they so desire.

A last point to make is that, at present, the government seems happy to ply its anti-asylum rhetoric while opening up the path, albeit on a limited scale, to economic immigration—a topic on which it remains largely silent, as if this debate occupied a separate discursive universe from asylum. However, bringing in 'desirable' economic migrants, for instance from eastern Europe, while simultaneously promoting a political discourse of anti-asylum-seeker sentiments is a risky strategy. First, the new immigrants are likely to be indistinguishable in the public mind on streets and in supermarkets from their 'welfare scrounging' asylum-seeking counterparts, and are likely to face hostile receptions from landlords and in public places. They are also likely to populate the same metropolitan sink estates where grievances already run high. Second, over the long term, establishing a political discourse that is hostile to the social costs of asylum-seekers may provide legitimacy to anti-immigrant political entrepreneurs.

It is not beyond the bounds of plausibility that, in an economic downturn, political entrepreneurs would point out that the new 'guest workers' and their families also compete with natives for jobs, welfare and housing. History tells us that guest workers and their dependants tend to stay. If immigration to Britain of this type continues on a significant scale, there will be a category of people, as yet unlabelled in the public discourse, with a status of rights between citizens and asylum seekers. Current government aspirations to deepen the notion of British citizenship, with citizenship classes and cere-monies, will not make the path to naturalisation easier. If the government faces a challenge from political opponents to its new labour migrants it will be much harder for it to defend the legitimacy of this group as a benefit to the national community when at the same time it stigmatises another group, asylum seekers, in a way that goes beyond the objective condition of their actual social costs.

Notes

1 The research findings are to be found in 'The Contentious Politics of Asylum in Britain and Europe', funded by the British Economic and Social Research Council R000239221; for details see http://www.leeds.ac.uk/ics/euro.htm.

2 See esp. Gary Freeman, 'Modes of Immigration Politics in Liberal Democratic States', *International Migration Review*, vol. 29, no. 122, Winter 1995, pp. 881–902, and 'The Decline of Sovereignty? Politics and Immigration Restriction in Liberal States', in C. Joppke, ed., *Challenge to the Nation-State*, Oxford, Oxford University Press, 1998.

3 Here see Thomas Faist, 'How to Define a Foreigner? The Symbolic Politics of Immigration in German Partisan Discourse', *Western European Politics*, vol. 17, no. 2, 1994, pp. 50–71; Dietrich Thränhardt, 'The Political Uses of Xenophobia in England, France and Germany', *Party Politics*, 1995, pp. 325–45.

4 A more detailed presentation of these research findings is given in Paul Statham, 'The Role of Public Debates and the extent of "Europeanisation" within British Immigration and Asylum Politics: Some Empirical Findings', paper presented at the 1st Pan-European Conference on European Union Politics, held by the Standing Group of the European Consortium for Political Research, 2002. This is available in pdf format at http://www.essex.ac.uk/ECPR/standinggroups/eu/index.htm.

5 The newsprint mass media are taken as the main source for the public sphere, as the events and outcomes within many semi-public and non-public spheres are also reported here. It should be noted for purposes of interpretation that this method brackets out journalistic opinion on events, and, following the protest event analysis method from social movement research, collates a record of public events where political demands are raised by collective actors within a specific issue-field. The present data are based on every second issue (Monday, Wednesday, Friday) of the *Guardian* for Britain from 1990 to 1999. The reliability and validity of these sources were checked and confirmed by comparisons with several other national news-papers. For further details on method, see Ruud Koopmans and Paul Statham, 'Political Claims Analysis: Integration Protest Event and Political Discourse Approaches', *Mobilization: The International Journal of Research and Theory about Social Movements, Protest and Collective Behavior*, vol. 4, no. 2, 1999, pp. 203–22.

6 These findings appear in a more detailed form in Paul Statham, 'State Policies,

Political Discourse and "White" Public Opinion on Ethnic Relations and Immigration in Britain: Pushing the Borders of "Extremity"', paper presented to the joint sessions of workshops at the European Consortium for Political Research, 2001, available in pdf format at http://www.essex.ac.uk/ECPR/events/jointsessions/paperarchive/grenoble.asp?section=14.

7 See e.g. Richard E. Dawson and Kenneth Prewitt, *Political Socialization*, Boston, Little, Brown, 1969.

8 See the classic approach by Robert Merton and Patricia Kendall, 'The Focussed Interview', *American Journal of Sociology*, vol. 51, 1946, pp. 541–57, which has been advanced by David E. Morrison, *The Search for a Method: Focus Groups and the Development of Mass Communication Research*, Luton, John Libbey Media, 1998. Also relevant is the social movement approach by William A. Gamson; see his *Talking Politics*, Cambridge, Cambridge University Press, 1992.

9 The findings here are based on six focus groups, which were professionally randomly recruited, according to the following characteristics of ethnicity, gender, age and location: 6 white, 3 male, 3 female; 2 of each age cohort 16–24, 24–45, 45+ years; 3 Bradford, 3 Catford (SE London). There were between 8 and 11 participants in each group. For further details on method see Statham, 'State Policies, Political Discourse and "White" Public Opinion on Ethnic Relations and Immigration in Britain'. This research continues.

Immigration and the Politics of Public Opinion

SHAMIT SAGGAR*

ANTI-IMMIGRATION political sentiment has been a familiar feature of British public opinion on and off since the 1960s. In certain periods it has been a predictable element in electoral contests. The cumulative result has been that its existence, and the unspoken boundaries such opinion creates, have come to be assumed as a factor in modern British politics. It has led to the 'race card' thesis by which public attitudes against further immigration have been viewed—and accepted—as a semi-permanent feature of the political land-scape.

By the late 1970s, this doctrine appeared to underscore party competition in Britain. Elsewhere, in countries facing large-scale immigration pressures, the race card was also thought to be a powerful veto on parties seeking office, and could be utilised relatively easily by parties wishing to exploit this truth. In the 1990s Californian Republicans calculated that such sentiment could be deployed to hurt their Democratic opponents. The Australian general election of 2001 underlined the capacity of a centre-right incumbent coalition to gather votes inexpensively on this issue—and to succeed, unexpectedly, in holding on to office. Recently, anti-immigrant and anti-immigration sentiment has also had a profound impact on electoral politics in several west European countries.

Debates have persisted in Britain on the nature, scale and impact of the race card dividend. The Crossman diaries, published in 1977, furnish one of the most succinct accounts of the political imperatives of anti-immigrant public sentiment. Writing of the watershed developments surrounding the 1968 Kenyan Asian crisis, in which the Labour Home Secretary Jim Callaghan took unprecedented action to curtail the right of British Asians expelled from Kenya to enter the UK, he reported that: 'Mainly because I am an MP for a constituency in the Midlands, where racialism is a powerful force, I was on the side of Jim Callaghan.'[1]

The seminal account of issue-voting, *Political Change in Britain*,[2] highlighted the party context within which anti-immigration fears could be mobilised. By accusing the other party's candidate of being soft on immigration, leading politicians were able to extract an electoral dividend that held no obvious short-term costs. Enoch Powell's intervention in 1968 denouncing the two-party conspiracy of silence on immigration may have led to his immediate

---

* The views expressed in this paper are purely personal and do not reflect statements of UK government policy.

© The Political Quarterly Publishing Co. Ltd. 2003

178 Published by Blackwell Publishing Ltd, 9600 Garsington Road, Oxford OX4 2DQ, UK and 350 Main Street, Malden, MA 02148, USA

dismissal from the Conservative front bench; but in the minds of voters this episode appeared to reinforce the perception that the Conservatives, alone, understood the make-up of public attitudes on the issue. Two studies of the 1970 general election suggested that the unexpected victory of the Conservatives was at least partly due to the impact of the party's perceived tougher stance on immigration.[3]

This essay will review past and current trends in public attitudes towards immigrants and immigration in Britain. There is a widely held assumption that governments have only limited scope to engage the public in rational debate on future options. This is said to condition the level of support that can be won—or criticism that can be advanced—in the name of liberalising immigration policies. The essay examines the origins and evidence for such an assumption and links this to public attitudes on issues of ethnic pluralism.

Comparative evidence is also reviewed, often pointing to the persistence of strong streaks of anti-immigration sentiment in major developed countries of immigration such as Australia and France. However, such popular attitudes have been the subject of intervention by political leadership, producing both a softening (Republican leadership under George Bush Jnr) and hardening (Austrian junior coalition participation in government under Jörg Haider) of sentiment. The essay concludes with a discussion of immigration politics in UK and the long-term capacity to foster support for a managed migration policy agenda.

The profit in following the crowd

Three essential prerequisites govern the likelihood of the race card being played effectively.

Significant majority opposed

First, the evidence must show that public opinion on immigration is clearly skewed in one direction. In the main, this has meant clear majorities stating that they are opposed to further immigration in general or certain categories of immigration in particular (such as family reunification, primary labour migrants or asylum seekers). The 1970 British Election Study reported that four-fifths of voters described themselves as hostile to further immigration. There was no mistaking this clear message. Snapshots taken in later decades have revealed a notable dilution in this majority.

The views of US citizens on aspects of immigration control are revealing here. Contrary to many perceptions, a generally strongly pro-immigration elite political culture has sat alongside fairly evenly divided public opinion. A Zogby poll in May 2002 reported that 58 per cent of Americans favoured admitting fewer immigrants each year, whereas 30 per cent approved of keeping immigration at current levels and 6 per cent supported admitting more immigrants each year. Previously, a poll for *USA Today*/CNN by Gallup in October 2001 showed a similar proportion in favour of decreased immigration alongside 30 per cent endorsing present levels.[4]

The point that should be stressed is that even this level of hostility is rather short of the sharply skewed public opinion that would be required to enable large-scale issue voting to impact on electoral outcomes. There are, nationally at least, simply too many dissenters who would be alienated if the views of the anti-immigration majority held sway for too long. The rather different immigration history of the US accounts for the generally more favourable views towards immigrants than found in Britain, a point drawn out more fully in Susan Martin's essay in this volume.

Alignment between party and voter preference

A second point to be made is that securing a long lead in public opinion is far from enough to make the issue pay. It is also necessary that potential voters internalise the belief that one of the major party choices is aligned more closely with their preferred position. An anti-immigration majority in opinion matters little unless voters have an outlet for this sentiment.

By the early 1970s, the Conservatives had succeeded—with or without any deliberate effort—in persuading an overwhelming and decisive majority of the electorate that they were 'tougher on immigration' than their Labour opponents. Whereas the Conservatives' electoral edge over Labour on immigration amounted to 13 percentage points in 1966, this had swollen to a massive 53 points by 1970. 'The party of Powell' is how voters appeared to see the Conservatives, regardless of the party leadership's efforts to the contrary.

Electoral saliency

Neither of these conditions will matter much unless the issue has high electoral saliency. The issue of immigration must be one that is of high concern to voters and will be used to reward and punish parties. In that sense, it is important to see the electorate as driven essentially by rational choice considerations. Voters will know what they want and do not want, will have a clear sense of which party will most likely deliver this preference and, crucially, will feel sufficiently strongly about these matters to act on them in determining party choice. If voters behave in such an instrumental manner, there is little room for loyalty between voters and parties. The incentives for parties to follow the crowd are simply too great to ignore. Party strategists may of course dismiss this evidence, but they will not do so lightly.

The 1970s were an era in which immigration had indeed emerged as a highly salient issue. Some two-thirds of voters reported that it was one of the two or three most important issues facing the country. Their concern was placed in a wider context of bleak attitudes towards race in general. By 1979, around a third of voters reported that 'recent attempts to ensure equality for coloured people had gone too far.'[5] Strangely and rather against the tide, the issue declined rapidly in its saliency during the early 1980s. By 1983 it was barely visible on the radar of the general election campaign, whereas in 1979 it had been a major battleground question between the parties.

An important caveat needs to be attached to the application of this established, issue-voting model to immigration in the UK today. In the past it may have been possible to draw broad generalisations regarding immigrants. Prior to the 1990s, immigration was effectively a codeword for the large-scale settlement in Britain of New Commonwealth British citizens, chiefly from South Asian and Caribbean sources. Indeed, this traditional immigration question was frequently collapsed together with issues of race and ethnic diversity.

Over the course of the past decade, a clear shift in the number and composition of immigrants and in the political debate about migration has occurred in the UK. Labour migrants, asylum seekers and undocumented illegal flows have combined to establish something of a 'new immigration issue', one which can often be distinguished from older immigration concerns.

It is not hard to identify the source of the new issue, given the public focus on the unprecedented increase in the number of asylum applicants (including dependants) from 28,000 in 1993 to 110,000 in 2002—and the much less well publicised rise in labour migrants to the UK. In 1995, under a Conservative administration, some 45,000 work permits were issued by the government, a figure which is anticipated to quadruple to 200,000 in 2003. Where possible it is thus helpful to note distinctions in public sentiment towards past and present migrants, as well as in attitudes towards core labour migrants on the one hand and asylum seekers on the other.

Contemporary public attitudes and party competition

At the time of writing (spring 2003) there is renewed press and public attention on the migration issue. This is reflected in three domains: the outlook of voters, the coverage of the mass media, and the responses of political parties and their leadership. There is once again some potential for issue voting on immigration, but in the main this has not had the impact it might have.

Some measures suggest that the issue has risen in importance: a *Times/Populus* poll in February 2003 reported that 39 per cent of members of the public regarded the number and flow of asylum seekers as 'the most serious problem' facing Britain.[6] A further 49 per cent felt that it remained serious but was eclipsed by more pressing issues.

Immigration is not always seen as a national issue. It can have both national saliency, in the sense that it contributes to an aggregated assessment of a government's track record, and also a local dimension that is shaped by the degree to which immigration impacts on local circumstances and political debate.

Only one area of the country (Kent) regularly gives immigration national and local importance when ranking local issues. The unique experience of this particular county—in which migrants who cross the English channel arrive—suggests not only that local circumstances shape the outlook of voters but also that this is a one-off effect, not necessarily connected to views on other issues. It highlights the possibility that it is growing competition for scarce public services, experienced near to ports and in the few designated areas to which asylum seekers are dispersed, that fuels public hostility. These are classic congestion effects with which governments are long familiar across many public services, and in Kent these have often been given an immigration face. The overall implication is that the majority of people in the UK are concerned about immigration despite the fact that they do not consider the issue to be directly affecting them at a local level.

The structure and direction of opinion are fairly skewed, although there are caveats to this characterisation. The February 2003 *Times*/Populus poll is a window into public sentiment, showing that hostility towards asylum seekers is conditional upon circumstances such as congestion effects in public services, and sits alongside a firm sense of fair play and burden-sharing. Some 78 per cent of members of the public agreed with the statement that 'It is right in principle for Britain to accept genuine asylum seekers but we have accepted our fair share and cannot take any more.'

Absence of party distinctions

Of course, underlying saliency and skewed public opinion matter, as we have seen, only to the extent that cross-party differences exist and can be exploited. To date, although there are some elements of substantive difference in the policy strategies of the major parties towards asylum seekers, it is not clear that a deep interparty distinction is felt or understood by the public. The same poll revealed that voters split fairly evenly in relation to which party stood the greatest chance of successfully tackling the asylum issue: 22 per cent stated that Labour was best equipped while 23 per cent took that view of the Conservatives; a similar proportion (21 per cent) felt the Liberal Democrats would do best. Interestingly, this left almost four-fifths without party moorings on the issue, implying that there is some scope for one of the major parties to establish a clear lead. The contrast with parties' rating on the 'old' immigration question during the 1960s and 1970s could not be sharper.

In the past immigration has only rarely served as a key, let alone the determining, issue at a general election. There is, however, evidence to suggest that public attitudes towards immigration shape and condition political outlooks and preferences leading to, and including, party choice. That said, there is genuine doubt that the causal relationship is quite so one-directional. An authoritarian–conservative political outlook may in itself be a factor that contributes to the saliency of issues such as immigration—alongside issues such as crime and punishment, homosexual and women's rights, and privacy and censorship.

Overall, it is widely assumed that immigration remains one of a handful of political issues that contain an inherent political advantage for parties of the right over parties of the left. This was confirmed by a MORI/One Nation poll published in 2000 which asked people which party had the best policy on twelve issues. Immigration and asylum seeking was found to be one of only two issues on which the Conservative Party had a clear lead over Labour.

Public attitudes are not merely the product of subliminal belief systems and values. It is important not to ignore the role played by events and the behaviour of political leaders themselves. Yet one of the most striking features of the research conducted in this area has been the limited acknowledgement of the part played by politicians. This is odd, since the role of the media is widely cited and assumed to be significant. Home Office research compiled in 2001 featured an analysis of newspaper articles about attitudes to immigrants and asylum seekers.[7] The study found that 53 per cent of sampled articles presented a negative view of immigrants, while only 25 per cent discussed the benefits associated with immigration. The vast majority of the articles—95 out of 106 (90 per cent)—focused on asylum seekers.

For political leadership, the risks are not confined to a backlash against a liberal stance. There is a further risk to be negotiated, namely the need for consistency in presenting an overall narrative that addresses equality through the prism of racial and ethnic diversity. The task of operating an effective immigration policy can add to the enormity of that basic task, where charges of expediency and duplicity are common.

British governments since the 1960s have been at pains to emphasise their commitment to the domestic integration of settled immigrant groups. In a salvo aimed at government ministers a generation ago, Bernard Levin crystallised this accompanying risk in terms which will have resonance today: 'You cannot by promising to remove the cause of fear and resentment fail to increase both. If you talk and behave as if black men were some kind of virus that must be kept out of the body politic, then it is the shabbiest hypocrisy to preach racial harmony at the same time.'[8]

Attitudes towards other minorities

There appear to be patterns in public attitudes in relation to groups that are thought to be politically unpopular. These patterns may usefully be described as forms of 'joined-up tolerance' and intolerance, particularly in relation to attitudes towards immigrant and ethnic minority groups on one hand and other socially contentious groups such as sexual preference minorities on the other.

A MORI survey for the Stonewall Citizenship project in 2001 noted that

64 per cent of respondents named at least one minority group towards whom they felt negative.[9] The most frequently cited groups were: Travellers/ Gypsies (35 per cent), refugees and asylum seekers (34 per cent), people from a different ethnic group (18 per cent), and gay or lesbian people (17 per cent). Further, 43 per cent said that they personally knew someone who is prejudiced against people belonging to a different ethnic group from their own. This is evidence of imputed prejudice, whereby hostility can be estimated via the perceptions of third parties.

Some 16 per cent of people expressed negative feelings towards three or more groups, suggesting that there may be a 'hard core' of prejudice among a small minority with a strong antipathy to any group perceived to be different. Overall it is fair to say that people who are prejudiced against one group are more likely than average to be prejudiced against other groups too. But some consistency also exists within positive public attitudes. The Stonewall survey found a fairly substantial 'tolerant' minority—36 per cent—who did not feel negative towards any group. This tolerant minority were more likely to be female and young, to have children, to be educated to A-level or above and, interestingly, to vote Labour.

The media (both broadcast and print) were confirmed by the survey as a powerful influence on people's attitudes. There was also evidence to point to a hierarchy in recognition of discrimination against particular kinds of group: 50 per cent said asylum seekers were likely to be discriminated against, followed by 49 per cent in respect to ethnic minorities, and 38 per cent citing Travellers and Gypsies.

The pattern may not stop there, but may extend to subtle, though generally under-reported, tensions between different immigrant groups. A survey by NOP in 1991 uniquely highlighted that Asian attitudes towards further waves of economic migrants and towards refugees were indistinguishable from those of their white counterparts. In previous eras, anti-immigration sentiment among segments of British Jewry has been noted, including hostility directed at unskilled arrivals from eastern Europe and Russia in the early twentieth century. Clear scepticism among African Americans directed against East Asian immigrants has been documented, particularly in cities rich in Asian immigration in the western and south-western parts of the US. In Britain today there are signs of hostility towards east European migrants, for instance among settled Caribbean groups. Much of this may be attributed to sharp competition at the lower end of the jobs and skills market, as well as to familiar congestion problems with public services in inner urban London.

Delving deeper into British public attitudes

Public attitudes constrain the scope of parties and governments. Certainly, policy proposals to liberalise areas of immigration policy will be highly circumscribed. Public opinion thus acts as something of an over-arching constraint on policy and political discretion. It is therefore necessary to scratch beneath the surface to assess how enduring the constraint is for population subgroups and in particular contexts.

Political rhetoric from mainstream frontbench politicians asserts that British public opinion is now largely tolerant and accommodating of immigrants and immigration. Naturally there are caveats to this broad claim, and many of these relate to the implicit understanding that the cultural pluralism associated with immigration is to be contained within fairly tight boundaries. The reality is that Britain still contains a significant proportion of people who express intolerant attitudes to migrants and ethnic minorities. Common majority sentiments identified in surveys are that 'there are too many [immigrants] in Britain,' that 'they get too much help,' that 'migration controls are insufficiently tight,' and that people polled 'feel less positive towards minority groups'. Between 63 and 72 per cent of adults expressed this sentiment in recent polls.

The public, however, have erroneous impressions of the number of ethnic minorities and migrants. In a MORI/*Reader's Digest* poll in 2000, the average estimate of the size of the ethnic minority population in the UK was 26 per cent of the population, despite the official figure (at that time) being closer to 7 per cent. When asked to estimate the proportion of the population consisting of migrants and asylum seekers, the modal estimate was 51 per cent; the actual figure was closer to 4 per cent. There is, additionally, confusion in public opinion among ethnic minorities, immigrants and asylum seekers, all of whom are frequently viewed as a single undifferentiated group.

Several polls carried out between 1998 and 2002 by MORI, NOP, Gallup and ICM found that respondents are significantly more likely to be hostile to migrants and minorities if they are older, poorer and less well educated, and live in northern England. Not surprisingly, those population subgroups that are more likely to be intolerant are also likely to have erroneous views of the size of minority and migrant populations. Tolerance correlates with high levels of ethnic pluralism in different parts of the country. Thus MORI data from 2000 showed that some 75 per cent of those in the north-east felt that too much is done to help immigrants, compared with just 39 per cent of those in London, where the proportion of ethnic minorities is much higher.

A factor that is clearly associated with current levels of intolerance towards immigrants has been the rising number of asylum seekers. Gallup surveys between 1989 and 1999 indicate that the rise in the number of asylum seekers has corresponded directly with significant rises in the indicators of intolerance. The percentage of the population that thought that there were 'too many immigrants in Britain' rose by 11 percentage points between 1990 and 2000 after a decade of slight decline. Strikingly, given the earlier discussion of issue saliency in contributing to issue voting, the ranking of how important people think immigration is compared with other 'problems' also rose, from seventeenth place in 1998 to sixth in 2000. While the 'old' immigration arguments over postwar New Commonwealth immigrants may have slipped off the table by the early to mid-1980s, this is strong evidence that this 'new' immigration issue has taken root in the fabric of British public opinion.

The role that attitudes towards cultural pluralism play in shaping these patterns should not be under-estimated. Evidence points to a persisting public scepticism. MORI reported in 2001 that two-fifths of respondents felt that 'immigrants should not maintain the culture/lifestyle they had at home.' Earlier evidence from the 1997 British Election Study showed opinion on this question as less relaxed: 71 per cent of white respondents signed up to the proposition that 'it is far better for immigrants to adapt and blend into society,' with only 23 per cent agreeing that 'it was better for immigrants to keep [their] customs and traditions.'

Given these nuances, overall positions on public opinion are hard to frame. Attitudes towards large-scale black and South Asian immigration stem largely from a past chapter in British immigration policy and experience. For the most part, public opinion appears to be able, and even willing, to distinguish between this earlier episode and more recent arrivals. British Election Study evidence from 1997 demonstrates that hard-line opposition to the legacy of black and Asian immigration stood at around a third of the white electorate.

While this hostility is not something to be dismissed, the evidence in 1997 did not point to an overwhelming anti-immigrant veto in public opinion. Indeed, a combined 60 per cent of white electors now thought that such immigration had benefited the country, or else were not prepared to commit themselves on this question. Translating this positive judgement into an equally sanguine view about asylum seekers, however, has yet to be achieved.

Impact of age and ethnicity

This softer position, not surprisingly, is correlated with age, but only to a degree. Those aged between 18 and 24 were typically no more likely than older age cohorts to think that such immigration had been very or fairly good for the country. However, the strong opinion that this had been a very bad thing for Britain was associated with older respondents: 17 per cent of those aged between 60 and 64 years held this view, as against only 5.9 per cent of those between 18 and 64. Older groups were also less likely to decline to commit themselves to a judgement, with a gradual increase in opinion that immigration had not benefited the country.

Not surprisingly, the black and Asian groups surveyed generally reported much more upbeat evaluations of the historic value of a particular immigration flow that had featured either themselves or their parents or grandparents.

The inference from this data might be that of a long-run decline in strident anti-immigrant sentiment. In May 2001 the *Guardian* newspaper reported an ICM poll in high-profile terms, as evidence of such a decline. It showed, for example, a strong majority in favour of loosening controls for immigrants with valuable skills that were in short supply in the UK, such as doctors,

Table 1: Do you believe that immigration by blacks and Asians has been good or bad for Great Britain?

	White	Indian	Pakistani	Bangladeshi	Black African	Black Caribbean
Very/fairly good	19.5	65.8	65.6	67.2	65.2	63.2
Neither good nor bad	41.1	23.7	17.9	17.2	22.0	21.1
Fairly/very bad	36.6	6.8	8.9	3.4	5.5	12.0
Don't know	2.9	3.8	3.7	12.1	7.3	3.6

Source: British Election Study, 1997.

nurses and teachers. It also showed that 51 per cent of respondents would support allowing unskilled economic migrants into Britain as long as it was done on a quota basis.

This evidence underlines the importance that public opinion attaches to maintaining control and to transparency. As before, important and familiar groups within the survey stood against this approach to managed migration. Those over 65 and social classes D–E particularly opposed unskilled immigration that was not governed by a strict quota system. A further condition that respondents attached to fresh immigration of any kind was that unskilled entrants should be permitted only if they have the financial means to support themselves. The poll also confirmed little demand for the abolition of all immigration controls among voters, with only 18 per cent in favour and 76 per cent against.

This disaggregation story can be taken further and applied to various kinds of immigrant groups. Countries and regions of origin are interesting conditioners in this respect, and it is far from true to say that negative sentiments are based purely on colour. East European groups are thought badly of, and yet they are white. In one poll by ICM in 2001, every age group disapproved emphatically of Romanians coming to live in their neighbourhood, while every group (except those over 65) approved of Chinese neighbours. The former group may have been interpreted as Gypsies with an attendant degree of core racism.

These results revealed very different attitudes to people of different national and regional origins, which could well be linked to racism, as well as reflecting the influence of the media. Every group of respondents (except social classes D–E) said they would approve of white South African asylum seekers coming to live in their neighbourhood. All groups (except those aged between 18 and 24) disapproved of Afghan asylum seekers coming to live among them, while every group without exception disapproved of Iraqi asylum seekers.

Such survey evidence itself does not immediately throw light on what accounts for these differences in attitudes. Clearly attitudes towards immigrant groups are complex, relying on more than simply opinions of racial, religious or cultural factors. Perhaps the most compelling reason comes from mass media images. Prominent parts of the print media have been consistently negative in their reporting of Romanian and Afghan asylum seekers, and since the first Gulf War these newspapers have featured generally negative portrayal of Iraqis.

Comparative patterns and lessons from Australia

Britain is by no means unique in containing strands of public opinion that have been hostile towards immigration. One of the theoretical aspects of the race card debate has been assessing the degree to which anti-immigrant public sentiment serves as an inbuilt electoral advantage to parties that are either on the right or have been able to align themselves with centre-right public sentiment.

Historically, the electoral dangers of this situation were brought home to the British Labour Party by the Smethwick by-election disaster in 1964, in which the successful Conservative candidate ran an overtly racist campaign, described by Randall Hansen in his essay in this volume. In recent years, similar confrontations have been observed in a range of countries including Australia, France, Austria, Denmark and the Netherlands.

The case of Australian federal politics, culminating in the November 2001 general election, is particularly striking. The surprise win and margin of victory of the incumbent Prime Minister, John Howard, was widely thought to have been linked with a hardening of public opinion on refugees in the couple of months leading up to the election. In late August 2001, the Australian and international press seized on the spectacle of a shipload of Afghan refugees seeking to enter the country's territorial waters. The fate of the SS *Tampa* and its human cargo of 438 asylum seekers quickly became a touchstone for Australian public opinion towards unregulated and uncontrolled refugee settlement in which the strength of hostility intensified.

A week into the *Tampa* crisis, as a second boat loaded with refugees attempted to land on Australian territory, voter attitudes to immigration became very revealing. Some 51 per cent of those aged between 18 and 34 reported that the issue would be very important in shaping their vote, 46 per cent of those between 35 and 49 took the same view, and as many as 53 per cent of 50s and older also said immigration would be very important. The comparable numbers three months earlier had been 27 per cent, 27 per cent and 34 per cent respectively, showing a dramatic short-term escalation in issue saliency. At the height of the crisis, a Newspoll survey showed the direction of public opinion to be skewed on a colossal scale: between 85 and 90 per cent of all age groups declared their support for a policy of turning back all boats carrying unregulated asylum seekers.

The final element in this familiar model was the capacity of the electorate to recognise clear policy differentiation between parties—and in some cases between politicians—on the substantive issue. In this respect the federal election presented an opportunity for further distance to open up between the ruling coalition National and Liberal parties on the one hand and the Australian Labor Party on the other. In the event, the Labor opposition came under irresistible pressure to try to match the government's hard-line stance. Prime Minister Howard and his immigration and defence ministers set the standards of their populist position by declaring the administration would intervene proactively to prevent refugee ships approaching the Australian mainland.

This position was partly accounted for by the considerable electoral damage that had previously been inflicted on the national governing and opposition parties by the populist crusade against immigration mounted by Pauline Hanson's One Nation party. Hanson had drawn huge crowds and a million votes (out of 12 million) in 1998, and yet three years later the government's tougher stance on immigration had succeeded in shrinking her support to just 4 per cent.

The outflanking of One Nation on the right created an equally large dilemma for the Labor leader, Kim Beazley. At first, Howard accused him of 'walking both sides of the street' on the issue, opening up Labor's vulnerable flank by portraying the party as weak and ineffectual on illegal immigration. This accusation contained depressingly similar notes to the criticism levelled at Britain's Labour Party during its own opposition wilderness years between 1979 and 1997. During the campaign itself, Beazley surrendered principled or ideological ground for short-run tactical reasons that yielded few dividends in public perceptions.

In his attack on the government Beazley declared that 'at the heart of this election campaign is a giant lie.' Nevertheless, he pledged to uphold the policies out of which that lie emerged. He reiterated his vow that a Labour administration would continue to turn back 'boat people' and retain the government's border protection legislation that authorised the use of military force against refugee boats. Among all age groups, and among both male and female voters, the coalition was seen as the 'best party' to handle immigration by more voters than had been the case just three months previously. At the same time, immigration climbed from fourteenth place to ninth among fifteen issues.

By pursuing a campaign theme of national security, founded on immigration concerns and defence from terrorist attacks, the incumbent party persuaded Australian voters to throw sufficiently more support behind it. Of course, the galvanising role played by Australian talk-back radio and the impact of a multifaceted defence issue, as well as the unpredictable legacy of Hanson, should not be understated. This combined scenario amounted to a near-classic test case of the race card hypothesis by which a slim victory was snatched from the jaws of possible defeat.

Such circumstances are, however, relatively uncommon, and it is rare to see any single-issue effect across a national election. Moreover, the implication behind this case was that a broad reservoir of soft opposition to immigration already existed in Australian public opinion. The general election and its preceding events had galvanised this into a firm-to-hard flow of votes based on particular circumstances. Anti-immigration public sentiment, in other words, was an important necessary precondition of 'race card'-style issue voting, but the other elements in an overall sufficient set of conditions were met from different sources.

European xenophobia and responses

Recent European anti-immigration sentiment is a more complex and nuanced phenomenon. The recent rising tide of support for anti-immigration parties and politicians in European countries has been widely commented upon, and has helped to establish an impression that far-right, xenophobic parties are on the march. It was clear, for instance, that controlling immigration and asylum had shot to the top of the agenda of the June 2002 Seville summit of EU leaders, as Claude Moraes explains in his essay above. By the time these leaders met, the Danes, French, Dutch and Austrians had all experienced significant advances by far-right parties.

As the essay by John Lloyd in this volume shows, within continental Europe the recent rise of the far right displays various distinctions and discontinuities. Moreover, within some European societies, such as Germany, opinion continues to recognise the economic benefits of immigration, while in others, such as Spain, the negative association of immigration with rising crime is particularly stark. Each country, indeed, contains elements of positive economic and negative social concerns.

The Danes elected into office in 2001 a centre-right coalition containing the small but popular Danish People's Party with a clear anti-immigration mandate. The Austrian Freedom Party, led by the turbulent Jörg Haider, succeeded in joining a centre-right coalition in 2000. France witnessed the widely unpredicted presidential run-off in 2002 between the far right Front National candidate, Jean Marie le Pen, and the incumbent Jacques Chirac. Le Pen's party had enjoyed significant electoral backing on the immigration issue since the 1980s.

The picture in the Netherlands posed something of a contrast. Dutch society experienced a dramatic challenge to its image as a peaceful, tolerant nation that had historically provided a welcome to immigrants. The second place ranking of Pim Fortuyn and his PFL party in the 2002 general election introduced doubt over the country's liberal credentials. Interestingly, as Lloyd recounts, the Fortuynists attacked the perceived intolerance and moral absolutism of Islamism, claiming that it was an affront to the Dutch tradition of cultural and social pluralism, secularism and tolerance towards different lifestyle choices. Finally, Italian national and regional politics continues to be identified with strong support for anti-immigration parties and factions such the Alleanza Nazionale and the Liga Nord.

Public attitudes in each of these countries have inevitably varied in character and significance. However, all of the cases have in common some elements of popular feeling against different aspects of the immigration question. In the Netherlands a defence of putative existing cultural norms was the prism through which popular sentiment was refracted, whereas in France the question has been part of a longer-established set of anxieties about the settlement and integration of large immigrant communities such as Algerians.

That said, there is a striking feature throughout in that all these far-right parties have based their appeal on some form of betrayal thesis, dwelling on the lack of accountability of existing political elites. Party leaderships, so the argument goes, have been insulated from popular opposition to immigration by ethnically, culturally and religiously distinctive groups. Although party memberships have been better at assessing this feeling, elites have often completely misjudged not just the direction of opinion but also its intensity. Inward-facing conspiracies of silence have been the outcome, in which mainstream parties—and even the mainstream media—have been reluctant to discuss immigration.

This betrayal argument was of course initially deployed most effectively by Enoch Powell in British domestic politics in the late 1960s. His critique of mass black and Asian immigration, though pronounced, was widely thought to be the sole characteristic of Powellism. In fact this is probably a mischaracterisation, because Powell's outspoken views on race and immigration served to eclipse his scathing attack on the Labour and Conservative parties for neglecting the immigration question altogether. Decisive, unplanned policy had been preceded and followed, he complained, with little or no regard for the need to consult with, or be guided by, public opinion.

Betrayal of this kind clearly resonated with the popular mood surrounding his 1968 intervention. The period between 1965 and 1975 is one in which a two-party consensus operated to depoliticise race and immigration issues. One—unintended—outcome of this agreement was the greater scope it gave to polarised voices and political movements (such as the Anti-Nazi League) and the electoral rise of the far right (such as the British National Front) during this era. The clear and rather more transparent determination of the Conservatives to address the immigration issue after 1975 at least partially accounts for the waning of support for extremist parties towards the end of the 1970s. The fate of the FN in France recently, and of the NF in Britain in the 1970s, both imply that, subject to a willingness by mainstream parties to engage public concerns about immigration, European far-right forces are toxic yet containable.

Marching out of the immigration cul-de-sac

In August 2000, addressing the Republican Party convention in Philadelphia, George Bush Jnr called for an end to elements of his party's traditional hostility towards immigration and immigrants. In doing so, he cited three core arguments: that 'nativist' politics went against the grain of a proud nation that had been built by immigrants; that a pro-market party could not argue for strong restrictions on immigration on social and cultural grounds; and finally that anti-immigration politics were not as electorally popular as some had claimed. Indeed, the Bush campaign and later his administration stressed that anti-immigration messages were often poor political messages, citing the demise of Governor Pete Wilson's Republicans in Californian state politics, as well as the burgeoning scale of the Latino vote in the nation's sunbelt states.

California's Proposition 187, which created a state-run screening system to prevent illegal aliens from obtaining welfare and medical benefits, had been an important landmark in both state and national politics. Its successful passage suggested that deep-seated anti-immigration sentiment could be mobilised against the backdrop of steadily increasing flows of legal and illegal immigration, public worries about the associated congestion effects and an undercurrent of racial exclusion. In his publication *The Death of the West*, Pat Buchanan (a former Republican challenger for the party's presidential nomination) claimed that rising levels of immigration killed the Reagan coalition. In particular, he cited the 1965 Immigration Act, which opened the door for greater levels of non-European immigration, as directly responsible for breaking 'the GOP [Republican Party] lock on the presidency'.

The Bush leadership initiative may have caught some observers by surprise, given the party's apparent flat-footedness in the face of the Clinton Democrats' appeal to a wide range of social groups in the US. Bush's background as a Texas governor may have played an important part in exposing conservatives to the scale of demographic change that had already come about through immigration. Moreover, the appetite for additional labour recruited through immigration (as opposed to harnessing under-employed segments of the existing domestic population) is a strategy particularly favoured by business interests as well as geographical constituencies in the west and south-west of the country.

All told, the boldness of the August 2000 speech in Philadelphia prompted the *Wall Street Journal* to publish an editorial heaping praise on Bush for marching the Republican Party out of the anti-immigration cul-de-sac it had entered twenty years earlier. One US commentator, Daniel Griswold, has described effectively the underlying dilemma facing the American mainstream right:

Conservative Republicans face a clear choice when it comes to immigration politics. They can follow the lead of President Bush, who has sung the praises of immigrants and sought to create a more welcoming legal path to the United States for those seeking a better life through peaceful work. Or they can follow the likes of Pat Buchanan, Pete Wilson, and Tom Tancredo back into the political wilderness.[10]

By contrast, the Bush Republican initiative on immigration has placed the spotlight firmly back on the tortuous position of Britain's Conservative Party. While not opposing the present Labour administration's concerted increase in labour migration, it is noticeable that they have not championed this approach as US conservatives have tended to do. In part this is testimony to the continuing legacy of Powellites on the social authoritarian wing of the party, many of whom are concentrated among the party's influential rank and file membership. However, it is also a contrast that can be explained in terms of the dominance of the social and cultural, rather than economic, frameworks within which British party politics routinely considers the politics of immigration policy.

Closing comments

The sobering model of issue voting has tended to dominate discussion of the impact of immigration on British public attitudes. In the past this has proven to be reliable in highlighting the particular circumstances under which party competition is affected. It has been less valuable in providing insights on the extent to which mainstream parties have simply responded to or been the driver of populist opinion on this issue.

As this essay has argued, issue voting has been notably deficient in explaining the contextual position of the immigration issue alongside voters' broader assessment of the performance of parties. Such an approach has the benefit of viewing immigration not as a narrow concern indelibly driven by attitudes towards race and ethnicity (though these links clearly remain), but rather as a further illustration of managerial competence as the central prism through which voters view political and party choices. Indeed, as some parties have succeeded in neutralising populist sentiment on immigration, it has to be said that this has been achieved on the basis of a view of the electorate in highly instrumental and unsentimental terms.

There are few certainties in British politics about the nature and deployment of the race card. The traditional view emphasised the exposed weak flank of the Labour Party and implied that votes could be gathered cheaply by the Conservatives on this issue. A Conservative populist trump card is not felt so keenly now; nor is the idea that immigration naturally serves to sap the strength of Labour. Immigration is no longer an electoral albatross simply and solely for the left.

The picture today is a more complex one, in which broader assessments are made about the managerial competence of parties with, it must be said, heavy discounting against past broken promises and the exaggerated claims for the future made by some political leaders.[11] The work of Sanders and colleagues has shown that voters attach more importance to delivery on classic performance-type issues, of which controlling immigration is an obvious example.[12] In addition, evidence from MORI surveys indicates that asylum is among the range of issue concerns that most frustrate voters and fuel their lack of faith in parties keeping promises.[13] The implication is that managerial competence is a central prism through which voters view a variety of choices, including those in areas, such as immigration, that have been historically framed by clear positions informed by ideology. Immigration matters as an issue, but it matters above all else because of what it suggests about a party's broader ability to deliver.

The ability to *deliver* on immigration is thus perhaps what matters to voters—and indeed parties—most of all. This simple statement could not be more problematic, since it reminds us of the inherent difficulty in managing immigration. It is widely accepted that it is not possible to control precisely who enters, or indeed who leaves. Much of this volume is addressed towards ways in which migration could be managed more effectively and, to the extent that this increases public confidence in the competence of governments on this issue, concerns will be diffused.

The level of control achieved, however, is unlikely to match what the public and their voices in the press expect. Thus, governments will always be vulnerable to a high degree of public scepticism over their basic competence in this field. The only remaining point of hope, then, is to shift underlying, longer-run public attitudes towards a more favourable understanding of the benefits of immigration as against the costs. The extent to which public opinion now acknowledges the benefits of the postwar migration from the Commonwealth suggests that, over time, it is not beyond the bounds of possibility that this could be achieved.

Notes

1 R. Crossman, *Diaries of a Cabinet Minister*, vol. 3: *Secretary of State for Social Services 1968–70*, London, Hamish Hamilton/Jonathan Cape, 1977, p. 676.
2 D. Butler and D. Stokes, *Political Change in Britain*, 2nd edn, London, Macmillan, 1974.
3 D. Studlar, 'Policy Voting in Britain', *American Political Science Review*, vol. 72, 1978, pp. 46–72; W. Miller, 'What Was the Profit in Following the Crowd?' *British Journal of Political Science*, vol. 10, 1980, pp. 15–38.
4 http://www.fairus.org/html/04120604.htm.
5 Quoted in S. Saggar, *Race and Representation*, Manchester, Manchester University Press, 2000, p. 190.
6 *The Times*, 12 Feb. 2003.
7 'Public Attitudes and Immigration', Economics and Resource Analysis Unit, Home Office, April 2001.
8 Quoted in *The Times*, 14 Feb. 1978.
9 MORI Stonewall Citizenship Project on prejudice in Britain (May 2001).
10 http://www.nationalreview.com/comment/comment-griswold112002.asp.
11 H. Clarke, D. Sanders, M. Stewart and P. Whiteley, 'Britain (not) at the Polls, 2001', mimeo; G. Evans, 'In Search of Tolerance', *British Social Attitudes: the 19th Report*, Aldershot, Dartmouth, 2002.
12 D. Sanders, 'Economic Performance, Management Competence and the Outcome of the Next General Election', *Political Studies*, vol. 44, 1996, pp. 203–31.
13 MORI Socioconsult, 1999; GB Monitor; *Britain beyond Rhetoric: Delivering Equality and Social Justice*, survey commssioned by the CRE, London, MORI Social Research Institute, 2002.

Immigration, Citizenship, Multiculturalism: Exploring the Links

WILL KYMLICKA

MOST Western democracies are having to rethink their approach to citizenship to respond to the challenges raised by migration. There are growing numbers of migrants in most Western countries, and these migrants often retain close ties with their country of origin. What are the implications of these facts for citizenship?

Some commentators argue that in a world of migration, we must recognise that the whole idea of 'national citizenship' is increasingly obsolete. On this view, we need to develop a new way of assigning rights and responsibilities, perhaps based on international law and human rights norms, that does not presuppose that immigrants will or should become 'national citizens'.

Others argue, on the contrary, that the increasing ethnic and religious diversity within modern states requires a more active effort by the state to construct and sustain a sense of common national citizenship. Feelings of solidarity and common values, which could perhaps be taken for granted in a period of greater ethnic and religious homogeneity, must now be actively promoted by the state, in part by emphasising the centrality of common citizenship. On this view, learning to live with diversity requires a 'revaluation of citizenship'.[1]

Viewed in this context, the recent changes in citizenship policy in the United Kingdom are instructive. They fall squarely into the 'revaluation of citizenship' approach. The British reforms have occurred at two levels. First, there are changes in the actual rules and regulations regarding the acquisition of citizenship. In particular, there has been the specification of language tests for naturalisation, and the introduction of citizenship ceremonies and oaths. Second, there are changes in discourse or rhetoric. In particular, citizenship is now being described as an important value and identity. The public promotion of the value of citizenship, and its internalisation by individuals, is said to play a vital role in ensuring 'cohesion' and 'integration'. The introduction of national citizenship education into the prescribed school curriculum is another manifestation of this 'revaluation of citizenship' strategy.

These changes to citizenship policy have been controversial. Some critics accuse the government of abandoning a commitment to multiculturalism and replacing it with an old-fashioned goal of assimilation. The British government officially denies this. It argues that, on the contrary, a strengthened commitment to citizenship will help generate respect for diversity and build a culture of tolerance. On this view, the revaluation of citizenship does not require devaluing multiculturalism, but rather provides the only sustainable

© The Political Quarterly Publishing Co. Ltd. 2003
Published by Blackwell Publishing Ltd, 9600 Garsington Road, Oxford OX4 2DQ, UK and 350 Main Street, Malden, MA 02148, USA

basis for a successful multiculturalism. Some defenders of the policy, however, acknowledge that the policy involves a 'retreat from multiculturalism'. They are unapologetic about this, since they view multiculturalism as both morally unjustified and pragmatically a failure.[2]

So we have a range of contending views. In an age of migration and transnational identities, should national citizenship be de-emphasised or revalued? And if the latter, does revaluing citizenship require de-emphasising multiculturalism, or can national citizenship and multiculturalism support each other?

In this essay, I want to use the British reforms as a starting point for reflection on the links between immigration, citizenship and the accommodation of ethno-cultural diversity. I will begin by comparing the British debate with similar debates in North America. In each context, the policies and politics of immigration, citizenship and multiculturalism are inextricably linked. However, the links among these policies differ from one country to another, and these variations help to explain the politics of citizenship reform.

What is striking in the North American context, in comparison with Britain, is the relative lack of controversy about citizenship policy in the narrow sense: that is, the basic rules and regulations regarding the acquisition of citizenship. I suggest that this relative consensus reflects the particular way that citizenship policy relates to, but is also distinguished from, policies on immigration and multiculturalism. I then consider how the configuration differs in Britain, and why this results in greater controversy over citizenship policy.

Citizenship policy in North America

From a North American perspective, there is nothing in the new British legislation that is unfamiliar or surprising. The basic rules and regulations regarding the acquisition of citizenship are in fact quite similar to the Canadian model. Language tests, citizenship ceremonies and citizenship oaths are all well-established features of Canadian citizenship procedures, as they are in the United States. This is not accidental—the UK White Paper that in 2002 proposed the citizenship reforms specifically cites Canada as a model for its approach.

Moreover, these aspects of citizenship policy are widely accepted within both Canada and the United States. Indeed, I would go so far as to say they are almost completely uncontroversial, even among immigrant groups themselves. I cannot think of a single major immigrant organisation that has contested the legitimacy of the naturalisation tests in either country. And the citizenship ceremonies are positively cherished by immigrants as both a symbol of acceptance and an occasion for celebrations with family members, neighbours and co-workers.

Why are these policies uncontroversial? Why are naturalisation tests and citizenship oaths not perceived as potentially exclusionary or assimilationist? After all, many ethnic groups in North America are highly vocal and well organised, and are not shy about complaining about aspects of life they find discriminatory or offensive.

Since I know the Canadian case best, I will focus on this first. To my mind, there are at least five overlapping reasons that explain the relative consensus on citizenship policy in Canada. First, the requirements for naturalising are not onerous or burdensome—they essentially involve a modest residency requirement (three years), a language test, and a (simple) test of knowledge of Canadian history and institutions. The language component is likely to cause the most anxiety for some immigrants, but it is not a difficult test, and it is intended that the immigrant be able to pass it with a modest good-faith effort. Moreover, those immigrants who have a special hardship in learning the language, such as the elderly, are exempted from the test. We can compare this to the situation in Estonia after it regained independence in 1991, when the Estonian language test was set so high that the ethnic Russian settlers practically had to become professional linguists to become citizens.

Second, becoming a Canadian through naturalisation is not perceived as the first step towards assimilation, or as requiring renunciation of one's previous national identity or loyalty. This is reflected both in the official acceptance of dual citizenship, and in the public policy of multiculturalism. Both policies acknowledge that 'being Canadian' is not an exclusive identity, and accept that immigrants are likely to have dual identities and loyalties.

Canada has a particular advantage in this respect, in that few immigrants view the adoption of a Canadian identity (or Canadian citizenship) as somehow a betrayal of their original country. Because Canada is not a former imperial power, and has not engaged in historic acts of overseas conquest or colonisation, few immigrants see any inherent antagonism between loyalty to Canada and loyalty to their home country. Acknowledging loyalty to Canada is not seen as bowing to a former enemy or former master, and no immigrant group (to my knowledge) discourages its members from taking out Canadian citizenship. So dual citizenship and dual loyalties are relatively uncontroversial from both the government's and immigrants' perspective.

Third, public resources and encouragement are provided to help immigrants meet these modest requirements. There are publicly funded language training classes, for example, as well as citizenship promotion campaigns, informing immigrants about their right to naturalise, and encouraging them to do so. To my mind, the presence of such public support is a key test of whether citizenship rules are used as a tool of inclusion or exclusion. Once again, we can compare the Canadian case to Estonia. The Estonian government, far from providing its own funds to help the Russians learn Estonian, initially rejected an offer of EU funds to support language-training classes (although it subsequently accepted). In this case, it was clear that Estonia did not want its Russian settlers to become citizens. In the Canadian case, public funds are spent to encourage and facilitate naturalisation.

Of course, even with modest requirements, allowance for dual citizenship and public support, there will always be some immigrants who are unable or unwilling to meet the requirements of naturalisation. However—and this is the fourth factor that defuses controversy—the legal status of non-citizens is quite tolerable. They have equal access to civil rights (freedom of speech and association), social benefits (such as public health care and unemployment insurance) and the labour market (except for a few civil service positions), as well as the full protection of strong anti-discrimination laws regarding housing and employment. Non-citizens cannot vote, and in principle face the risk of deportation if convicted of a serious crime. But in general, their position is neither legally precarious nor socially stigmatised.

These first four factors help to remove potential sources of controversy or opposition. However, whether or not people find a policy objectionable is not decided just by looking at the details of the proposal. It is always viewed in a larger historical or comparative context, and assessed by how it fits into a larger trajectory. Is the policy moving us closer to, or further from, the sort of country we want to be, or admire? More specifically, people ask whether the policy represents a step forward or backward compared to earlier policies within the country, and/or compared to policies in other countries that are viewed as successful models. Put simply, is the policy moving in the right direction?

This leads to the fifth and final factor that helps defuse controversy in the Canadian context. The trajectory of citizenship policy in Canada, since the 1960s, has clearly been towards greater openness. This is reflected most strikingly in the repudiation of older, racially biased policies that made it difficult for non-whites to gain admission to Canada, or to become citizens. It is also reflected in the acceptance of dual citizenship and the adoption of multiculturalism. So there is no basis for immigrant groups to feel nostalgia about past policies, or to fear the general direction of citizenship policy.

This is reinforced by the fact that, in Canada, the most obvious reference point for comparison is the United States. The US is not only a powerful and omnipresent neighbour, but is seen by most immigrants as the very model of an open country of immigration. Yet in all of the respects I have just mentioned, Canadian citizenship policy is more liberal than US policy. In the United States, the residency period is longer (five rather than three years); the language tests are more demanding; dual citizenship is not formally permitted (although it is now informally accepted); there is less public funding of language training; there are no public campaigns to promote naturalisation; and the commitment to multiculturalism is less explicit. By comparison, then, the Canadian policy appears quite progressive to most immigrants.

These five factors help to explain why citizenship policy is relatively uncontroversial in Canada, at least among immigrant groups. But why is it not more controversial among the native-born majority? Why do they not see the trajectory of citizenship policy as 'too soft' on immigrants, making citizenship 'too easy', and going 'too far' in catering to the interests of immigrants rather than the native-born majority? There are periodic complaints along these lines, but they have not gained any political traction in Canada. For example, a minor dispute arose about residency periods when newspapers reported that some Hong Kong immigrants were applying for citizenship after three years even though they had spent virtually all of that time in Hong Kong, looking after businesses they had retained there. The government subsequently tightened up the rules so that now immigrants can apply for citizenship after three years only if they have actually resided in Canada for most of that time.

In general, however, the basic outlines of the current citizenship policy are not disputed by any of the major political parties, or by any significant proportion of public opinion. Part of the explanation is a rather crude self-interest. Canada is competing for highly skilled immigrants with other Western countries, and studies show that Canada's reputation for openness to newcomers is a factor that sometimes leads immigrants to choose Canada even when they would earn less there than in the United States or UK (and have to suffer through the Canadian winter). Government officials and business leaders do not want to lose one of the areas where Canada has a competitive advantage in recruiting the most desirable immigrants.

There is also a widespread perception in Canada that it is a good thing for immigrants to become citizens. When immigrants gain the psychological and legal security that comes with citizenship, they are more likely to put down roots, to contribute to local community initiatives, to care about how well their children are integrating, to invest in the linguistic skills and social capital needed to prosper, and more generally to develop stronger feelings of Canadian identity and loyalty. Naturalisation is not seen only as giving greater protection to immigrants, but also as protecting the larger society's investment in immigrants, making it more likely that the money spent recruiting, settling and training immigrants will have a payoff for the larger society.

Put another way, citizenship policy in Canada is seen as a mid-point in the integration process, not as the end-point. Unlike some west European countries, Canada does not see citizenship as a reward for, or recognition of, complete integration, of the sort that can be attained only after many years. Rather, it is seen as recognition of a good-faith effort to start that process of integration, and as encouraging and enabling further integration. This basic conception of the function of citizenship policy is, I believe, essentially uncontested in Canada.

This is not to say that there are no controversies in Canada around issues of migration and integration, or that there are no perceptions among native-born citizens that Canada has gone 'too far' in admitting immigrants, and is 'too soft' on them once here. For example, many native-born Canadians complain about the alleged rise in fraudulent refugee claimants. (Conversely, many immigrants bitterly complain about the difficulty in gaining recognition of their professional qualifications.) I will discuss some other controversies below. But these issues are disconnected from the issue of the rules and requirements for acquiring citizenship, on which there appears to be a fairly broad consensus.

A similar set of factors explains why citizenship policy is relatively uncontroversial in the United States. It is true that the American policy, while quite open in comparison with most Western countries, is less open than Canada's or Australia's. However, Americans do not generally compare themselves to such countries. Rather, they judge their policies in terms of their own historical trajectory. And on this score, the current American policy is more open than older policies that were racially biased and rejected the idea of dual national loyalties.

The main exception to this generalisation (to which Susan Martin refers in her essay in this volume), is the Welfare Reform Act of 1996, which cut back on the social entitlements of non-citizens, and thereby put them in a disadvantageous position. Precisely because this can be seen as a deviation from the larger historical trajectory, it was very controversial, and has as she explains been effectively nullified by subsequent court decisions.[3]

Citizenship debates in the UK

Let us return now to the British reforms and the controversies they have raised. Of the five factors I have identified as defusing controversy in the North American context, which are similar in the British context, and which are absent or less salient?

It seems to me that several of the factors are quite similar. In particular, the requirements for naturalisation are modest; dual citizenship is allowed, public support is provided to enable immigrants to meet these requirements, and the status of non-citizens is reasonably well protected.[4] Indeed, in all of these respects, the British policy is highly comparable to that of the United States and Canada. These factors would all suggest that the British government is not seeking to discourage or inhibit immigrants from becoming full and equal citizens, nor to stigmatise those immigrants who reject or defer naturalisation.

Why, then, are the reforms controversial? One difficulty is that Britain's imperial past makes the issue of naturalisation and dual loyalty more difficult. Some ex-colonial immigrants may resent having to express loyalty to their former masters. Others may resent the implication that they need to be resocialised into British culture, given the fact that they were born and raised in societies whose legal, political and educational institutions were designed by their British imperial masters. Yasmin Alibhai-Brown, for example, suggests that some Jamaican immigrants view themselves are 'more British than the British'.[5]

For these and other reasons, issues of oaths of loyalty and naturalisation requirements may be more sensitive for ex-colonial immigrants to Britain than for immigrants to Canada. We see a similar phenomenon in respect of

Algerian immigrants in France, or Korean immigrants in Japan, where some immigrant organisations describe the act of naturalisation as a betrayal of their home country.

By itself, this imperial legacy would probably fade over time. However, in the British case it is compounded by the fifth factor I listed earlier: the trajectory of citizenship policy. In the North American context, as we have seen, the current citizenship rules express a repudiation of earlier policies that were clearly assimilationist (for instance, in prohibiting dual loyalties) and racially biased (in the privileging of white European over non-white immigrants).

In the British context, by contrast, the trajectory of citizenship policy is more complicated. Indeed, some commentators argue that the trajectory is precisely the reverse. What was originally a very open citizenship policy in the UK has become progressively more assimilationist and more racially biased. In the 1950s, migrants from former British colonies had the right to move to Britain, and automatically to gain the same citizenship status as native-born Britons. When large numbers of non-white immigrants unexpectedly started to exercise that right, however, there was a rapid move to close the doors to immigration, and to impose new rules and requirements that delayed the gaining of full citizenship. Moreover, this closing of the door was not seen as race-neutral. While it has become more difficult for non-white ex-colonial migrants to gain admission to and citizenship in Britain, access for European (that is, predominantly white) immigrants from other EU countries has been maintained, and indeed enhanced.

In this sense, one can see the trajectory of immigration and citizenship policy in the UK as increasingly exclusionary and racially biased. In so far as this is how the trajectory is perceived, immigrant groups worry about what will come next. If the new policy is part of a larger trend to make Britain less open to non-white immigrants, perhaps tomorrow the government will forbid dual citizenship, or substantially increase the residency requirement, or restrict refugee asylum, or weaken anti-discrimination laws, or follow the Dutch policy of forcing adult immigrants to attend compulsory 'integration' classes that teach the national language and 'European' values.[6] What will be the next step down the slippery slope to exclusion and assimilation?

Some commentators dispute this description of the trajectory of UK policies. Randall Hansen, for example, has argued (elsewhere) that, in so far as the current policies can be criticised, the problem is not with citizenship policy per se. He argues that it is perfectly legitimate and fair for Britain to impose residency requirements and language tests on immigrants, as even the most open and liberal of immigrant countries do. This, by itself, manifests no racial bias. He acknowledges that there is a plausible case to be made for greater non-European immigration to Britain, or for a more generous or humane system of responding to refugee claims. But he insists that these disputes over whom to admit into the country as immigrants and refugees are separable from decisions about the rules of naturalisation, which he views as eminently fair and liberal.[7]

In one sense, I think Hansen is quite right. Viewed in isolation, citizenship policies in Britain are fully compatible with liberal values, and fall well within the range of acceptable practices, even good practices, of Western democracies. However, people do not view citizenship policies in isolation. They interpret citizenship policy in the light of larger trends regarding the acceptance of newcomers and the accommodation of diversity. And since immigrant groups in Britain feel insecure about these larger issues of admission and integration, they question the motivations for the new citizenship policy.

A three-legged stool

To put the point another way, we can think of immigration, citizenship and multiculturalism as a three-legged stool, each leg of which supports (or weakens) the other two. Where one leg is weak, people begin to worry about the motives and consequences of the other two legs as well. Conversely, confidence in one leg can help generate optimism and trust in the other two.

We can see this quite clearly, I think, in the Canadian context, where potential concerns about citizenship policy are defused or pre-empted by the strong state policies on immigration and multiculturalism. For example, there is a very broad consensus in Canada on a proactive policy of high immigration. The current goal is to admit 1 per cent of the population each year, or 300,000 people, as new immigrants. To be sure, this policy is not unanimously supported. One of the five major parties (the Canadian Alliance) has contested it, and is therefore often called the 'anti-immigration' political party. But it is worth noting that the Alliance proposal is to cut immigration in half, to 0.5 per cent per year, which is roughly the current American rate of immigration. So the spectrum of political opinion on immigration in Canada varies from those who think Canada should be tied with Australia for having the highest per capita rate of immigration in the world, and those who think Canada should be tied with the United States for having the second-highest per capita rate of immigration in the world. The more general principle that Canada is and should remain a country of immigration is uncontested.

There is also stable majority support for federal multiculturalism policies to accommodate immigrant groups better once they are admitted. These policies impose on public institutions an obligation to reduce barriers to immigrant participation and more accurately to reflect the diversity of the population.[8] Multiculturalism policies may be more controversial than the high-immigration policy, although recent polls suggest they retain broad popular support (over 80 per cent).[9] In any event, the commitment to multiculturalism is not only enshrined in legislation (the 1988 Multiculturalism Act), but in fact constitutionalised, in section 27 of the 1982 Constitution, as well as having been part of the education curriculum for over twenty-five years. So it is now a deeply embedded part of the legal and political framework in Canada.

These strong public commitments to immigration and to multiculturalism serve to reduce fears that citizenship policy will be used as a tool of exclusion or assimilation. After all, if the Canadian government or populace were suddenly to become much more exclusionary or assimilationist, this shift would manifest itself first in the immigration and multiculturalism legs of the stool. If Canadians became less accepting of the presence of non-whites in their society, they would reduce the high intake of immigrants. If they became more assimilationist and less accommodating of ethno-cultural or religious diversity, they would backtrack on the multiculturalism policies. So long as those two legs remain strong, however, then immigrant groups are unlikely to view citizenship policy as posing a threat of exclusion or assimilation.

Conversely, the fact that immigrants to Canada express support for the basic principles of the citizenship policy helps sustain support for its immigration and multiculturalism policies. If immigrants disputed the necessity of learning an official language, or of swearing an oath of loyalty, or if they simply tended not to naturalise, then the majority group might worry that high immigration and multiculturalism policies would destabilise the country. The fact that immigrant groups endorse the citizenship policy, and have very high rates of naturalisation (much higher than the United States), provides reassurance to the majority group that immigrants want to contribute to the country, not undermine it. So the mutual support between the citizenship leg and the immigration/multiculturalism legs runs in both directions.

In the British context, by contrast, there is no strong visible public commitment to either immigration or multiculturalism. On the contrary, there is if anything a consensus against (non-European) immigration. To put it crudely, many people in Britain believe that it was a terrible mistake to have admitted and granted automatic citizenship to so many non-white immigrants in the 1950s and 1960s, but luckily the country woke up in time and adopted more restrictive admissions and naturalisation policies, and must remain vigilant against the threats and burdens posed by unwanted illegal immigrants and 'bogus' claimants to refugee status.

Similarly, there is no legal or constitutional commitment to multicultural-ism in Britain. There are many de facto forms of multicultural accommodation at various levels of government and within many public institutions, but there has been a reluctance to make this a matter of official public policy.[10]

Under these circumstances, neither the immigration nor the multicultural-ism leg of the stool provides much reassurance to anyone who fears a slippery slope towards exclusion and assimilation. Neither dispels worries that Britain's commitment to the acceptance and accommodation of non-whites is fragile and/or half-hearted.

This may help to explain why the same moderate, liberal citizenship policies that have proven uncontroversial in North America have been more controversial in Britain. In the 2002 White Paper on migration, the British government drew upon Canadian experiences with naturalisation rules and citizenship oaths and ceremonies. These are described (rightly, I think) as working well in Canada. But part of the reason for their success in Canada is that they are cushioned or framed by a strong public commitment to immigration and multiculturalism. Britain has adopted the citizenship leg of the stool, but not the other two legs, and the resulting package may be less stable, or at least more controversial.

This suggests that Joppke and Morawska are wrong to suppose that the 'revaluing of citizenship' strategy competes with or contradicts a commitment to multiculturalism.[11] On the contrary, in an age of migration, the revaluing of citizenship strategy may work best when it is combined with a visible public commitment to multiculturalism. Conversely, multiculturalism policies may work best when they are combined with a visible public commitment to the revaluing of citizenship. This indeed is one of the clearest flaws in the sort of 'multiculturalism' policies originally adopted in countries like the Netherlands or Germany, which were disconnected from any attempt actively to promote naturalisation and citizenship identities.

Moving forward?

If the analysis so far is correct, then the success of efforts to revalue citizenship in an age of migration will depend not just on the nuts and bolts of citizenship policy, but also on broader attitudes towards immigration and multiculturalism. The likelihood of gaining a strong public consensus on citizenship policy may depend on developing a stronger consensus on immigration and multiculturalism (and vice versa).

I think the British government is in fact well aware of this. An interesting aspect of its approach, articulated in the White Paper, is its attempt to encourage greater openness to higher levels of immigration. It argues that skilled immigrants are important to the economy, and that there is no alternative but to loosen the rules that enable employers to bring in immigrants. Similarly, it affirms the commitment to accommodating immigrant identities, and the importance of learning to live with ethnic and religious diversity—indeed, the subtitle of the report is 'Integration with Diversity'.

Some cynics view these comments as window-dressing to hide what is fundamentally an exclusionary and assimilationist approach adopted to appease anti-immigrant public sentiment. But they may be genuine attempts to modify, and not just appease, anti-immigrant sentiments: gentle nudges trying to push British public opinion towards greater acceptance of the merits, and the inevitability, of immigration and multiculturalism.

What is striking, however, at least from a North American perspective, is how timid and cautious these statements are. The White Paper reads as if the government were terrified of provoking a backlash against even these modest affirmations of immigration and multiculturalism, and so hedged them with multiple qualifications and safeguards.

For example, it emphasises that skilled immigrants can come only to fill a specific job vacancy that cannot be filled by a British resident. In the United States and Canada, many immigrants are admitted without a job arranged in advance, and the evidence suggests that this results in a net increase in jobs. But the British government apparently felt that the public would not accept increased immigration if there were any possibility that immigrants would take jobs from residents, even if this cost were more than outweighed by the creation of new jobs. They want to present increased immigration not as a policy in which the benefits outweigh the costs, but as a policy in which there are no costs. The prospect that an immigrant might be allowed to come or to stay without a specific job is implicitly condemned as a grave mistake, if not a threat to the very fabric of society.

A similar tone pervades the discussion of the measures the government will adopt to root out illegal immigration and fraudulent refugee claims. Here again, the prospect that some poor Chinese economic migrants may slip through the border, or may succeed in a fraudulent refugee claim, is presented as a threat to the nation. To be sure, a government has the right and the responsibility to secure its borders, but it is difficult (for me) to see how several thousand bogus refugees or illegal immigrants are a threat to the state or society. Many countries have functioned perfectly well with much higher levels of 'irregular' migrants in their midst.

Similarly, the government's endorsement of 'diversity' is almost painfully cautious, beginning with the decision to avoid any use of the term 'multi-culturalism'. Its proposals emphasise that citizens can be expected to tolerate newcomers only if their own identities are 'secure'. The implication is that while public institutions should perhaps do more to accommodate immigrant groups or to reflect the ethnic diversity of the population, native-born British citizens will not be expected to make any changes in their own habits, practices or identities. Here again, the idea of respecting diversity is not defended as something whose benefits outweigh its costs, but rather as something that costs nothing to native-born citizens, and asks or expects nothing from them in terms of adaptation.

This is reflected in the feverish response to the Parekh Report, which had the temerity to suggest that British citizens might need to rethink what it means to be 'British', so as consciously and decisively to repudiate its historic racist elements.[12] The press reaction, on both the left and the right, was almost universal condemnation. The idea that multiculturalism might require individuals in the dominant group to re-evaluate (and hence temporarily destabilise) their inherited identities, heroes, symbols and narratives is apparently unthinkable.

In all of these respects, the White Paper's support for immigration and multiculturalism is muted almost beyond recognition: death by a thousand qualifications. This may well reflect an accurate realpolitik assessment of what the British public will accept. Perhaps this is the limit of what could be said in defence of immigration and multiculturalism without triggering a backlash that would be capitalised on by far-right anti-immigrant groups. Recent events on the continent show that this is not a far-fetched scenario, and it would be irresponsible for governments to ignore this possibility. Britain has been spared the worst forms of this hateful far-right politics, and Home Secretary David Blunkett and others are clearly concerned to ensure that they do nothing to provoke it.

And yet one cannot help thinking that there is more the government could do to encourage a more open attitude towards newcomers and ethno-cultural diversity. There is a fine line between honestly acknowledging the existence of public fears and unintentionally reinforcing them. The tone of the British approach suggests that a single false move on issues of immigration, determination of refugee status or citizenship could be fatal, as if it were potentially catastrophic to admit a few too many skilled immigrants, or to accept a few too many dubious refugee claims, or to have too many immigrants with substandard English skills. It suggests that there is no margin for error here, no room to undertake bold experiments or creative initiatives on issues of immigration, citizenship and multiculturalism, since the consequences of failure would be disastrous. This sort of tone can only heighten public anxiety about the issues.

My own view, by contrast, is that there is considerable room to undertake a variety of policy initiatives, some of which will work, others not, without endangering the fabric of society. Successful policies are often built on lessons from past failures, and we need therefore to be prepared to risk failures, and to give citizens the confidence that the risks are manageable and worth taking.

This sort of public confidence is crucial to the successful management of issues of immigration, citizenship and multiculturalism, as Shamit Saggar argues in his essay on public opinion in this volume. A recent study of immigration and refugee policies in nine industrialised countries concluded that the reason why some countries had not faced a crisis over such policies was the 'self-confidence' of the public. In some countries, citizens trusted that whatever problems arose in the admission or integration of immigrants and refugees could be managed. As a result, problems that in other countries led to a far-right backlash and/or ill-conceived restrictive legislation were dealt with in a sober and pragmatic way.[13]

Seen in this light, the British approach has a paradoxical quality. By acknowledging the anxiety of the public on these issues, it may help pre-empt a far-right backlash. Moreover, its specific citizenship reforms are moderate and pragmatic. However, I wonder whether it will do much to instil the public confidence to experiment with the sorts of initiatives relating to immigration and multiculturalism that are likely to be needed in our new age of migration.

Notes

1 For a classic statement of the 'transnational' view, see Yasemin Soysal, *Limits to Citizenship*, Chicago, University of Chicago Press, 1994. For a reaffirmation of the 'national' view, see the essays in Christian Joppke and Ewa Morawska, eds, *Toward Assimilation and Citizenship: Immigrants in Liberal Nation-States*, London, Palgrave, 2003.
2 For an example of the critique, see Les Back et al., 'New Labour's White Heart: Politics, Multiculturalism and the Return of Assimilation', *Political Quarterly*, vol. 72, no. 4, pp. 445–54. For the government's position, see the White Paper entitled *Secure Border, Safe Haven: Integration with Diversity in Modern Britain*, London: Stationery Office, 2002. For the claim that revaluing citizenship requires the retreat from multiculturalism, see Christian Joppke and Ewa Morawska, 'Integrating Immigrants in Liberal Nation-States: Policies and Practices', in Joppke and Morawska, eds, *Toward Assimilation and Citizenship*, pp. 1–36.
3 See Gary Freeman, 'Client Politics or Populism? Immigration Reform in the United States', in V. Giraudon and C. Joppke, eds, *Controlling a New Migration World*, London, Routledge, 2001.
4 On how naturalisation requirements in Britain compare with those in other Western democracies, see Patrick Weil, 'Access to Citizenship: A Comparison of Twenty-five Nationality Laws', in Alexander Aleinikoff and Douglas Klusmeyer, eds, *Citizenship Today: Global Perspectives and Practices*, Washington DC, Carnegie Endowment for International Peace, 2001, pp. 22–3. On how the status of non-citizens in Britain compares with that in other European countries, see Harald Waldrauch, 'The Legal Integration of Immigrants in Europe: Measuring the Rights of Migrant Workers and their Families in Seven European Countries', paper presented at conference on 'Immigration and Human Rights', Contemporary Europe Research Centre, University of Melbourne, Nov. 2002.
5 Yasmin Alibhai-Brown, *After Multiculturalism*, London, Foreign Policy Centre, 2000. Some members of substate national groups in Britain—e.g. the Scots and Welsh—may also have reservations about emphasising Britishness. A similar issue arises even more dramatically in Canada with the Québécois.
6 On the new Dutch policy, see Alfons Fermin, *The Justification of Mandatory Integration Programmes for New Immigrants*, ERCOMER Research Paper 2001/01, Utrecht, European Research Centre on Migration and Ethnic Relations, 2001; Hans Entzinger, 'The Rise and Fall of Multiculturalism in the Netherlands', in Joppke and Morawska, eds, *Toward Assimilation and Citizenship*, pp. 59–86. This may seen like an extreme scenario, but it is worth noting that many commentators lump together the new Dutch and British policies as two examples of the same trend towards revaluing citizenship by repudiating multiculturalism.
7 See Randall Hansen, 'British Citizenship After Empire: A Defence', *Political Quarterly*, vol. 71, no. 1, 2000, pp. 42–9.
8 For a description of multiculturalism policies in Canada, see Will Kymlicka, *Finding Our Way: Rethinking Ethnocultural Relations in Canada*, Toronto, Oxford University Press, 1998.
9 See ACS/Environics, 'Public Opinion Poll', *Canadian Issues*, Feb. 2002, pp. 4–5. This poll found 82 per cent support for multiculturalism as a federal policy. The most extensive study of popular opinion on multiculturalism policies is Angus Reid

Group, *Multiculturalism and Canadians: Attitude Study*, Ottawa, Multiculturalism and Citizenship Canada, 1991.

10 For a discussion of the implicit commitment to multiculturalism in Britain, see Adrian Favell, *Philosophies of Integration: Immigration and the Idea of Citizenship in France and Britain*, New York, St Martin's Press, 2001. For a plea to make it more explicit, see the Parekh Report: Commission on the Future of Multi-Ethnic Britain, *The Future of Multi-Ethnic Britain*, London, Profile Books, 2000.

11 See Joppke and Morawska, 'Integrating Immigrants in Liberal Nation-States'. For a more detailed discussion of the link between citizenship and multiculturalism, see Kymlicka, *Finding Our Way*, chs 1–5.

12 Commission on the Future of Multi-Ethnic Britain, *The Future of Multi-Ethnic Britain*.

13 Wayne Cornelius, Philip Martin and James Hollifield, eds, *Controlling Immigration: A Global Perspective*, Stanford, Stanford University Press, 1997, p. 14.

Index

Abraham, Spencer 143, 145
Afghanistan 85, 93, 101, 109
Ajami, Fouad 95
Albania 86
Algeria 94
Alibhai-Brown, Yasmin 94, 200
Amsterdam Treaty 107, 116, 117, 121, 127
anchor ethnic communities 41
Angola 78
anti-discrimination legislation 32, 93, 103–4
anti-elitism 12, 90
anti-semitism 12, 91–3
armed conflict 10, 41, 76, 97
asylum 1–2, 5, 9, 10, 11, 13–14, 16–17, 20, 35–6, 75–87, 142, 153
    anti-asylum rhetoric 163–76
    costs 8, 11, 33, 83
    in developing countries 4, 11, 76–9
    in industrialised countries 81–7
Ataturk, Kemal 100
Australia 43, 51, 57, 85, 89, 178, 188–90, 202
Austria 26, 88, 124, 128, 178, 188
    Freedom Party 88, 89, 123, 190
    People's Party 89

Baganha, Maria 161
Baltic states 89
BBC (British Broadcasting Corporation) 108
Beazley, Kim 189
Belgium 26, 89, 117
    Vlaams Blok 88, 123
Berlusconi, Silvio 88, 89, 101
Bin Laden, Osama 93,100
birth rates 27, 36–7
Bivand, P. 68
Blair, Tony 32, 85, 166–7
Blunkett, David 91, 166, 206
Bommes, Michael 159
border controls 53, 82, 83, 117, 128, 129
Borjas, G. J. 66, 67

Bosnia-Herzegovina 76, 80–1, 93, 101, 109, 118
Brimelow, Peter 137
British Election Study 179, 186
Buchanan, Pat 192
Bush, George, Jr 18, 140, 179, 191–2

Campaign to Free Campsfield 173
Canada 43, 51, 57, 66, 95–6, 98, 205–19
    citizenship 196–200, 202–3, 204–19
Cato Institute 136
causes of displacement 3–4, 40–1, 48, 75–6
Cerdeira Report 127
Chechnya 101
Chinese Exclusion Act, 1882 135
Chirac, Jacques 190
Chiswick, B. 65–6
Chrétien, Jean 96
citizenship 7, 18–19, 30, 31, 95–8, 195–206
colonial migration 26–7, 28, 102–3, 200–1
Commission for Racial Equality 111, 113
Commission on Islamophobia 113
Commission on Multi-Ethnic Britain 113–14
Commonwealth Immigrants Act 1962 28
Commonwealth Working Holiday Scheme 62, 71
complementarity 61
Cornelius, W. 155
Côte d'Ivoire 78, 80
Croatia 86
Crossman, R. 178
culture 95–8
Czech Republic 89, 128

demographics 3, 10, 49–51, 69–71
Denmark 26, 88, 89, 156, 160
    Danish People's Party 88, 90, 123, 165
Dhondy, Farrukh 111
distributional effects 45, 61–2
dual citizenship 197, 200
Du Bois, W. E. B. 114

Published by Blackwell Publishing Ltd, 9600 Garsington Road, Oxford OX4 2DQ, UK and 350 Main Street, Malden, MA 02148, USA